The Myth of
Homeland Security

The Myth of
Homeland Security

Marcus J. Ranum

WILEY

Wiley Publishing, Inc.

Vice President and Executive Publisher: Robert Ipsen
Publisher: Joe Wikert
Executive Editor: Carol Long
Developmental Editor: Nancy Stevenson
Editorial Manager: Kathryn A. Malm
Senior Production Editor: Angela Smith
Text Design & Composition: Wiley Composition Services

Library of Congress Cataloging-in-Publication Data:

ISBN: 0-471-45879-1

Printed in the United States of America

10 9 8 7 6 5 4 3 2 1

To Katrina and the herd, all my love.

To my parents, my deepest thanks.

Contents

Acknowledgments

Sincere thanks to Carol Long and Nancy Stevenson, without whom this book never would have happened.

To the many good people at USENIX and other conferences, who listened and argued, thanks for the sanity-check.

About the Author

Marcus J. Ranum is a world-renowned expert on security system design and implementation. He is recognized as the inventor of the proxy firewall, and the implementer of the first commercial firewall product. Since the late 1980s, he has designed a number of groundbreaking security products, including the DEC SEAL, the TIS firewall toolkit, the Gauntlet firewall, and NFR's Network Flight Recorder intrusion detection system. He has been involved in every level of operations of a security product business, from developer, to founder and CEO of NFR. Marcus has served as a consultant to many FORTUNE 500 firms and national governments, as well as serving as a guest lecturer and instructor at numerous high-tech conferences. In 2001, he was awarded the TISC "Clue" award for service to the security community and also holds the ISSA lifetime achievement award.

It's Another Code Orange Day

As I write this, I'm sitting in a restaurant in a major U.S. airport, eating my breakfast with a plastic knife and fork. I worked up quite an appetite getting here two hours early and shuffling in the block-long lines until I got to the security checkpoint where I could take off my shoes, remove my belt, and put my carry-on luggage through the screening system. Of course, I had to take my laptop out of my bag, but not my digital camera or the backup FireWire hard disk I travel with.

The nice people from the Transportation Safety Agency in their uniform white shirts are professional and cool. They're a big improvement over the screeners in the past who could hardly speak English or who chatted about their personal business the whole time while they perfunctorily waved people through the checkpoint.

Once I'm done eating my breakfast, I'll show my government-issued ID one more time as I board a plane with the new armored cockpit doors. My plastic knife and fork are, presumably, to keep me from successfully assaulting the plane. I've noticed I've developed a new nervous tic: As I stand in security lines, I constantly pat myself down to make sure I'm not carrying any metal. I'm caught in the mechanism of a multibillion-dollar airport security apparatus that, as far as I could discover, has never actually caught a terrorist or prevented a terrorist incident.

WHAT'S GOING ON HERE?

What's going on? It's homeland security. Welcome to the new age of knee-jerk security at any price. Well, I've paid, and you've paid, and we'll all keep paying — but is it going to help? Have we embarked on a massive multibillion-dollar boondoggle that's going to do nothing more than make us *feel* more secure? Are we paying nosebleed prices for "feel-good" measures?

WHO AM I?

I'm a security practitioner; specifically, I'm an Internet security and computer systems security designer. I work in a fascinating field that is utterly unforgiving of mistakes: The computer hackers who probe e-commerce sites are invisible, plentiful, motivated, and merciless. Because computers don't have *feelings*, it doesn't *matter* if they appear to be secure, or make their users feel confident and protected. The only thing that works is keeping the bad guys out 100 percent, 24/7, 365 days a year. Antiterrorism is exactly the same: There are no prizes given for second place. Ninety-nine percent isn't good enough.

To build good security systems, I had to learn how to think about broad problems as well as their implementation details. It's kind of a process of automatically prioritizing solutions to security problems in order of how effective they're likely to be, how much they cost, and so on. So when I started running into the Department of Homeland Security, I got curious and instinctively started chewing over the details of some of the silly stuff I saw going on at the airport and on the television. Of course, that was just the tip of the iceberg. I guess you could call this book an exploration of the gigantic submerged mass that represents the true problem of homeland security.

INTO THE RABBIT HOLE

This book was painful to write. By nature, I am a problem solver. Professionally I have made my career out of solving complex problems efficiently by trying to find the right place to push hard and make a difference. Researching the Department of Homeland Security, the FBI,

CIA, INS, the PATRIOT Act, and so forth, one falls into a rabbit's hole of interdependent lameness and dysfunction. I came face to face with the realization that there are gigantic bureaucracies that exist primarily for the sole purpose of prolonging their existence, that the very structure of bureaucracy rewards inefficiency and encourages territorialism and turf warfare.

CHASING THE TRUTH

When I first started thinking about homeland security, I thought it would be a simple problem of assessing whether or not the Department of Homeland Security was a good idea. I had no awareness that our personal security is probably more dependent on keeping the Palestinians and Israelis from killing each other than on keeping people with weapons out of airplane cockpits.

This book was also painful to research. Unlike a lot of people, I've actually *read* the PATRIOT Act and the Homeland Security Act. I'm not sure I was able to grasp much from those documents other than that they are huge, complicated, and terribly, terribly obscure. I read other people's interpretations of them as well and was surprised to find that most people overlook the parts that don't fit their preconceptions and take the rest out of context to suit their particular political or financial agenda.

I recall, as I read the Department of Justice's reasoning for the PATRIOT Act, and the ACLU's analysis of it, my sense of reality began to dissolve — were they even talking about the same document? I could only conclude that both were too busy grinding their particular axes to spend any time searching for truth. After I got further into it, I started to wonder if there was any truth to be found.

WAS THAT TWEEDLEDEE OR TWEELEDUM?

I did a lot of my research using the Internet. One of the great things about the Internet is that you can find any information you want. *Even if it's wrong.* And sometimes it's contradictory. So I was careful about sources; I didn't take anything for granted and tried to find corroboration for facts. I double- and triple-checked. I read a couple bookshelves of books. The more I read and researched, the less I knew, it seemed.

There are some things I couldn't find out because nobody seems to know. I have friends who were also important resources for me, so I bought them lots of beer and asked a lot of questions. The whole time, I searched for *impressions* of broad trends, rather than *evidence*.

For example, I tried to find out how many different databases the FBI maintains that contain terrorism-related information. Even the FBI appears not to know — which is a really interesting thing, in and of itself. I had to write whole sections of this book based on partial information. But this book is not intended to be a history text or a reference. I'm making some inflammatory observations; I don't want you, the reader, to ignore the substance of what I have to say by getting bogged down in the details of my research. So I didn't quote sources. When you read a piece of legislation, and the ACLU says one thing about it and the Department of Justice another, what's the point in citing your sources?

Remember, we're living in the middle of history as it's being written. Fifty years from now, historians will be able to dissect events with greater accuracy, once the dust has settled a bit and the hidden agendas have been uncovered a bit more. So remember: *There is no reality down here in the rabbit hole.*

FOR THE RECORD . . .

In the course of writing this book there were a few sources that I remember thinking I'd like to share with my readers. These are the *fun* and *interesting* ones and don't represent anything like a complete list. If you enjoyed parts of this book, or found parts of it thought-provoking, you might be similarly pleased or provoked by some of these:

Secrets and Lies, Digital Security in a Networked World, by Bruce Schneier (John Wiley & Sons, 2000) ISBN# 0471253111

Invasion: How America Still Welcomes Terrorists Criminals & Other Foreign Menaces to Our Shores, by Michelle Malkin (Regnery Publishing, 2002) ISBN# 0895261464

Wedge: From Pearl Harbor to 9/11 — How the Secret War between the FBI and CIA Has Endangered National Security, by Mark Riebling (Touchstone Books, 2002) ISBN# 0743245997

Lic 2010: Special Operations & Unconventional Warfare in the Next Century (Brassey's Future Warfare Series), by Rod Paschall (Brasseys Inc., 1990) ISBN# 0080359825

Wilderness of Mirrors: Intrigue, Deception, and the Secrets that Destroyed Two
of the Cold War's Most Important Agents, by David Martin (The Lyons
Press, 2003) ISBN# 1585748242

The Consequences of Permissive Neglect, by James Bruce (www.cia.gov/
csi/studies/vol47no1/article04.html)

Most of the Web searching I did was part of a chaotic whirlwind of
followed hyperlinks. But a few sites stick out as having interesting and
very cool information:

www.cryptome.org	John Young's web archive
www.cia.gov/csi/index.html	CIA's Center for Study of Intelligence
www.fas.org	Federation of American Scientists

IN A PERFECT WORLD

Once I digested everything I could, I started trying to think of something concrete and helpful to offer. After all, nobody reads a book like
this because he or she expects the author to shrug and say, "Hey, it's an
unsolvable problem. It's just too big." But that just might be the path of
intellectual honesty. So I've organized this book around broad topical
areas, which represent what I see as the crucial pieces of the whole
picture.

At the end of each chapter, I've included a few observations about
how I think things could be done differently in a perfect world. I've
tried to tread the fine line between idealism and useless complaining.
Do I think it will actually be done that way? No. Am I issuing a call to
action? No. Some of the things I think would happen in a perfect world
may already be happening right now. Others may happen in their own
good time, as a result of pressures that arise. Perhaps, in a perfect world,
someone who reads this book will be in a position to provide a positive
nudge in the right direction at the right time, and we'll get there a little bit sooner.

GETTING STARTED

Now it's your turn to discover many of the surprising and disturbing
things I've spent the last several months of my life unearthing about

homeland security. Sit back and enjoy the show provided courtesy of the Department of Homeland Security. Buy the plastic sheets and the duct tape. Take your shoes off before you go through airport screening. Call the Department of Homeland Security's 800-number if you see signs of potential terrorist activity. Let's all take a look behind the curtain and see if we can make some sense of this concept we call homeland security.

1

Homeland Security: A Convenient Invention

A friend was listening to a baseball game on the radio a few weeks ago. As the fans were going into the stadium, the announcers explained that "for security reasons" they could no longer bring bottles and cans through the checkpoints. Was this an attempt to prevent a terrorist disguised as a fan from hijacking a stadium with the jagged end of a broken bottle, or was it an obvious and insultingly stupid attempt to increase the revenues of in-stadium drink sellers?

Homeland security is not a game for amateurs or the impatient. This is a scenario that involves complex challenges, from finding ways to stop terrorists from hacking into secret databases, to developing new procedures for airline security, communicating with the public about threats, and tightening immigration policies.

In this chapter I take a look at how we got where we are today. Jump on board the scare and hype bandwagon and get a taste for where we might all be headed.

INFORMATION WARFARE: THE INTANGIBLE THREAT THAT KEEPS ON GIVING

To understand how we got where we are today, take a step back in time. It's the early 1990s; the Cold War is ending and suddenly a lot of people are talking about the "peace dividend." Of course, politicians, bureaucrats, and Beltway bandits are busy positioning themselves to grab a chunk of any windfall that might come. Nobody is quite sure what is going to happen, and many folks in the information security and computer security fields are wondering if their research grant money is going to dry up and blow away.

What's a warrior to do when the enemy packs up and closes operations? Simple: *Generate worry about an intangible threat.*

ALL ABOARD THE SCARE AND HYPE BANDWAGON

When it came to casting the part of Intangible Threat, information and technology, two linchpins of the 1990s, seemed to be likely candidates.

In 1994, Winn Schwartau, a charming rogue, wrote a blockbuster book called *Information Warfare: Chaos on the Electronic Superhighway*. It hit a nerve. This was during the height of the early dot-com boom, and the book filled readers' eyes and minds with visions of stealthy international cyber ninjas and countries brought to their knees by teenaged hackers working for ideological extremists.

There were visions of aircraft falling out of the sky because their command systems had been wiped with pulses of directed radiation and government agencies collapsing when a pimply-faced subculture hacked into their information resources.

The spooks who were looking at budget cuts had found their foe. Best of all, because it was a nebulous foe — a threat that didn't really exist — it had advantages: It could not be beaten, could not surrender, and could be ascribed awesome, superhuman powers.

HACKER, CRACKER . . . WHATEVER

Immediately after Schwartau's book came out, conferences devoted to information warfare began to crop up and more books were published on the topic. Eventually, congressional hearings were held on the threat, featuring suit-wearing, longhaired hackers who announced that they could "take down the entire Internet in minutes," assuming they wanted to.

Otherwise sensible people made comments such as "If an info war attack took down the AMTRAK train scheduling systems, the U.S. economy would grind to a halt in three days." Of course, these comments completely ignored the fact that AMTRAK strikes and track outages lasting weeks had already failed to have a noticeable effect on our economy.

> **" You could feel the bandwagon rocking from the sudden weight of all the bodies climbing onto it. "**

Researchers having anything to do with computer security rushed to change the titles of their grant proposals to contain the words "Information Warfare." You could feel the bandwagon rocking from the sudden weight of all the bodies climbing onto it.

you should know

Today, strategic think tanks write scholarly tomes on information warfare, and the term is in widespread use. A search on Amazon.com's site returns over 70 pages of book titles matching the search term "information warfare." This shows a tremendous amount of interest in a form of war that doesn't have a whole lot of substance.

There are a few interesting aspects of the information warfare scare that are worth noting:

- The term information warfare is used so broadly that it can cover everything from crank calls and email spam to destructive attacks against physical components of online systems.
- The antagonists are so vague and ill-defined that anyone, ranging from a nine-year-old hacker to a government-sponsored researcher, can be an information warrior.
- None of the world-class scarifying events that have been projected has ever really happened. When minor information faux pas have occurred — for example, pieces of the Internet went down or Web sites were deliberately crashed — most of the victims reacted with bland indifference rather than panic.

INFORMATION WARFARE IN THE TRENCHES

Here's an interesting paradigm: As soon as someone conceives of a possible weapon that could threaten our security, the military creates defenses against that weapon. Once there's a defense in place, someone almost inevitably feels compelled to build the weapon itself. In other words, conceiving of a defense against a possible threat will automatically encourage someone to make that threat a reality.

So, the information warfare scare-hype gave birth to any number of organizations that build defensive information warfare capabilities — as well as stimulating shadowy efforts to build offensive information weapons. Thus, information warfare may become a self-fulfilling prophecy as some clever hacker comes up with an offensive to match our defense.

What would an offensive information weapon look like? Probably a lot like the kind of stuff we're already dealing with. Right now the Internet is rife with worms, viruses, and Trojan horses. While we may not be dealing with it 100 percent effectively, these kinds of threats haven't exactly crippled our information economy, yet, or even slowed it down.

A huge amount of money has been spent on ameliorating the threat of information warfare. In general, that money has been spent on a mix of initiatives that are either (1) a complete waste of time, (2) useful basic research, or (3) improvements to infrastructure.

> " *Perhaps the best description of the information warfare defense process is a kind of Chicken Little make-work program for Beltway bandits and high-tech firms.* "

Taxpayers can take refuge in the hope that the information warfare fad, so far, has simply been a very inefficient vehicle for funding research in computer security and systems and network management, as well as an excuse for buying lots of new PCs for government workers. Perhaps the best description of the information warfare defense process is a kind of Chicken Little make-work program for Beltway bandits and high-tech firms.

BANDWAGON ON A ROLL

The information warfare movement is a good example of how scare and hype bandwagons get rolling and take on a life of their own. In a lot of ways, the information warfare scare-hype bandwagon is like the terrorism scare-hype bandwagon, except that, so far, the former has just been a waste of money.

Unfortunately, unlike cyber ninjas, terrorists are a real threat. Most people don't immediately withdraw from the economy and head for the hills when their email is inaccessible.

THE EMPTY PROMISE OF EMERGENCY RESPONSE

Once you've got the public good and scared about a threat, the first thing they'll ask is "Well? Isn't someone going to *do* something about it?" (The other common American refrain is "There ought to be a law.") Once everyone was good and scared about information warfare, organizations quickly flocked to embrace the new cash cow.

THE BEGINNING: CERT

Early adopters included the various Computer Emergency Response Teams. The granddaddy of such teams was the original CERT, from Carnegie-Mellon University. CERT was founded in 1988 with funding from Defense Advanced Research Project Agency (DARPA). Its stated goal was to act as a coordination center in the event of future Internet attacks and outbreaks, such as the 1988 Morris Internet worm.

CERT was hugely successful in drawing attention to itself. While it never accomplished a whole lot, it had a highly visible team of experts that gave lots of good talks at conferences and became expert media-handlers and an excellent source of quotes for journalists. The level of attention the first CERT received spawned a raft of imitators, both at home and abroad. Many government agencies founded their own CERTs — not because they needed them, but because being part of a CERT was a virtual ticket to all the conferences you wanted to attend.

Pretty soon, there were meetings where CERT organizers could go to learn how to run CERTs. Meanwhile, networks kept getting hacked, and the state of network security remained pathetic. Eventually, a lot of the early CERT founders made their reputations and went to startups during the mid-1990s. If all the CERTs ever accomplished anything, I'm damned if I know what it is — but a lot of beer was consumed in the process.

STAYING ALERT?

During its early days, the CERT's charter was primarily to educate organizations about the need for computer security and to work with vendors to fix glaring bugs in their software. The CERT's main vehicle for getting the message out was security alerts.

Alerts are a critical aspect of the whole emergency response scenario, as well as a hugely important aspect of this particular scare and hype bandwagon. In 1998, the year it was founded, CERT released only one alert — about the Morris worm — adhering to a long-standing tradition among alerting agencies of only issuing alerts after it is too late to do anything about them.

you should know

During the course of this book, you will run into countless cases where alerts are issued and they're either ignored or are simply too late. They are useful, but only within a very narrow window of time, and only if you're in a situation where you can actually do something about the threat.

The CERT was supposed to act as a sort of Internet Center for Disease Control (CDC), but that doesn't really make sense in an environment where a problem (such as a computer virus) can transmit without you getting near another person who is infected. In fact, in this case, the means of transmitting the alert is one of the carriers for the disease. It would be like getting a letter in the mail from the CDC saying, "Be alert. There is anthrax in the mail. Do not open any envelopes." Most online security alerts are sent via email — a popular avenue for hacking attacks and a transmission medium for many viruses.

Emergency response is not something that works through warnings; it is something that works through preparedness. This is especially true when the threat is terrorism or another form of sneak attack. By definition, the attack is a surprise, and any warning that is issued will simply serve to confuse the people who are trying to deal with the problem.

> **" Emergency response is not something that works through warnings; it is something that works through preparedness. "**

The military has always understood this, and that's why emergency drills are a way of life on naval vessels. Sailors understand that "general quarters" means "get to your assigned post and deal with problems you see there, be prepared to do other stuff if told to, and stay out of the way if not."

When you're driving down a road and see a sign that reads "Falling Rock," you're receiving a useful warning to help you practice preparedness: Presumably you're going to be more ready to dodge large moving objects, and unmoving objects that are sitting in the road. Generalized warnings, such as the FBI's antiterrorist warnings, are like seeing a sign by the side of the road that reads "LOOK OUT." Look out for what? Should I speed up, or slow down? Should I call someone on my cell phone? Or get out of my car and run for cover? In fact, I'm more likely to ignore the sign and turn up my radio a notch; at least if danger is present, I can hum along.

PREPARED FOR ANYTHING . . . OR NOTHING

Preparedness is critical for dealing effectively with virtually any kind of surprise. As societies are repeatedly forced to deal with many new types of nasty surprises, they quickly evolve responses and people become prepared to use them.

In the United Kingdom the Provisional IRA planted a car bomb at Bishopsgate in 1993. An observant local police officer identified the vehicle as suspicious and began a response within two minutes of the terrorists leaving the vehicle. The police began taping off a cordoned area within minutes, and the IRA actually called in a warning *after* the police had already begun to respond to the weapon. Existing evacuation plans prepared by local businesses were invoked, and the police were able to almost completely evacuate the buildings in the area before the bomb exploded. Preparedness showed in the fact that the police were thinking about car bombs rather than parking tickets, the police had bullhorns, the businesses had plans, and the civilians reacted rapidly and in a disciplined manner.

Imagine a similar incident in a U.S. city. Some employees would remain at their desks and not take the situation seriously. Other people, inspired by curiosity, would stand in the middle of the evacuation path trying to get a look at the bomb. And, of course, a camera crew from a local TV station would get itself blown up while asking people on the scene, "Do you think the terrorists were *serious* about a bomb being in that car?" Such attitudes change rapidly with experience. Compare the Israeli and British popular media attitudes to terrorism if you want a perspective on the difference between us and countries that have truly internalized the terrorist experience. In the United States we simply haven't had enough time and contact with terrorism for it to sink in. I'm not saying 9/11 was unimportant, but there is a major difference in the cultural attitude of a society that lives with a constant threat of terrorism at home and one that is still surprised by it.

FIGHTING THE LAST WAR

There's an adage in military theory that says "armies always prepare to refight the last war." It's generally spoken as a criticism of stodginess in military thinking. But unless you're able to anticipate new methods of warfare on a regular basis, there is no alternative.

Being prepared to fight the last war is certainly better than being prepared to run around flapping your arms and shouting "The sky is falling!" In fact, preparing to fight the last war at least shows an awareness that you may need to fight. On a more practical level it shows an awareness you'll need somewhat up-to-date equipment, well-trained troops, and a familiarity with the latest tactics. The drilled-in reactions to a car-bomb threat will not serve effectively against a biological weapons attack, but the discipline required to respond to the threat, and perhaps some of the tools available, might.

HEY, WHAT ABOUT US?

As the United States prepares to deal with homeland security, there will be any number of organizations attempting to boost their budgets and importance by preparing to lead responses to incidents as they occur. Oddly enough, to date, the most fundamental component of response — disciplined and thoughtful civilians — has been left out of the equation.

Those who grew up in the late 1950s and early 1960s recall how we mindlessly performed air-raid drills against possible nuclear attack. We performed fire drills in schools at various grade levels. The time it took for us to evacuate the building was always too long, but it was always shorter than it would have been if we had never performed a single readiness drill.

This preparedness is the point of incident response organizations. The poor ones exist to increase their funding by issuing alerts to exaggerate their importance. The good ones teach people response procedures for categories of problems within their purview.

These organizations are prepared to act as the coordinating locus in their area of expertise. They are also prepared with appropriate lines of communication that work during the duration of the emergency.

you should know

The CDC has the necessary contacts within the media to be able to issue necessary instructions in the event of a plague. But do they waste people's time with weekly plague-level alerts as the FBI has done post-9/11? No. For one thing, the folks at the CDC have a pretty good sense of the damage a pointless panic can cause.

THE NICHELESS NATIONAL INFRASTRUCTURE PROTECTION CENTER (NIPC)

The National Infrastructure Protection Center (NIPC) is an example of an organization that has had problems finding an effective niche. It was established by the FBI — basically it *is* the FBI — with a broad charter but no actual ability to execute. Its mission: "To serve as the U.S. government's focal point for threat assessment, warning, investigation, and response for threats or attacks against our critical infrastructures. These infrastructures, which include telecommunications, energy, banking and finance, water systems, government operations, and emergency services, are the foundation upon which our industrialized society is based."

But if you look closely at what NIPC can actually do, its authority extends to releasing alerts, "coordinating," and "sharing information." In other words, it relies on other people to tell it what's going on, and then it hopes to turn that information around quickly enough to issue an alert to those who have not already succumbed to the threat.

One audit performed by the Government Accounting Office (GAO) found that NIPC issued many of its incident warnings after the incidents — especially the spread of computer viruses and worms — had occurred. Lots of organizations already knew they had massive-scale worm attacks under way because their network connections were clogged with worm traffic in the form of millions of email messages generated by self-propagating attack programs. NIPC's alert was drowned out by the flood of emails that crashed servers worldwide. (Unfortunately, there is no Internet equivalent of a bullhorn, such as the British Police used in the Bishopsgate bomb incident.)

> " *One audit performed by the Government Accounting Office (GAO) found that NIPC issued many of its incident warnings after the incidents had occurred.* "

NIPC typifies a number of other problems that exist with incident response organizations throughout the government. NIPC has

- A lack of staffing and expertise.
- A confused position within governmental structures, especially with regard to relationships between the FBI and the National Security Council (NSC).
- A lack of credibility with the private sector.

Somebody Forgot to Train the Staff...

There's a saying in the military: "You fight the way you train." Well, what does that say about how well you fight if you're basically untrained? Lack of staffing is usually synonymous with lack of expertise. In fact, if your staff members don't know what they're doing, it doesn't matter how many of them you have (clueless × 1,000 still equals clueless).

The NIPC was originally funded in 2000 with $27 million and 200 FBI agents. In the private sector, substantial, successful companies have been founded with far less. Indeed, that level of staffing is comparable to the funding and head count of many software security companies, such as those that produce Internet firewalls and antivirus software. Two hundred employees is only "lack of staffing" if the lack of expertise is severe.

The NIPC was initially forced to train its staff by inviting outside Internet security experts in as unpaid guest speakers and instructors. This resulted primarily in NIPC's educational input coming from the marketing departments of vendors who were hoping to influence federal security procurement efforts.

Being Left Out of the Pecking Order

Organizational confusion is another major problem bedeviling many government organizations. It most acutely strikes those groups that are chartered to "coordinate" but have no actual management authority over the things they are supposed to be coordinating.

> " How is the NIPC supposed to make a positive impact when the only way they can bring about change is by asking nicely? "

How is the NIPC supposed to make a positive impact when the only way they can bring about change is by asking nicely? Further, because NIPC is supposed to work with the private sector, there is a huge problem because private-sector organizations are often technologically ahead of NIPC. But even within the federal government, nobody knows if they have to listen to NIPC — or, more precisely, they're sure they *don't* have to listen to NIPC, which makes NIPC into a vestigial organization that can't do much more than issue bulletins.

NIPC — Who??

Last, but far from least, is the lack of credibility many federal agencies have with their private-sector counterparts.

While many commercial firms had problems with some of the outbreaks of Internet worms such as CodeRed and Nimda, a large number of them had adequate protections in place, and many even had antivirus response procedures. Many commercial antivirus products had released signatures to detect and block the worm before the NIPC's alert was issued. So, for a large number of private-sector organizations, the entire alert was a nonevent.

Many of NIPC's alerts are essentially derived from the alerts issued by commercial product manufacturers, which makes private-sector organizations wonder if NIPC exists to do much more than to paraphrase and summarize alerts that have already been issued by commercial antivirus or security companies.

How does this lack of credibility come about? Why is NIPC recognized as a failure even by the government, when the CDC is a highly respected organization? It's simple:

- Government can only dominate an agenda when they clearly monopolize expertise.
- An organization can lead only when it is ahead; in this case, the government would have to be ahead of the private sector, and it's not.

The CDC operates in an area where there *are* no private-sector competitors. In areas where "to provide for the common defense" obviously holds, the private sector has a history of letting the government lead. National-level response to disease outbreaks and biological warfare are closely related topics that most people clearly expect our government to take the lead in. Information technology, and use of near-cutting-edge information technology, is not something most people expect the government to be good at.

Indeed, the government's entry into cyberspace has been slow and fraught with embarrassing faux pas. During the early 1990s, when many Americans were jumping onto the Internet with both feet, most federal employees' email addresses ended in "@aol.com." Many senior and motivated law enforcement personnel purchased their own computers so that they could begin to learn cyber forensics because the desktop systems available to them were barely powerful enough to run word processors.

WHERE DID ALL THE COMPETENT PEOPLE GO?

These observations about government efforts at mastering technology are not intended to belittle the incredible efforts of the small but diligent number of federal workers who struggled and overcame the technological backwardness of the government. Long, hard hours of self-training brought many FBI and Department of Defense computer experts to skill levels meeting or exceeding those of their private-sector peers.

In fact, many of those federal experts were unable to resist the lure of healthy raises and stock equity offered by Internet security startups during the late 1990s. After years of working on a shoestring in a management structure that was stifling, a lot of motivated people left government employment and earned healthy fortunes by doing so.

Many federal agencies are using hopelessly obsolete computers and software — yet somehow the federal government still spends massive amounts on information technology. My guess is it's not being spent well.

9/11 AND THE BANDWAGON TAKES OFF

The homeland security bandwagon lurched into gear after 9/11. In many respects, it was a perfectly natural reaction to the fear and confusion caused by the terrorist attacks. Practically the first thing out of everyone's mouth was "How could this have happened?" The second was "How can we keep it from happening again?"

The media only added to the hysteria, and it was clear that *something* was going to have to be done, whether it made sense to do it or not. So the bandwagon began to roll, accelerating through 2002 to become a bureaucratic and financial juggernaut of epic proportions.

Three different segments were fueling the bandwagon:

- The media asking "What is going to be done about this?"
- The government looking for an answer to the media's question
- Vendors of security solutions looking for an opportunity to make money off the whole thing

Each of these groups' concerns is *perfectly valid*, but because of the vested interest each has in the outcome, it's nearly impossible to get a sensible answer.

you should know

See Chapter 10 for more about security vendors and their role in homeland security and Chapter 8 for a closer look at the media.

THE MEDIA'S QUESTION

The media, of course, doesn't really want definitive answers to the problem of homeland security. In fact, the media is probably happier with unanswered or unanswerable questions, since those make for better stories and provide a good forum for endless pundits to discuss endless questions endlessly.

You've doubtless heard the theory about the infinite number of monkeys typing at random and how they'd eventually re-create *Hamlet*. Media pundits probably couldn't accomplish that much; remember, their role is to clarify divisions and present opposing views. A cynic might call that "sowing discord."

The media's role in getting the bandwagon rolling was primarily that of acting as Monday morning quarterback — searching for the "could have dones" and "might have beens" that would have prevented the act of terrorism in the first place. The media sells 20/20 hindsight; after all, when was the last time you heard CNN say "Today, a potentially disastrous

> *" The media sells 20/20 hindsight. "*

situation was staved off years in advance because of some sensible decisions that were made by a federal agency"?

In fact, the media was in a perfect position to get the bandwagon rolling by simultaneously asking "How could this have happened?" and "What is the government going to do about it?" casting the onus of response clearly on the administration. After all, the pundits were the ones who implied something was wrong when President Bush didn't immediately drop everything (he was visiting a children's school when notified of the attack) and rush to do something. The very same pundits would have implied something was wrong about how President Bush "panicked and fled" if he had immediately run from the school children, jumped on Air Force One, and headed to Washington.

One person's panic is another person's resolute action; one person's disinterest is another person's deliberate action in the face of a crisis.

MEDIA VERSUS BUSH

I think the Bush administration did about as good a job as could be done handling the 9/11 crisis. President Bush basically said: We are going to learn what happened, we are going to study matters, we are going to decide on an appropriate response, and we are going to enact that response. That's actually what leaders are supposed to do in time of crisis.

But we had a media that wanted dramatic, drastic action; they wanted to stampede into doing something — *anything* — but at the same time they were standing by to enthusiastically second-guess anything anyone did. The media even second-guessed itself — anything to fill the vast, uncertain, nervous emptiness between advertisements.

> " *The media even second-guessed itself — anything to fill the vast, uncertain, nervous emptiness between advertisements.* "

I recall one TV show where an expert was talking about horrible scenarios and how easily terrorists could do tremendous amounts of damage. One listener sent a feedback email asking if it was a good idea to discuss such things — whereupon the talking head who fielded the question proceeded to describe, "Oh, there's lots worse things I could have said! For example . . . blah blah blah." Another talking head was quick to take up the baton by asking, "Does the media sometimes err in what we divulge?" That's sort of like asking the town gossip to tell you which person in town talks too much. It was a relief to see that CNN at least implemented a policy of not reporting on operational details during the most recent Gulf War, when Geraldo Rivera revealing troop locations on live TV was more the kind of grandstanding I'd come to expect of the media.

IN A PERFECT WORLD

Poor government technology infrastructure, emergency response systems that don't extend to the general populace, and at-risk public buildings don't bode well for effective homeland security. What could make a difference?

ENSURING CYBER SECURITY

Cyber warfare, if it happens at all, is going to mostly damage systems that are insecure, poorly designed, and badly managed. The *single best* security technology for improving the attack resistance of a system or network is a good system administrator who understands security and is motivated to keep his or her systems safe. Unfortunately, we've come to accept poorly secured systems as a matter of course.

TAKING EMERGENCY RESPONSE SERIOUSLY

To me, emergency response is the one ray of hope in the whole homeland security mess. If you practice reacting sensibly to one kind of emergency, the discipline of the drill will stand you in good stead even in a completely different kind of emergency. Practiced responses go a tremendous way toward reducing the hand-flapping and hair-pulling that takes place during the first few minutes of a disaster. Indeed, if there's one expenditure in the entire homeland security budget that I support absolutely, it's the money set aside for more training opportunities and drills for first responders.

I'd even go so far as to say that we should consider establishing civilian emergency drills and procedures so that civilians learn the basics of their evacuation procedures and the basics of how to respond to the current threat models. Fire drills really *do* save lives. The same applies to computer security incident response: Teach people useful things to do in the event of a fast-spreading worm or virus, and suddenly it's a lot less of a panic and media circus. Of course, such drills and procedures must be well designed and presented to the public in a disciplined and thoughtful manner. And I'm not talking about having some idiot go on CNN to tell everyone to stock up on bottled water, tape, and plastic sheeting.

Another tremendously valuable side effect of performing response drills is that it teaches people *whom to listen to* in the event of a problem. Right now, most Americans wouldn't have a clue what to do if their local police told them one thing, CNN said a different thing, and the Department of Homeland Security told them another. One of the first things I remember from my grade-school fire drills was learning that "when there's a fire alarm going off, listen to the fireman." I'm terrified that if there is a severe national level incident, we'll get nothing but

> " 'We're from the government and we're here to help' is only comforting if it's not accompanied by contradicting messages from 15 different sources at once. "

conflicted messages and turf wars as various government entities try to stake their claim to being the ones best suited to help. "We're from the government and we're here to help" is only comforting if it's not accompanied by contradicting messages from 15 different sources at once.

2

A Multitude of Myths

I mproving the antiterror status of an entire country is a project that requires more than sound bites and posturing; it requires rethinking how we do a lot of things. The risk of failure is high; the media is always hungry for a disaster story to splash all over the evening news, and the enemy truly is unrelenting and doesn't play by the rules.

The people in the brave new homeland security world definitely have their work cut out for them. But with all that work to do, why does myth building seem to be the first thing on their agenda?

WHAT, EXACTLY, DOES HOMELAND SECURITY CONSIST OF?

People have a desire to make complicated things simple and simple things complicated. On one hand, the truly big problems (like securing a country the size of the United States) have so many variables our minds probably cannot comprehend them all. On the other hand, simple problems (like losing weight by burning more calories than you eat) seem to inspire far more complex answers than are really necessary.

Now that the problem of homeland security is a hot topic, we're going to be deluged with answers that are simple, obvious, and wrong. There is no *single* simple thing we can do to give our homeland security. There's no *single* place we can monitor to keep the bad guys out, nor a *single* thing we can do that will make it all right.

Take a look at some of the components of homeland security to understand how overwhelmingly difficult it will be to make significant progress in each of these areas.

THE MYTH OF THE SECURE CITY

If you think securing an airplane is hard, pause for a second and consider the differences between an airplane and a small city or even a single building. It is vastly easier to secure a plane than a town. Airplanes have one or two entry/exit points, while towns and buildings have many. Airplanes have a small number of people passing through them, relatively speaking, and all the passengers have at least arguably some kind of identifiable reason for being there. Not so with a city. If it weren't for the fact that terrorists make mistakes and get sloppy just like everyone else, we'd probably never make much progress in defending towns and public places.

Terrorists appear to fall prey to fads or get stuck in methodological ruts, just like nonideological serial killers. One result of this tendency is that their choice of targets and method of attack become recognizable over time, allowing the good guys to adapt their threat model. In fact, if it weren't for the fact that these bad guys become set in their ways, they'd probably be nearly impossible to defeat. From the terrorists' viewpoint, they want their methods to become a signature that helps identify them by their actions. If we ever ran up against terrorists who used different forms of attack against every target they attack, they would be extremely difficult to catch without resorting to long-term infiltration of their organizations.

You Get a Roll of Plastic, and Some Tape . . .

In 1995, Paris, France, was besieged with a series of bombs placed in public locales. The bombs were constructed with gas canisters and placed in touristy locations in wastebaskets; this scenario became a "signature" of the bomber and caused considerable reaction, primarily in a policy of sealing and removing public wastebaskets.

However, removing wastebaskets was an effective reaction to only a very small piece of the overall problem. In the larger scheme of things, what was to keep the bomber from putting the bombs someplace else?

Palestinian suicide bombers have raised the ante by making their own bodies the hiding place for explosives. In the wake of terrorist truck-bombs used against U.S. embassies and the Oklahoma City bombing, a number of buildings in the United States began to sport large landscape rocks and walls to prevent people from parking vehicles too close. For example, the Capitol in Washington, D.C., suddenly sprouted large concrete floral planters that block roads that go close to the building. That may help until the attackers decide to start hiding bombs in hot-dog carts pulled into building courtyards at lunchtime.

The National Security Agency's headquarters near Laurel, Maryland, grew an extra circle of landscaping rocks, each weighing about a ton, behind its chain-link fence. That probably will prevent someone crashing a truck full of explosives through the fence, but what about a truck full of explosives following a stolen bulldozer? Security, as many practitioners will tell you, is all about raising the bar to the highest practical level and no higher. Nothing will ever be perfect; we need to accept that sufficiently motivated attackers will always be able to outsmart a static defense.

When anonymous letters full of anthrax spores began to appear in the U.S. mails, letter handlers began wearing gloves and masks to open the mail. United Parcel Service and Federal Express package handlers did not. Reactive measures are only effective against the current fad in attacks, regardless of the logic of such a reaction. If terrorists take to using rocket-propelled grenades (RPGs) against buildings, expect buildings to begin sporting chain-link fences and expect the terrorists to almost immediately find another method of attack.

> " When anonymous letters full of anthrax spores began to appear in the U.S. mails, letter handlers began wearing gloves and masks to open the mail. United Parcel Service and Federal Express package handlers did not. "

Buildings and Cities at Risk

As you can see from the preceding examples, physical security on land is a problem somewhat akin to securing airplanes, except that, unlike an airplane, a typical building has a larger number of possible entrances. Usually, we only think of the entrances that are aboveground, but most urban targets also have a huge number of below-ground access points. Major urban areas such as New York or Paris have miles of underground passageways that lead from one building to another. The only identification that you need to prove that you belong down there is a telephone worker's uniform and a crowbar.

When you move from a single building to an entire city, the challenge becomes truly daunting. The 2002–2003 New Year's celebration in New York City was unmarred by terrorist incidents. According to statements from local law enforcement, tactical sharpshooters monitored the rooftops, and manhole covers within a certain radius of Times Square were temporarily welded shut. Presumably, other unspecified security measures were also put in place. All in all, New York City's response shows some signs of having been thought out fairly well; but once again the reaction was primarily against the known threat model.

When you start thinking about how to defend national monuments or large buildings against devoted attackers, it's hard not to get depressed. How do you deal with infiltrators on the cleaning staff? Do you check their trash carts for explosives? What do you do about the air-conditioning repairman? Do you examine the pressurized coolant canisters to make sure there are no anthrax spores? Do you require background checks on all the telephone maintenance workers, plumbers, and roofers? Are building managers willing to pay three to four times current prices for such services to cover the increased cost of performing background checks and hiring bonded firms that guarantee employees without criminal records? Would any of that actually help?

The Myth of the Sneaky Terrorist

When you hear law enforcement portraying the opposition as nearly inhumanly intelligent, that should be a warning to you that the cops are flailing in a sea of incompetence. Basically, nobody likes to admit that they were asleep at the switch — it's much more palatable to have been overcome by a deadly genius with overwhelming powers. Enter the myth of the sneaky terrorist.

Just How Smart Are These Guys?

In late December 2002, the FBI announced a nationwide alert involving several men suspected of having infiltrated the country through Canada. Several days later, the alert was cancelled. Apparently, the alert was triggered by an informant (a smuggler) who had purportedly

SECURITY 101

Security is all about understanding the benefit (if any) you gain depending on which steps you take. One of the fundamental dynamics of security is that what you're trying to do is to make the most *cost-effective* choices that provide the desired protections against an expected level of attack.

Figuring out the possible attacks and their severity, as well as possible responses, is part of a process called *risk assessment*. Basically, you weigh the damage that particular attacks would do against the likelihood of their success. This allows you to begin to prioritize your defenses appropriately. This mixture of threats and likelihoods is also sometimes referred to as a *threat model*. Essentially, it's the set of assumptions under which we're operating, and it's — by definition — based on only the things we can imagine. In other words, it's heavily dependent on past experience.

Another important thing to understand is the difference between *risk reduction* and *risk mitigation*. In the reduction case, you're accepting that something might still go wrong, but you are trying to reduce its likelihood. In the mitigation approach, you're trying to reduce that likelihood to zero. As you can imagine, the closer you want to put the likelihood of something going wrong to zero, the more expensive it is. That's why nuclear reactors are really expensive, whereas portable gas-powered generators are relatively affordable. The cost of failures in one case is a lot lower, as is the cost of basic safety protections.

When looking at failure modes, you can judge based on whether things go wrong in a favorable way or a disastrous way. The failure modes of a nuclear reactor are carefully constructed to tend to lead the system to fail in ways that are safer than the alternative. When we are thinking about homeland security, the *fail-closed* security approach would have us favor restricting access to a "need to be there" basis: If you don't know who someone is and can't ascertain whether he's a threat, don't let him near the building or on the plane. The *fail-open* security approach accepts that we'll just have to fall victim to periodic successful attacks before we can update our threat model.

helped the infiltrators across the border. The FBI later concluded that the informant had made the story up in order to get off the hook for a charge of smuggling. Why would terrorists really feel the need to hire smugglers to get into the United States from Canada when they could steal or otherwise obtain a passport from a visa waiver country? On one hand, it's nice to see the FBI is looking at new threat models for how terrorists might enter the country, but on the other, you've got to wonder why they went public with such a tenuous lead.

The truth is that the terrorists do *not* show signs of being all that smart. Osama bin Laden, the terrorist mastermind, used to use a satellite telephone to carry out regular conversations with family and friends. At the National Security Agency's headquarters in Ft. Meade, Maryland, tapes of bin Laden were a popular "show and tell" item for VIP visitors.

Bin Laden relied on the satellite system for years until word that he was being watched and tracked leaked out. In terms of espionage, that oversight is *not* supersmart and sophisticated. You might think that an evil genius like bin Laden would have done a little research on his enemy's capabilities before selecting his phone service. (Then again, what does it say about our own team's abilities that when bin Laden escaped from the mountains of Tora Bora, it was apparently thanks in part to one of his bodyguards acting as a decoy by carrying a satellite telephone.)

Don't Blame Us: He's Just So Brilliant

In the computer security arena, where I come from, the FBI constantly panders to the press by portraying the hackers they are up against as "brilliant" or "geniuses" or "whiz kids." In fact, a lot of the hackers are simply persistent and are going up against defenses that are incredibly weak and poorly maintained.

How smart, exactly, were the 9/11 terrorists? Now that facts are coming to light about their activities leading up to the attack, it seems kind of amazing that they weren't caught. Why did we fail? Because senior FBI field agents raised red flags about people trying to learn how to fly 747s but not land them, and senior bureaucrats in the FBI's Washington headquarters told them to be quiet and forget about the whole thing.

Bin Laden has now "gone low-tech" according to experts and security pundits. The same pundits, mind you, who probably blathered about how the NSA was listening in on his satellite phone and who warned him off in the first place. It's hard to tell who's the stupidest operative in the flock of turkeys that's flapping around the whole terrorist debacle.

Silent throughout most of this are the real spies: the KGB, NSA, CIA, and so on. Those folks understand operational security, deep cover, and covert communications. Compare how the Soviet spies operating within the United States handled their communications with how Al Qaeda operates, and you'll get a better idea what the FBI is *really* up against.

KGB agents frequently communicated with their handlers by leaving messages in carefully prearranged locations, hidden in innocuous-looking objects. Field agents' handlers were often protected against the agent's being compromised by a level of "cut-outs" — individuals who didn't know the contents of the messages they were carrying but who were responsible for carrying the unopened message from one delivery point to another.

> 66 *The terrorists aren't sneaky, or even brilliant. They're just smarter than the FBI.* 99

Real spies use encryption, not satellite telephones and clear communications. Real spies disguise themselves as innocuously as possible; they don't appear on videotapes at terrorist training camps firing AK-47s into the air. Real spies, not coincidentally, are a hell of a lot harder to catch than terrorists. The terrorists aren't sneaky, or even brilliant. They're just smarter than the FBI.

CYBER SECURITY: THE MYTH OF THE FIREWALL

Computer security is another area where there has been a great deal of hype, specifically surrounding cyber attacks. Largely, cyber terrorism is a nonthreat, which is a good thing, because most organizations' defenses are essentially vaporous.

Internet firewalls consist of a technology designed to block and mediate access between a private "secure" network and a public network like the Internet. Most organizations install a firewall and forget about security because it's now a solved problem. The situation is reminiscent of the U.S. taxpayer, who knows there are border patrols and the INS and hears about deportation, but doesn't realize that the INS has lost track of hundreds of thousands of deportees within our own borders.

The typical computer network's security is comparable. Once you get behind the firewall, you'll find a large loosely managed network of computers with secret data available to anyone who gains access.

The Mess behind the Wall

In security audits of corporate networks, I've generally found that every single system on the network can reach every other one to a sufficient degree that a clever computer user could access significant data with a little effort. That means if you walk into the lobby and borrow the receptionist's system, you can access the mainframe in the basement. Usually, if you look in the receptionist's desk, you'll find the necessary password written on a Post-it note someplace. Like the mythical sneaky

terrorist, it doesn't take a great deal of skill to be a sneaky cyber ninja:
You just walk in the door.

Hackers call this "social engineering" — the art of appearing to
belong where you don't so that you can get your victim to grant you
levels of access you don't deserve. Many of the current crop of hacking
tools combine social engineering with other forms of attack. The sim-
plest and nastiest I've seen lately is a fake email that claims to come from
customer service at eBay.com. The email asks the recipient to please
click on the URL below to verify and update their account information. The URL, of course, asks the victim to provide his or her eBay user
ID, password, and credit card number. Similar hacking tools convince
the victim to run an executable file, then tunnel out through network
firewalls from behind, allowing the hacker an easy portal through even
the best-configured corporate security.

Another example of technology that topples the network firewall is
wireless networks. Recent advances in networking have made wireless
networks extremely popular, giving rise to a new fad among hackers
called "war driving." When war driving, hackers drive around with a
wireless computer searching for new base stations that are not secured.
It doesn't require brilliance, just patience, electricity, and gasoline. Typically, a war drive through a busy high-tech area will yield dozens of
accessible networks full of interesting materials to browse.

So, what's the point of having a firewall if you've got wireless
networks? You might just as easily ask what's the point of having a
border patrol if anyone can get a visa by asking nicely. The answer to
both questions is, because it offers the appearance of security; and the
appearance is all we can afford because the substance is too expensive.

It's Not My Job

Many organizations that set up firewalls never communicate the basics of
preparedness to their employees. They never tell them what they need to
do to keep the network secure. Or, worse yet, they may delegate authority for bits and pieces of the entire network's security to individual
departments.

Imagine how secure a national border would be if each airport
could implement its own passport controls, issue its own visas, and
perform its own customs baggage checks.

That kind of random chaos is what a typical large corporate
network resembles. There may be a dozen firewalls, one at each point
connecting to the Internet, but each firewall is configured differently

and managed by a different security administrator. Each administrator may have discretion for the security policy (the passport checks and baggage checks of the networking world) on their own access point. On top of that, local administrators can bury the cost of a $100 wireless access point in their budget and open up a wireless border that has no security at all, anytime they like.

When an organization gets hacked, there is almost always a renewed interest in security, and a crackdown on the access point by which the hackers gained ingress. Does this sound similar to the national security approach post–9/11? It should. Building a secure network is a complex problem requiring strong fundamental designs and a great deal of discipline and common sense. All three of those things are lacking in Washington, D.C.

> " *Building a secure network is a complex problem requiring strong fundamental designs and a great deal of discipline and common sense. All three of those things are lacking in Washington, D.C.* "

THE LAMEST OF THE LAME: GOVERNMENT SYSTEMS COMPUTER SECURITY

Some of the worst computer security in the world is that used by the U.S. federal government. Amazingly, many people in the private sector believe it is good — or at least better than it really is. That's because Hollywood almost always represents government (CIA and NSA computers, particularly) as supersecure, with capabilities right out of science fiction novels, and because law enforcement represents hackers as a whole lot more skilled than they really are.

Real computer security experts get a chuckle out of movies like *Mission Impossible* in which the computers are protected with elaborately layered defenses: Most really important government data can be found on clunky last-generation PCs, usually running an older version of Microsoft Windows. KGB mole Aldrich Ames pillaged some of the country's most sensitive secrets off of exactly such systems — nothing like what you see in Hollywood's productions.

The reality of the computer security scene is *not* a bunch of brilliant cyber ninjas going after heavily defended government systems. The real-

ity is a bunch of bored teenagers using well-known attacks against poorly
defended systems managed by undertrained and poorly motivated civil
servants. These are the same civil servants whose main defenders are
undertrained computer-illiterate FBI agents who regularly confuse the
Internet with AOL and often barely know how to use email.

THE GOVERNMENT AND TECHNOLOGY OXYMORON

One area of government security that is confusing is the separation
between *classified* systems and *sensitive but unclassified* (SBU) systems.
Whenever CNN reports that hackers broke into Pentagon/military systems, the response is invariably "We have closed the hole. This was not
a significant attack because no classified materials were accessed." What
nobody ever seems to acknowledge is that the government's logistical
systems, payroll systems, military purchasing and planning, shipping,
medical, enlistment, and similar systems are all SBU. In other words, that
stuff is just as important as the classified stuff; it's just not classified.

Administrators of classified computers have special rules for how the
data they maintain is accessed and managed. In order to get to those systems, you need the proper clearances. But classified systems have still had
serious security problems, and usually those problems are the result of
insiders.

Former CIA Director John Deutch downloaded unspecified classified
materials to his home computer in order to make it easier to work from
home. President Clinton issued him a presidential pardon to prevent further digging into this embarrassing issue. A lower-level civil servant would
have faced criminal charges for such deliberate violations of security rules.

you should know

The option to getting proper clearances is to be a KGB mole like Aldrich
Ames, who, once he had access to CIA's classified systems, was able to download and sell huge amounts of information. In fact, the data Ames accessed
was so classified that nobody appears to know what he was able to download and CIA had to negotiate with Ames to learn just how badly he had
screwed them.

It is on sensitive but unclassified systems where the government's
security is truly woeful. The Pentagon's network has been compromised
by teenaged hackers literally dozens of times in the last 10 years. Of
course, none of those attacks was acknowledged as significant because no

"classified" materials were accessed.

In a recent incident, hackers demonstrated to the *New York Times* that they could hack into military logistics computers and arrange the purchase and shipment of parts, including vehicle components and weapons parts.

> ❝ *The Pentagon's network has been compromised by teenaged hackers literally dozens of times in the last 10 years.* ❞

One would expect that after a few incidents such as this, there would be an overall housecleaning in the network's security. In fact, what usually happens is that a scapegoat is found and the situation continues as before.

you should know

I don't know about the last few years, but as recently as 1996 I know the Pentagon's backbone network was un-firewalled and accessible to the Internet. I'm surprised that the 14-year-olds even thought it was enough of a challenge to break into.

BLAME IT ON THE WEB

Federal government computing has made the news in the area of security over and over again in the last 10 years, as federal agencies have explored the possibilities of the Internet.

The Department of the Interior's Bureau of Indian Affairs was ordered to take its computers off the Internet. This occurred after comprehensive audits related to a court case found that the Bureau was in contempt of court by not correcting egregious security flaws they had been aware of for years.

Recently, Secretary of Defense Donald Rumsfeld issued a directive that government agencies need to be more careful about what they publish on the Web so as not to aid terrorists. This was in response to a constant problem the feds discovered: Al Qaeda had plans for this building, or that landmark, or the other military communications system, all downloaded from helpful government sites.

But blaming the Web is silly; this is the same approach the FBI used when it announced that Timothy McVeigh had probably gotten his

---

ATTEN...TION!

Back in the early 1990s when I was doing an information-gathering survey on government Web sites, I found the complete training materials for U.S. Army field intelligence officers, available for anonymous download from Fort Huachuca, Arizona. If Osama bin Laden had access to that material, his insomnia would have been cured forever.

Basically, the government is rediscovering what it should have known all along: Loose lips sink ships. And data from loose lips travels very fast and anonymously over the Internet. Just so you can sleep tonight, you'll be glad to know that the materials were taken down a few years ago.

---

bomb-making knowledge off the Internet. Didn't they know that the Government Printing Office used to offer a handy printed pamphlet on making high explosive fuel/nitrogen mixtures such as were used in the Oklahoma City bombing?

No Simple Solutions

Why is government computer security so bad? Unfortunately, it's a complex problem and there is no single place you can point to as a root cause.

During the 1990s anyone with information technology skills was likely to hear the siren call of a 30 percent raise if he or she moved over to the private sector to take a job with a dot-com. The remaining information technology managers in the federal sector were either dedicated civil servants or people who had taken the job in order to boost their résumé with some on-the-job training so that they could go to a dot-com in a few years.

> **" The government's computer systems resemble a hodgepodge of incompatible networks, each a separate fiefdom with its own rules and security practices. "**

Additionally, government computing is bereft of standard practices, except in handling classified materials. So, organizations pretty much do what they feel is appropriate, whether it is or not. Some, like the Bureau of Indian Affairs, do nothing about security and claim they lack the budget. Others have fairly good security. But all in all the government's computer systems resemble a hodgepodge of incompatible networks, each a separate fiefdom with its own rules and security practices.

you should know

In the military, there is also a lack of standards. This is made worse by the fact that, as enlisted personnel rotate through duty stations, they know that they need to just hold things together for a couple of years and it'll be someone else's problem. In nonmilitary agencies there are always contractors to blame: contractors who are happy to fix the problem in return for a fat contract.

Please don't believe the Hollywood images of how government computer security works. Next time you see Tom Cruise hanging over a pressure-sensitive floor in *Mission Impossible*, picture instead Aldrich Ames calmly sitting at a terminal downloading megabytes of data and walking out of the building with it stored on a floppy. Next time you hear about brilliant hacker whiz kids, just picture the kids you sometimes see at arcades who go and hit the coin return button on every vending machine: Sooner or later they get a couple of quarters.

Computer security isn't rocket science; it's just that those who don't do it very well want you to think it is so they can cover up the fact that they don't even handle the basics right.

IN A PERFECT WORLD

Keeping safe in an imperfect world requires a lot of different efforts, including civilian involvement in emergency response and better government information security. Promulgating myths doesn't help. What could?

PROTECTING OURSELVES

What can we do about all the buildings, monuments, and cities? Honestly — not much. Telling people that the terrorism alert level is *orange* today is a complete waste of time because it doesn't convey any sense of purposeful action. Perhaps, when we're at code orange or higher, we should have weekly evacuation drills or civilian response drills. The bottom line here is that if we want to implement civil defense, we need to get our civilian populace involved.

I'm always hesitant to look at Israel as an example of how to do things, but the truth is that their civilian populace is *involved*. Many of the suicide bombers that detonate themselves off-target have done so because someone noticed they were acting suspiciously and grabbed them or called the police. I hope and pray that the U.S. civilian populace

SOCIAL ENGINEERING: THE ART OF JUST WALKING IN

When you "social engineer" someone, you fool them into granting you access based on telling them what you think they want to hear. Famous hacker Kevin Mitnick talks about social engineers who would get Pacific Bell telephone operations staff to change numbers or give them access to systems by calling the private maintenance numbers and telling them "I'm 25 feet up a pole right now and can't get to my equipment; can you put a change through for me, please?" Because the hackers were calling on the right line, had a plausible excuse, and weren't threatening, they usually got their way. (Kevin has recently published *The Art of Deception* from Wiley Publishing, Inc. — a provocative and interesting account of some techniques of social engineering.)

Along those same lines, a terrorist showing up and asking for asylum in the United States would probably get it, especially if he said he was fleeing prosecution by Al Qaeda. He might even get a protective detail and a limousine.

Social engineering *always* works best against large, decentralized target organizations that do not coordinate communications internally. This applies whether the target is a corporation or a government agency. One of the popular techniques of social engineers is to call one department or branch and get a name and title of a key person, then use that name and title to convince somebody at another department that they're legitimate. Then they just ask for information the person they are impersonating would have a right to obtain, such as how to access the department network from their laptop computer.

So how do we prevent social engineering as a way of improving our homeland security? It's a nearly impossible task, unless you're part of an organization where responsibilities are very clearly delineated and there are no across-organization authorities you can appeal to.

is never involved to the point that the average Israeli is — the emotional and political scars are appalling and will last for decades.

IMPROVING OUR GOVERNMENT'S IT

The way to defend against information warfare is to shut up about it and start demanding that our government's computers and critical infrastructure be maintained at even a *minimal* level of security. It's been tried before — attempts to mandate computing standards for secure computing have all failed in the past. It's time to stop playing around and start

3

The Politics of Homeland Security

Somehow I have gotten on a "homeland security" conference's emailing list. About once a month I get invitations to attend this important conference: "The Grants Workshop will provide the attendee with important information about federal agency plans for over $3 billion in grants to first responders for training, communications, and outfitting. Attendees will learn where the funding is located, how to apply for and win grants, and how to survive the audit process." In other words, it's an entire conference devoted to teaching Beltway bandits and bandwagon-jumpers how to get their slice of the homeland security pork.

As you can surmise from the title, this chapter looks at politics. Like many people, I am uncomfortable with simplistic models of politics that suggest there are only two legitimate points of view. Reality isn't that simple; why should people insist on polarizing even the most centrist issues?

For that reason I like to avoid writing about politics because it tends to obscure issues behind party ideologies. I'm nonideological, so as you read this don't try to shoehorn my views by thinking "Marcus must be a closet Republican/Democrat." In fact, I hold views at both ends and the middle of the political spectrum.

So, for the rest of this book, I will try to avoid references to political parties and pay attention to the *significance* of individuals' actions and motivations.

Really, that's all that matters anyway.

A POLITICAL FOOTBALL FROM DAY ONE

Most Americans probably don't realize that the Bush administration didn't come up with the idea for the Department of Homeland Security. It was one of those political footballs that took on a life of its own until it could not be ignored.

HOMELAND SECURITY — HMMM...HOW WOULD THAT WORK?

Senator Joseph Lieberman proposed the Department of Homeland Security in October 2001, following the 9/11 attacks, as a crucial action that should be taken to help protect the country against further terror threats. The White House initially rejected the proposal, but responded with its own plan to establish a DHS in June 2002. The first shots in a long drawn-out war of wrangling had begun.

Should we automatically assume that the original proposal was politically motivated? We can never know. But we can ascribe a lot of the subsequent twists and turns in the DHS story to pure politics. For one thing, the proposal for DHS had come from one of President Bush's opponents in the last presidential election, and a likely potential candidate against Bush for the 2004 election.

> **" Basically, Lieberman's proposal created an infinite opportunity for second-guessing without having to actually take any responsibility for implementation. "**

Certainly, if Lieberman's proposal was politically motivated, it was a brilliant maneuver, because it forced the President to take on the issue while leaving him open to attack if DHS turned out to be less than successful. Basically, it created an infinite opportunity for second-guessing without having to actually take any responsibility for implementation — a "can't miss" situation for any politician.

BUSH PROPOSES

Initially, the creation of DHS was cast as a reorganization of existing capabilities, not an increase in the size of government. The timing of this announcement coincided with increasing criticism of the Bush administration for not acting on the homeland security issue, since appointing Tom Ridge (the former governor of Pennsylvania) as head of the Office of Homeland Security in November 2001.

The initial proposal from the President was vague and did not outline exactly which agencies and capabilities would fall under the new department. Presidential press secretary Ari Fleischer said the Office of Homeland Security would include elements of several government agencies and that it would take over border and transportation security and biological and chemical weapons defense of the homeland. This shift would also create a section to organize and analyze intelligence about potential attacks against the United States.

In the meantime, there were already other maneuvers under way: Namely, the USA PATRIOT Act, spearheaded by Attorney General John Ashcroft.

THE PATRIOT ACT: WHEN TOO MUCH IS JUST ENOUGH

PATRIOT stands for "Provide Appropriate Tools Required to Intercept and Obstruct Terrorism," a mouthful even for acronym-loving Washington.

The details of the birth of this act are today overshadowed by the controversy it has engendered. Here's a quick review of how it came about:

- A week after 9/11, Attorney General John Ashcroft met with House and Senate leadership to discuss the administration's views regarding new antiterrorism legislation.
- On September 24, 2001, the House Judiciary Committee held hearings on an early form of PATRIOT that was called the "Antiterrorism Act of 2001."
- After its formal introduction by Congressman James Sensenbrenner on October 2, it was passed October 25 and signed into law by President Bush the next day.

The PATRIOT Act was literally rammed through by lawmakers. For a law that later became so controversial to zip through the legislative process as it did is a testament to our elected leaders' desire to *do something* about terrorism. I suspect there was an awareness on their part that if the PATRIOT Act didn't go through quickly, they'd be tarred and feathered as "dragging their feet" on an important piece of antiterrorist legislation.

First Impressions

The public hue and cry about PATRIOT was immediate: The ACLU, librarians, and privacy advocates lambasted the new law as a first horrifying step on the way to a police state. But what really happened as a result of passing this act?

PATRIOT did two things: It furthered law enforcement's domestic surveillance agenda, and it rolled back a number of protections of personal privacy. For example, prior to the PATRIOT Act, school enrollment records were protected against access by the Department of Justice. So were many business records: It required a subpoena to get library records or bookstore purchase histories, for example. The act also considerably broadened law enforcement's powers to wiretap individuals who associated with suspected terrorist organizations.

In the face of a terrorist attack like 9/11, such broadened powers made sense. In fact, they probably made sense and would conceivably have helped fight terrorism prior to 9/11, had they been used effectively. What annoys me about the PATRIOT Act is the way it was passed.

Law enforcement has had a history of focusing on key legislative "wish-list" items and trying to grab them at each new opportunity, and the PATRIOT Act was opportunity knocking. For example, the FBI has been dying for a chance to "adjust" the country's laws so that it can more easily perform large-scale trawling through email.

Of course, what the FBI has been angling for all along is *blanket increases* in its authority to collect email. In fact, there are indications that in the past, the FBI has possibly played fast and loose with its *existing* capabilities for email traffic interception. A system code-named CARNIVORE was developed for the FBI's use in email collection and became public knowledge in 1999. Predictably, there were a lot of technical questions regarding CARNIVORE's capabilities. The FBI claimed CARNIVORE was only used with proper search warrants and that it only collected email from authorized targets. Technically knowledgeable computer networking specialists, however, pointed out that a system like CARNIVORE could easily perform very broad searches with no changes in its basic software.

you should know

I remember in the early days of the Internet explosion, FBI Director Louis Freeh was constantly harping on the threat of terrorists using email. Later, it became child pornographers and terrorists. While it is now apparent that some of the 9/11 terrorists and Richard Reid may have used email, it is very clear that child pornographers are much greater users of email than terrorists.

The FBI classified and obfuscated the details of CARNIVORE's function, and waited for the entire issue to go away, as it eventually did. 9/11 solved that problem for the FBI; under the PATRIOT Act, law enforcement has considerably expanded powers for surveillance. Included within the PATRIOT Act is the

> *" Included within the PATRIOT Act is the authority for the FBI to force businesses to turn over records on customers or clients. "*

authority for the FBI to force businesses to turn over records on customers or clients, including access to data on customer reading habits from bookstores and libraries.

you should know

During the Clinton/Lewinsky scandal there was an attempt to access records of Ms. Lewinsky's book purchases at a local bookstore. Presumably, this power got added to the "wish list" and tacked onto the PATRIOT Act.

SURVEILLANCE STATE?

The American Civil Liberties Union and privacy advocates see PATRIOT as a step along the path toward a surveillance state. PATRIOT expands exceptions to normal requirements to show probable cause in wiretapping; there is no longer any real need to show reasonable suspicion of criminal activity. More worrisome for civil libertarians, PATRIOT allows the government to conduct secret searches without informing the subject until long after the search has been executed.

Admittedly, these abilities are powerful tools that can be useful in cracking down on terrorists; they could also be useful for cracking down on whistle-blowers or political opponents, as happened during the Nixon administration and under the FBI of J. Edgar Hoover's time.

Unfortunately, surveillance and counterintelligence are two of the best tools for uncovering and countering terrorists. When you're dealing with organizations that are structured to resist infiltration, such as terrorist cells, it's *necessary* to be able to initiate secret surveillance and possibly secret searches, so that you can learn who contacts whom and when. The trick is to keep the net from getting flung so widely that innocent people's lives are ruined in the process.

This is an increasingly difficult trick when everything becomes computerized, information is widely shared, and the government's computers are involved. How many times have we heard about Internal Revenue Service employees being disciplined for accessing the private records of the rich and famous? How many instances have there been of Motor Vehicle Administration records being sold to credit bureaus, insurance companies, or private detectives? What will law enforcement do to compartmentalize information internally so that terrorists cannot tip each other off if they see traces that their coconspirators are under suspicion and are being investigated? These are problems that the intelligence community has had to deal with for a long time, and they aren't easy problems to solve. We want to allow our enforcers the powers they need without giving them free reign to create a police state.

AT A PRICE

The climate after 9/11 also provided a nearly unlimited excuse to ask for more money. PATRIOT included $200 million in additional emergency funding for the FBI. This money was provided to "support and enhance the technical and tactical operations" of the agency. This is the same agency that *already* had an Osama bin Laden task force of 26 people *prior* to 9/11. Apparently, more than support and enhancement is needed at the FBI.

PATRIOT did a few other things that were even more questionable. First, it amplified the Bank Secrecy Act to allow the federal government an even better window into people's financial relationships with their banks. The Bank Secrecy Act requires banks to report cash transactions of

> "This is the same agency that already had an Osama bin Laden task force of 26 people prior to 9/11. Apparently more than support and enhancement is needed at the FBI."

greater than $10,000. I'm still not sure why "Secrecy" enters into the name of the act, since it's primarily an attempt to prevent people from keeping gambling winnings, drug profits, and other windfalls secret.

you should know

Apparently, someone in the government has a degree in marketing, or is a master of Orwellian doublethink, to call a law that removes secrecy a "secrecy act."

The PATRIOT Act extends the large cash transaction reporting requirement to apply to most businesses. Money laundering *is* a serious problem, but the 9/11 terrorists were not laundering money. They never engaged in an activity that would have caused them to be reported under the Bank Secrecy Act. So what's going on?

In my opinion, law enforcement saw the events of 9/11 as a good lever to help them push through something they have wanted for a long time. It worked. Now every organization (loan offices, pawn shops, brokerages, travel agencies, horse traders, and vehicle sellers) must have anti–money-laundering procedures and practices in place or risk being put out of business. Fundamentally, piggybacking one agenda atop antiterrorist legislation is deceptive, and it treats the citizens of the United States as dupes. Sure, it happens all the time, but that doesn't make it right.

DOMESTIC TROUBLES

The main concern civil libertarians raise about PATRIOT is that it permits the Secretary of State to designate foreign *or domestic branches of foreign* groups as "terrorist," thereby unlocking a lot of legal artillery that can be used against those groups.

Under PATRIOT, organizations that have ever resorted to violence can be targeted, and individuals assisting those organizations may be deported. I'm not sure how much of a threat deportation is, given the sorry state of the Immigration and Naturalization Service (INS), but it'd be a shame to be made an example of for having donated money to, for example, People for Ethical Treatment of Animals or an anti-abortion group.

There is no notification requirement for changing the status of an organization. If the Secretary of State decided tomorrow that the ACLU was a terrorist organization, none of its financial supporters would have any way of anticipating that they could instantly be considered enemies of the state.

It gets worse: This terrorist status can be applied retroactively. Ten years from now, someone might be deported for having donated to an organization that later changed its methods and resorted to violence, or splintered into several organizations, one of which resorted to violence. Basically, this provision of PATRIOT amounts to "guilt by association," which is a dangerous legal precedent and is something we hoped the United States had put behind us following McCarthyism.

I HAVE A LITTLE LIST...

On December 21, 2001, the Secretary of State issued a list of 39 organizations that were designated as terrorist. On the surface, it's a pretty good list, including organizations like Hizbulla and the Continuity Irish Republican Army. So, is this list of terrorist groups vital to our national security and are the civil libertarians just a bunch of whining leftists who need to shut up and stop impeding the war on terror? It's hard to tell.

There are precedents for misusing legislation aimed at the bad guys. The Racketeer Influenced and Corrupt Organizations (RICO) Act of 1970, for example, was aimed at organized crime, but has been used against anti-abortion activists. Several members of Operation Rescue, an anti-abortion movement, were found guilty on 21 counts of extortion. Regardless of how you feel about the abortion debate, I think it's pretty clear that, in this case, RICO was stretched a bit from its original purpose.

Without too much creative thinking, one could see how PATRIOT could eventually be used as a means of mass-deporting entire groups that become unpopular at a later date. You might think "but that couldn't happen here" — until you realize that a lot of Germans probably thought the same thing in the late 1930s.

PATRIOT AND IMMIGRANTS

PATRIOT also permits indefinite detention of immigrants without charging them for a terrorist-related crime. Basically, the way it works is that if Joe Immigrant is detained and the Attorney General chooses not to charge him with a terrorism-related crime, *but* Joe has a visa status problem (such as an overstayed visa) and his country doesn't want to take him back, he can be tossed into a bureaucratic limbo where he can languish for a very long time at the public's expense.

There has been a lot of commentary on this issue; media coverage regarding the negative effects of the PATRIOT Act has focused on students who were questioned and detained, or "innocent" illegal aliens who had been detained because their visas had expired.

The concerns, however, are real: Nobody likes being questioned by people in uniform. A lot of the concern may be motivated by fear for the well-being of our domestic tourism industry or the side effects on labor costs if summer workers from Mexico cannot get employment visas. There are so many special and contradictory interests that it's extremely hard to figure out who is genuinely concerned about the moral plight of innocent immigrants, and who is concerned about the potential impact of the PATRIOT Act on their wallets.

In fact, a lot of people voice concern that PATRIOT indicates the beginning of a police state. What a lot of people seem to be ignoring is that illegal aliens or people who've overstayed their visas are committing a federal crime. It's certainly not the same as being a terrorist — but come on, already! — it's not the same as being completely innocent, either. There are a lot of countries in the world where you can be "disappeared" for smaller crimes; I think the United States is incredibly forgiving on this particular issue.

> " What a lot of people seem to be ignoring is that illegal aliens or people who've overstayed their visas are committing a federal crime. "

Many illegal aliens cannot be repatriated because their home countries *won't take them back*. A lot of them are nasty individuals you wouldn't want in your neighborhood. For example, of the 40,000 criminals Fidel Castro allowed to "emigrate" from Cuba, several thousand settled in Union City, New Jersey, and were responsible for nearly one third of the felonies committed in that area during the mid-1980s.

In the city of San Diego 26 percent of all burglary arrests and 12 percent of all felony arrests involve illegal aliens, who are estimated to compose less than 4 percent of the total city population; yet these individuals are seldom deported, or if they are, they return quickly to our country.

It's extremely hard to sort out what's going on, because most of the sources of information on this topic have some kind of axe to grind. Both sides of the issue emphasize only the information that supports their viewpoint, rather than keep an evenhanded perspective.

CLOSING THE OPEN GOVERNMENT

The Freedom of Information Act has often been used to investigate the doings of the Federal Government. FOIA was enacted following some of the more egregious secret activities of the intelligence community during the 1950s and 1960s. Shadowy actions by the intelligence community and the FBI led to a justified concern that there was insufficient transparency in the actions of the government. FOIA allows a citizen to request information and documents from federal agencies, and to receive those documents promptly and accurately except where the information is classified.

Part of the purpose of the FOIA was to allow an individual to see what information the government kept on him or her, as well as to access other public records. Primarily, FOIA was a reaction to the fear many Americans had of J. Edgar Hoover's notorious FBI files: Nobody knew what was being kept on whom, and it seemed like the best solution was to allow citizens to request copies of their own files.

you should know

I tried to find any history of a terrorist using the FOIA to get his or her FBI record, but it doesn't appear to have happened.

Of course, the agency receiving an FOIA request has a certain amount of leeway regarding how the request is fulfilled. I've seen documents returned from National Security Agency FOIA requests that have 90 percent of the text marked over to make it unreadable. In past administrations, however, FOIA has been taken seriously and has been an invaluable tool for historians, researchers, and hobbyists who like to learn about the government's activities. Indeed, the Clinton administration made a considerable push to declassify a large number of previously classified documents (mostly from WWII and the early Cold War) for historians and researchers. Prior to 9/11 the climate for FOIA was pretty favorable.

Attorney General John Ashcroft released a Freedom of Information Act memo in October 2001, explaining how the administration should interpret FOIA requests. The memo could be interpreted as encouraging agencies to default to withholding information as long as there is a sound legal basis for doing so. The previous FOIA memo, from former Attorney General Janet Reno, implied that unless there was foreseeable harm, the Justice Department would not defend an agency's choice to withhold information. This shift in position actually concerns me more than the PATRIOT Act, because it's highly likely that with an open government, abuses will eventually come to light. Cutting back on FOIA means it's easier for the government to abuse PATRIOT and cover its tracks. That is a worrisome combination.

What most of us forget is that we're surrounded by history as its happening; future generations will have a more distant perspective with, hopefully, better, or at least different, information with which to reconstruct events. Just as our understanding of the Bay of Pigs operation during the Kennedy administration is profoundly different from most American's view of it at the time, I suspect that political historians of the year 2050 will have a different view of PATRIOT and FOIA in the mid–twenty-first century.

> **" The trick is to make sure that there is still a United States of America in 2050, and that it's still the 'land of the free and home of the brave.' "**

The trick is to make sure that there is still a United States of America in 2050 and that it's still the "land of the free and home of the brave."

PASSING THE HOMELAND SECURITY ACT

It's a given that anything that happens in Washington, D.C., is going to be political, especially if it involves billions of dollars in expenditures. Homeland security is no different.

Homeland security represents the biggest reorganization of government since WWII. In the face of that reorganization the feds are acting just like department heads in a company undergoing a merger/takeover: Everyone is jockeying for position to make sure that his or her position is safe and that the layoffs happen to their enemies.

But within the chaos, just how did the Homeland Security Act, which started its life as a 35-page document, turn into a pork-laden political football? Whose political agenda does it serve? And how did all that pork ever pass through Congress?

PORK AND TAXES

As mentioned earlier in this chapter, the first version of the Homeland Security Act (H.R. 5710) was 35 pages long. By the time everybody had thrown his or her interests into the balance, it finished weighing in at 485 pages.

Piggybacking various agendas in a popular bill is normal in our political process, but it makes you wonder how many of our elected representatives actually *read* 485 pages of bureaucratese before voting for or against it.

There are lots of parts that appear to have been added to appease someone with a particular axe to grind. For example, there's section 601: Treatment of Charitable Trusts for Members of the Armed Forces and Other Governmental Agencies. Section 601 consists of pages 208 to 215 and describes how Johnny Spann Patriot Trusts are to be administered.

Johnny Spann was the CIA officer killed in Afghanistan early during the operations within that country in 2002, which made him an instant hero. What does the Johnny Spann Patriot Trust have to do with improving homeland security? Well, it's hard to tell. It appears to have more to do with improving the financial security of certain people. Basically, this trust allows the creation of tax sheltered charitable funds, a nice benefit for the wealthy. Charitable trusts allow the wealthy to generate income and avoid capital gains taxes by giving valuable assets to a charity, and then receiving a "management fee" of up to 15 percent from the charity for managing those assets. Over the lifetime of a charitable trust, it's possible to make more money than the original endowment.

you should know

Basically, this clause in the Homeland Security Act allows the wealthy to pocket an extra 5 percent in the name of Johnny Spann, a government agent who died in the line of duty.

For example, if you put $100,000 into a charitable trust, under a private foundation that invests it in something that returns 10 percent per year, in seven years, the trust will have $200,000. Then, as manager of the trust, you can begin to pay yourself 15 percent, or $30,000/year while the principal of the trust continues to grow. You've also got relief from various taxes. It's a tax shelter that has allowed a lot of wealthy families to avoid inheritance taxes and large capital gains taxes.

This portion of the act is *not* about securing our homeland from terrorism. You can easily guess why it's buried in the middle of the document, where most readers will have already fallen asleep before they get to it. Thus, our lawmakers act to protect our country — the well-to-do parts, anyhow. By naming it for Johnny Spann, it's an act of patriotism, so if someone like me points out that it's a tax shelter, he can be accused of being "unpatriotic" for attacking a charity that was intended for the poor widows and orphans of civil servants and soldiers.

Certainly, the Spann charitable trusts will eventually put money in hands that appreciate it, but in the meantime Congress is up to its usual sneaky tricks, hiding behind a mockery of patriotism.

> **" *Congress is up to its usual sneaky tricks, hiding behind a mockery of patriotism.* "**

SQUABBLING GALORE

There was considerable posing and posturing in Congress about the Homeland Security Act and the pork hidden within it prior to its passage. But exactly how much pork was there and where was it hidden? Typical of Washington, the resulting law still has plenty of pork in it, in spite of all the complaints. I'm sure if you challenged a congressperson on the issue, he or she would explain that some "compromises were necessary in order to get such an important piece of legislation completed," the compromises in question being the congressperson's morals.

First and most striking, none of the posturing about pork mentioned the new charitable trusts, because everyone, Democrat or Republican, has wealthy friends or wealth of their own. No, they found other things to point at and squabble about.

The main topics of debate centered on these three issues:

- Liability protection for drug companies against litigation related to drugs produced or deployed for antiterror activities
- Liability protection for technology companies producing antiterror products that have been approved by the Secretary of the Department of Homeland Security
- $500 million in funding for Homeland Security Advanced Research Projects Administration (HSARPA) directed toward Texas A&M University and other Texas universities

Who's Liable?

These three items are certainly weighty issues, but only if you're interested in playing partisan politics. Initially they were portrayed as pork because they excused manufacturers from liability, and presumably those manufacturers stood to benefit. But if you step back from the politics and read Section 863, it basically says that the government is offering indemnity protection for manufacturers of approved security systems that are bypassed and turn out not to be foolproof. In plain terms: If a terrorist manages to concoct a new form of bomb that gets past an explosives detector, the explosives detector manufacturer cannot be held liable for the damages from the bomb.

Considering that it came from Washington, this thinking is surprisingly sensible. Imagine if an airplane was blown up and bomb detectors were in use but didn't detect a bomb. The manufacturers of the bomb detectors would be sued for hundreds of millions of dollars by the bereaved relatives of victims and their greedy lawyers. Even if it was later discovered to have been a different type of attack, the manufacturers of the bomb detectors would probably have already been put out of business defending themselves legally. Never mind the claims of pork; I think this is actually common sense: It recognizes that no security system is 100 percent perfect and that the threat model changes. Indemnifying manufacturers against changes in the threat model or even misuse of their products in the field is a good idea. Of course, it's legislation, and legislation is open to interpretation. You can be sure that some day, some company will try to escape responsibility for negligence by trying to shelter itself under the liability protection in the Homeland Security Act.

you should know

The potential for lawsuits is extraordinary when you consider that someone can be sued simultaneously for attempting to protect passengers and failing in the attempt. Where does this stop? If we really want to start suing for negligence, how about the INS, for "losing" 300,000 illegal aliens who have been designated for deportation, or the FBI for having a 26-person "Osama bin Laden task force" for years prior to 9/11 that failed to do anything useful. For that matter, it's probably not too late to file suit against the government prior to World War II, for failing to correctly handle Hitler diplomatically and costing a lot of American lives.

The same logic holds true with the provision for the antiterror drug liability. To hear the opponents of the Homeland Security Act, one would get the impression that the act offers broad indemnification to manufacturers of entire classes of drugs. That turns out to be cynical posturing: The act says basically that vaccine manufacturers can't be held more liable for problems with vaccines offered for homeland security than they are for other types of drugs.

The Lone Star State Makes Out

Another criticism launched against the Homeland Security Act was that $500 million in funding was earmarked for Texas A&M University to start a homeland security research center, and that this was pork tossed to President Bush's home state. As a taxpayer, I do find this kind of thing offensive. As a historian, I don't find it shocking.

Take, for example, Johnson Space Flight Center, a colossal mountain of pork that was conveniently located in Texas, the home state of then Vice President Lyndon Johnson who controlled the early appropriations for NASA. It's probably not possible to run a government without this kind of scratch-my-back-I'll-scratch-yours nonsense hidden implicitly or explicitly in every major appropriation.

> **" The pork posturing over Homeland Security was a case of the pig calling the breakfast meat 'bacon.' "**

Basically, the pork posturing over Homeland Security was a case of the pig calling the breakfast meat "bacon." I'm sure that no congressmen or -women would have complained had it been their states getting the pork. There isn't a single member of Congress who isn't showing profound hypocrisy if he or she accuses another of lining their constituents' pockets. None of them would have gotten to Washington if they hadn't already demonstrated an ability to bring home the bacon.

Of course, what they *really* should have been doing was trying to make a Homeland Security Act that would actually help secure the homeland. But that's probably an impossible goal.

IN A PERFECT WORLD

Politics are here to stay, and the homeland security effort will always be a political animal. However, there are some ways that, in an even marginally better world, we should be able to get things right at least once in a while.

BIOLOGICAL DILEMMA

Liability when dealing with biological issues is a tough "damned if you do, damned if you don't" situation for the federal government. Let's imagine that there is a smallpox outbreak and some federal workers die because they had not been treated with a vaccine prior to the outbreak. In our litigation-happy society, you can pretty much rest assured that there would be a massive number of lawsuits claiming the government was negligent by not providing the countermeasure beforehand. Indeed, the U.S. Postal Service is already dealing with lawsuits from individuals who may have been harmed by exposure to anthrax during the anthrax mail attack: The claim is that the Postal Service did not act quickly enough to protect its employees.

But *any* vaccine comes with the possibility of an adverse reaction, ranging from coming down with the disease to a simple or severe allergic reaction. So, suppose the government takes the other route and decides to inoculate all critical civil servants against smallpox, and several civil servants display allergic responses — once again, the lawsuits would begin to fly.

But there's an even worse and extremely possible scenario: Suppose there's a real biological attack and the government makes vaccine countermeasures available on an emergency basis. Some people will die from the biological agent. Some people might die from reactions to the vaccine. What's to keep the families of people who die from filing suit claiming that the vaccine, rather than the biological attack, was the cause of death?

At a certain point, Americans need to grow the hell up and stop holding the government responsible for everything that can possibly go wrong. One of the purposes of the government is to "provide for the common defense." But if there's ever a biological attack, it'll be the attackers' fault, not the fault of the government that failed to adequately protect everyone. That's what the word "surprise" in "surprise attack" means.

Frankly, it's shameful to me that our government needs to protect itself against lawsuits when it's actually trying to do something useful. Another indemnity provision in the Homeland Security Act, for example, covers federal air marshals and indemnifies them from liability arising from acts or omissions unless they are grossly negligent. It's nice to see that this was considered, but a sad commentary that it was necessary.

POLITICAL FOOTBALL

No matter what we do, political footballs will still be tossed hither and yon. They'll be in play as long as we allow politicians to play silly games and get away with it. I truly believe that the best way to improve our political leaders is to demand more from them: Cease accepting lip service and require that they exhibit the courage of their convictions. If their convictions appear to be only "get reelected at any cost," we don't need them and we have the power to get rid of them.

I find it personally ironic that the politicians of the last century whom I hold in the greatest respect are the ones whose agendas I disagreed with, but who held their own view of the world and stuck with it regardless of the cost. In that regard, I am quite impressed with President Bush.

THE PATRIOT ACT

The dynamic of the balance between the need for surveillance and individual liberties is never going to be a simple one to maintain. In a perfect world, the PATRIOT Act would never have been necessary or, once enacted, would never have been so broad in scope. So what can we do?

Reassessing Our Agenda

It's obvious that potentially hostile noncitizens are taking advantage of the huge opportunities and privileges that we extend to everyone in this great country. In that regard, the United States is practically alone in the world. I believe that the PATRIOT Act is a backhanded way of beginning to reassess the level of protection we are offering possibly hostile aliens within our borders.

I think that it's about time we consider doing exactly that. But if we're going to do it, let's do it openly, let's discuss it, and let's decide as a society whether the cost of evenhandedness and openness is too high. Citizenship is a privilege that I believe a lot of people have devalued by failing to cherish it. Am I a horrible person to think that, perhaps, it is acceptable that our government spy on visiting noncitizens under certain circumstances? I think we need to call the question and decide as a society, rather than allow special interests at the extremes of the political spectrum to continue to make the decision for us by manipulating our perspective through the media or by sneaking their agendas through under the guise of PATRIOTism.

Personally, I am deeply conflicted about the issues raised by the PATRIOT Act. I'm sure that a vast majority of illegal immigrants are not terrorists, but it's intellectual dishonesty to dodge around the fact that they are living and working illegally within our country and are a major crime and public resource problem.

Reading the Thing

I know it's a lot to expect when you're looking at a monstrously huge and incomprehensibly jargon-ridden document like the PATRIOT Act or Homeland Security Act, but in a perfect world, more citizens would accept their responsibility and read, study, and understand the significance of what is going on around them and act accordingly. If nobody reads these documents, it's easy for things to slip by under the radar screen. In fact, it is easy for people to distort and reinterpret the contents of legislation to suit their agendas.

When I discuss PATRIOT with friends, who are mostly "info-libertarian digerati" types, they are all horrified by the legislation. Of course, none of them has *read* it. They're all accepting the ACLU's interpretation of PATRIOT unquestioningly. As I researched this book, and read the PATRIOT Act, I sometimes wondered if I was reading the same document the ACLU was upset about. (Of course, the ACLU's role is to worry about the distant future impact of legislation like PATRIOT and the total effect of many such pieces of legislation on American society over time, so they often present the worst-case scenario.)

Let's face it: It would be a monumental understatement to say that the views expressed by the media are often distortions of reality. If more citizens actually *read* legislation, it would improve people's reading skills and possibly politician's writing skills.

PORK AND BEANS: JUST SAY NO

In a perfect world, of course, we wouldn't have pork-barrel politics. I would argue, however, that pork barrels are a necessary consequence of representative government. Totalitarianism is overkill if all you want to do is eliminate squabbles over preference in government spending. What we appear to have forgotten is that eternal vigilance is the *responsibility* of citizens in a democratic society. Mostly, it's our jobs to watch the chumps we elect and rein them in when necessary. That means that it's a citizen's duty to understand legislation and its political, financial, and moral impact. Keeping our elected leaders' hands out of the cookie jar is our job, and we citizens must show some self-discipline. Pork is still pork if it's going to the district where we live, and we can never forget that. No matter how you slice the pork, it's still coming out of our own pockets in the long run.

The Johnny Spann Trust legislation is emblematic of two other huge problems that are outside of the scope of this book. The first is how we construct legislation: It is ridiculous the way legislation gets tacked onto a bill as it works its way around Washington. Line-item vetoes aren't the solution; the problem is more profound, but eventually it will need to be addressed.

The second problem, of course, is the tax code and all the loopholes, special exceptions, and dodges that are built into it. We desperately need an injection of sense regarding how taxes are assessed and avoided. I see things like the Johnny Spann trust as minor symptoms of a much more severe disease that nobody in Washington wants to try to cure because a lot of people make their living off the fact that it exists.

4

The Homeland Security Shuffle

With a law as important as the Homeland Security Act, you'd think that the congressional debate would center on topics that had something to do with the question: *Does this help improve our homeland security?* Unfortunately, Congress was too busy counting pork and posturing over peripheral issues to ask that question. I suspect that if they had asked it, I wouldn't be writing this book.

So when it came time to put the reorganization of government that created the Department of Homeland Security in place, was it any surprise to discover the whole thing was built on sand?

POLLING AND POSTURING

Actually setting up the Department of Homeland Security was an exercise in typical Beltway inefficiency that stemmed from a range of factors. Funding and politics were lead players in the show.

REDUNDANCY MERGED

The battle over the Homeland Security Act was won (and lost) during the midterm elections of 2002. Post-election surveys clearly show that the war on terrorism was a *major* deciding factor in many voters' choices at the polls. The economy and jobs were the number one and two concerns in voter polls, but terrorism had a huge influence on how people voted. Improving homeland security was the single largest issue polls identified as a voter concern for the 2003 Congress. Do you think for a second that the feedback from the polls had no influence over how quickly the Homeland Security Act passed in 2003?

The sharpest disagreements between the President and Congress had to do with the President's desire for greater authority to hire and fire workers in the new, merged agency. The President also wanted authority to merge, reassign, and eliminate redundant agencies or offices *without* Congressional approval. That authority was really what the fight was all about, and what took six months of hard wrangling to resolve.

Consider the situation, briefly. The Department of Homeland Security represents the largest reorganization of government since the creation of the Department of Defense. DHS merges over 20 agencies representing 170,000 employees and a $38 billion budget into a single entity.

It's not even possible to analogize such a merger in terms of corporate mergers, but for the sake of discussion, imagine if McDonald's and IBM were to merge. Even two companies in such completely different markets would find that there are redundancies as a result of the merger. For example, both McDonald's and IBM have human resources departments, both have payroll processing, both have fleet vehicles and maintenance technicians, and so on. In a functioning corporate environment, market pressures and shareholder expectations would demand that, eventually, the managers of the combined new corporation would identify those areas of overlap and reduce head count to eliminate waste.

But that's not how it's done in government. In bureaucrat land, when you have two large organizations that merge, you don't lop off redundancy; you add a new layer of management and make it responsible for coordinating the redundant efforts so that departments don't step on top of each other too frequently. If IBM and McDonald's merged the way federal agencies do it, IBM would *also* start making hamburgers and McDonald's would start producing McPCs.

THE ENVELOPE, PLEASE

One of the most complex and confusing games that gets played in Washington is The Funding Game. It's easy to create an agency and assign it a requested budget, but it's another thing entirely for that budget to be enacted. Although the public may vote based on its gut instincts, there is often a long time between the elections and the legislation that results from them. During that time, various congresspersons and committee members can try to attach their favorite items to spending bills, in order to either increase or decrease spending, or otherwise tie the bill to projects that will be focused in their districts.

For example, much of the increased spending that fueled the Transportation Safety Administration (TSA) came from emergency funding enacted after 9/11. No matter how such funding is arranged, there is always a dynamic related to the creation of such security budgets. Briefly, the dialog goes like this:

> End Customer: "We need to secure [*whatever*]."
> Security: "That will require a budget of [*astronomical amount*]."
> End Customer: "But that's *astronomical*! Here, you can have [a *more realistic amount*]."
> Security: "OK, but don't blame me if it doesn't work because you didn't give me the money I needed."

We've already seen this play itself out with TSA. TSA's initial budget request nearly tripled in its first year, to a whopping $6 billion. When the House provided $4 billion of the requested funds, TSA's administration pointed out that this would likely result in lengthy waits at airports, which would, of course, be blamed on lack of funding. The implication is that a spectacular failure of security that might lead to another terrorist incident will always be laid at the feet of the cheapskates who didn't provide adequate funding.

> " " *A spectacular failure of security that might lead to another terrorist incident will always be laid at the feet of the cheapskates who didn't provide adequate funding.* " "

RUNNING THE NUMBERS

The DHS reorganization results in a structure that can be broken down into three categories:

- Stuff that might actually help
- Stuff that's basically government-funded research that may someday pay dividends
- Pork

Most of the items in the "Stuff that might actually help" category depend completely on execution. In other words, "If it's done right, it could be really useful." Unfortunately, we won't be able to make a judgment about that for a long time to come, if ever. But to put this spending in perspective, consider this: In the corporate world, imagine going to the CTO or CEO of a large company and asking for 14 percent of the annual budget to spend on things that just might work, if they're done right. Now, imagine if you were the project leader for a project that had consistently failed to accomplish significant milestones, and you made the same request.

LET'S TAKE A LOOK AT THE BUDGET

The budget requests for DHS are in, and many agencies show dramatic expansion in their funding over 2002. For example, the INS's new budget has been increased by about $600 million — an increase of 16 percent. The FBI's NIPC, by all accounts a failed effort, has been increased 60 percent, or nearly $50 million. The new Office of Federal Protective Service gets a $400 million budget to try to improve security at federal office buildings, admittedly a massive task. Animal and Plant Health Inspection Services, moved to DHS's Border Security Department from the Department of Agriculture, got a bit over $100 million in additional funding, increasing its budget nearly 25 percent.

you should know

The increased funding for Animal and Plant Health Inspections is a bit puzzling. APHIS is chartered with worrying about invasive plant strains or plant diseases, but even the most "far out" pundits have not postulated an attack on U.S. crops via some kind of Al Qaeda-bred hostile plant-eating insects. I'm figuring they must be headquartered in some congressperson's or other's district and it was a pork-for-votes type of arrangement.

The U.S. Postal Service requested $1.1 billion for postal homeland security but got none of it in the 2002 Department of Defense appropriations bill. Later, the House–Senate conference approved $500 million. This money was in addition to $175 million approved by President Bush after the 9/11 anthrax attacks. Presumably, a huge amount was spent on disinfecting the anthrax-contaminated postal facilities, and on rubber gloves. But are we safer?

BREAKING IT DOWN

Probably the best way to understand what's going on in the new DHS is to look at a breakdown of what the money is being spent on by area. This information has been provided by the Center for Arms Control and Non-Proliferation Terrorism Project.

Area of Expenditure	Percent of Spending
Border security	28%
Bioterrorism defense	16%
Aviation security (TSA)	13%
Dept. of Defense security at bases	13%
Supporting first responders	9%
Dept. of Justice law enforcement	5%
Air defense patrols	4%
Dept. of Energy security	2%
New technology	2%
All others	8%

At a broad level, this really looks pretty sensible. Bioterrorism defense is very high, considering that there has been no active threat in that area, but I'm actually happy that we're spending thought and effort on a potential threat; that's a pleasant change from the usual practice of scrambling to lock the barn door after the horse is out. The budget for supporting first responders includes $3.5 billion for training and equipment for police, firefighters, and emergency medical technicians. New technology includes computer security and entry–exit visa system automation.

Within the preceding categories, the expenditures are broken down in the sections that follow (note that these numbers do not total 100 percent because smaller categories have been omitted).

Border Security

Taking an ineffective, mismanaged bureaucracy and giving it more money is just a recipe for having a *larger* ineffective mismanaged bureaucracy, but here's how the numbers break out:

Border Security: $10.6 billion	
INS	46%
Customs	21%
Coast Guard	27%

One element in this spending is the entry-exit visa system, which is part of the "Smart Borders" Initiative. This $380 million project was created to allow the INS to implement a computerized border control system. What nobody mentions is that the INS already has spent billions of dollars on information technology to no apparent effect. In fact, the INS has deployed "smart" biometric visa cards, but not machines to read them. The INS has deployed the Interagency Border Inspection System (IBIS) database to track stolen passports, but workers don't have IBIS computer terminals to access the system.

After 9/11 the INS commissioner promised to have a computerized entry-exit system in place at airports and seaports prior to the end of 2003. At present, the system is still in the design stage. Is the DHS budget throwing more good money after bad? As a taxpayer, I can only hope they get it right, this time. If they can't, perhaps the government could replace INS's IT department with the smart twenty-somethings that built eBay and Amazon.com in a matter of months.

Of course, it doesn't matter how smart the borders become, unless we also get smarter about enforcing border security.

Bioterrorism

This appears to be a reasonable program for defense against a presently unknown threat. Funding research and development in preventing bioterrorism will help considerably with preparedness, assuming that there is sufficient time for such programs to begin to pay dividends. Here's how spending on bioterrorism is allocated:

Bioterrorism Defense: $5.9 billion	
Research and development	40%
State and local health systems	20%
Communications	7%
Biodefense equipment	6%
Pharmaceutical stockpile	5%
Center for Disease Control (CDC)	2%
Smallpox vaccines	2%
Food supply security	2%

Increasing state and local health systems' equipment levels and training for bioterror will pay potentially huge dividends if there is ever an attack. The pharmaceutical stockpile presumably consists of antibiotics such as Ciprofloxacin ("Cipro") that work well against anthrax.

you should know

Cipro got a great deal of attention during the post 9/11 anthrax attacks, but there are other broad-spectrum powerful antibiotics that are quite effective against anthrax.

Hopefully, some of the R&D money spent on bioterror defense will go toward attempting to determine a reasonable stockpile to build, rather than rolling out the pork barrel. The smallpox vaccine issue is a case in point. We're about to spend $100 million on smallpox vaccines in the face of considerable public discussion about the potential for smallpox being used as a bioterror weapon. At this time there hasn't been any intelligence released that indicates that smallpox is a likely weapon. Are we preparing to spend $100 million to calm down a media scare? Or will we learn years

> **" At this time there hasn't been any intelligence released that indicates that smallpox is a likely weapon. Are we preparing to spend $100 million to calm down a media scare? "**

from now that there was a real threat? Considering some of the other places and ways we're wasting our money, I think $100 million is pretty small change. And if nothing else, the R&D and equipment upgrades for local medical organizations will help stimulate the economy and the development of new medical tools and techniques.

Aviation Security

The whole $4.8 billion allocated to aviation security goes to the Transportation Security Administration. TSA's budget is expected to have $2.2 billion of its total funding paid by surcharges on air travel. Within the $4.8 billion budget of TSA are provisions to hire 30,000 employees to oversee security and screening, hire federal air marshals, and buy and install explosives detection machines.

Is TSA money well spent? Yes and no. In the past, when each airport hired its own security service from the lowest bidder, it's safe to say that airport security was a shambles. TSA has definitely improved the state of airport security, but is it worth $4.8 billion? It's highly visible, and it's the single area where most Americans see a renewed focus on security after 9/11. Its value as public relations is incalculable. But that's about it.

As discussed elsewhere in this book, the problem of airline security is one that's not going to go away and get better just because we threw a few billion dollars at it. On one hand, TSA is the centerpiece of the scam that is DHS. On the other, it's probably the only part of DHS that is new and has not yet become moribund.

WINNERS AND LOSERS

As soon as it looked like DHS was going to become a reality, the departmental jockeying had already begun. Only a small amount of this behind-the-scenes activity managed to break out into the light of day where the media could latch onto it.

BREAKING UP IS EASY TO DO

A typical episode in this scramble was an FBI "internal draft" memo circulated in November 2002, which observed that the Bureau of Alcohol, Tobacco, and Firearms was an ill-trained and sloppy organization that should be subsumed within the Department of Justice. This is the kind of behavior you see in a merger in a corporate environment, when the various departments immediately start scrambling to position themselves for the great reorganization.

As it happened, the FBI got its wish: The BATF has now been broken up into two organizations, one of which is under the Department of Justice (ATF) and another under the Department of Commerce (the Alcohol and Tobacco Tax and Trade Bureau, or TTB).

The FBI itself preemptively reorganized under a storm cloud of criticism. In June 2002, Coleen Rowley, a senior whistle-blower, got a great deal of press by going public with a memo to the FBI director documenting the extent to which the FBI had known and ignored signs leading up the 9/11 attack.

JUMPING SHIP

Other organizations were expected to be losers in the reorganization from early on. The INS is one example.

Shortly after 9/11, four Pakistani crewmembers on a commercial freighter jumped ship and disappeared into the United States. This produced a short tempest of criticism when the INS and customs admitted that, not only didn't they know where the crewmen had gone, but they had no procedure in place that could help them find the illegal aliens. Many government watchers assumed that the INS had a target on its back, and Senator Lieberman's first version of a Homeland Security Bill called for the abolishment of the INS and the transfer of its duties to the new DHS.

So it happened: The Homeland Security Act significantly reorganizes the INS. The INS is broken up to become part of two different agencies, the Bureau of Border Security, and the Bureau of Citizenship and Immigration Services. One potentially promising sign in this new structure is the creation of the Agency for Immigration Hearings and Appeals as a branch of the Department of Justice. At least in theory, with their better conduit to the FBI's databases of suspected terrorists, this new organization might be well positioned to handle appeals from individuals who are incorrectly denied visas, or who are slated to be deported.

With a total budget of over $10 billion, the lion's share of the budget for border security goes to INS. Only time will tell, but it looks as if rather than clean house at a dysfunctional agency, the DHS' approach is to simply increase their budget dramatically. Additional funding always helps well-managed government agencies, but unless this funding is accompanied with a major shake-up, it's money down the drain at the poorly managed INS.

THE BIG REORG

So, how did all this change end up? What, exactly, does the Department of Homeland Security look like today? Read on.

WHEN PIGS FLY

The Department of Homeland Security is made up of organizations pulled from the Departments of Agriculture, Commerce, Defense, Energy, Transportation, Treasury, GSA, Health and Human Services, and Federal Emergency Management Agency (FEMA). Structurally, the grouping of the member departments makes sense. Within DHS structure, there are departments of Border Security, Science and Technology, Infrastructure Protection, Emergency Preparedness, and the Secret Service. Branches of the Department of Justice that have been incorporated into DHS are the INS, the FBI's National Infrastructure Protection Center (NIPC), and the FBI's National Office of Domestic Preparedness.

> ## " The new DHS consists of an impressive group of organizations that are both blind and paralyzed. "

The Border Security department is really the only part of DHS that has any kind of enforcement authority to speak of, embodied in the Coast Guard and Customs. This lack of authority, in my mind, will doom the DHS to being an agency that is constantly struggling to carry out its mission against bureaucratic hurdles. Making the kind of changes that would bring a truly effective homeland security agency would overturn too many political applecarts and vested interests.

you should know

For some of my thoughts about how to fix this mess, take a look at the last section of this chapter, *In a Perfect World*.

The new DHS consists of an impressive group of organizations that are both *blind* and *paralyzed*. I'm not saying that DHS should have its own police force and intelligence agency, but it's going to be critical that DHS has effective, non–stovepiped access into the FBI and CIA, two organizations that historically have had trouble working effectively with *themselves,* let alone other organizations.

CONNECTING THE DOTS

One constant thread through the post-9/11 investigations was a lack of coordination and communication between the FBI and CIA (mostly, the lack of coordination and communication was internal to the FBI). If you look at the entire DHS organizational structure, however, the only agencies that could have helped prevent the 9/11 attacks would have been INS — or more specifically, an INS correctly functioning on information gathered by the FBI, and an FBI correctly functioning on immigration/visa data gathered by a functioning INS. Since the structure of DHS makes the relationship with the FBI purely one of "coordinating," there's no guarantee (or even implication) that communications will be improved between the INS and the FBI, unless this communication somehow magically arises out of the $380 million computer system the INS is going to try to implement. Somehow that strikes me as unlikely.

FIGHTING OVER WHERE THE TROUGH RESIDES

Selecting the location for DHS's headquarters has been another battle over pork. At 250,000 initial square feet of office space, the leased property would be able to hold a fraction of the total 17,000 Washington-area DHS employees. Obviously, there is a huge amount of money at stake. The economic impact on the district that houses DHS will be at least $100 million annually, possibly as high as $200 million. The resulting tax revenue could be as high as an additional $200 million.

The DHS's original headquarters is in a temporary space in northwest Washington, D.C. For full-time office space, the department is (as of this writing) leaning toward space in northern Virginia near Dulles Airport. Immediately after word of the North Virginia decision was released, the states surrounding Washington lashed out. Maryland members of the house complained that the selection process was biased toward Virginia and that they had not had enough opportunity in committees to remove bias (presumably "remove bias" is a code word for "bias it in our direction").

Other local politicians weighed in immediately that the offices should be "near a metro station" (i.e., in my district) or "in Washington, as befits such an important agency" (i.e., in my district).

you should know

Washington delegates were quick to point to federal laws and executive orders requiring that agencies give preference to Washington, D.C., when housing federal agencies. Lawsuits were threatened, press conferences given, and fingers pointed.

The argument followed that leasing the space in Washington would cost $25 million annually, whereas in Virginia it would cost only $20 million. It would cost about $18 million in Maryland, but — surprise — Maryland's representation is primarily Democratic, whereas Virginia's is Republican. Was it coincidence that Republicans were in control of the White House and Congress at the time the property was selected?

Of course, the location has very little to do with increasing

> **" Knowing that the pork is being carefully and wisely divided by our elected leaders should make you feel a lot safer from terrorism. "**

homeland security. Once again, it's all about making sure that the right debts are paid, the right backs are scratched, and the pork is divided up properly. Knowing that the pork is being carefully and wisely divided by our elected leaders should make you feel a lot safer from terrorism.

IN A PERFECT WORLD

In a perfect world, our politicians would understand the expression "clean house." When businesses make profound structural changes to attempt to cure dysfunction, it's not pretty, but it usually gets results. The DHS reorganization isn't going to get results, because the same people who were running things badly before are expected to run them better in the future. That simply doesn't add up. In a perfect world, for example, the entire management structure of the INS would have been gutted, along with its entire information technology branch.

Occam's razor needs to be applied brutally to some of these agencies: "Entities should not be multiplied unnecessarily" applies to bureaucracies, their computer systems, their infrastructure expenditures, and their methods. There are appalling levels of redundancy across federal agencies. Attempts to "reinvent" government have been made in the past, and resulted in even bigger bureaucracies and more paper. That's backwards progress, and it happens because every time it's been tried, everyone wants to make sure there aren't any losers, only winners.

> " Responding to incompetence by increasing its funding is not going to make it turn into competence; it's going to produce bloated incompetence. "

To reinvent something, you need to start over, step back, and design new management processes that have built-in efficiencies. Responding to incompetence by increasing its funding is not going to make it turn into competence; it's going to produce bloated incompetence. I'd be impressed with the DHS reorganization if I heard on CNN that the entire INS had been fired.

5

Running for the Border: Immigration

T he United States shares lengthy borders with Canada and Mexico. The southern border with Mexico is staffed with an average of one immigration agent per thousand feet. The northern border with Canada, on the other hand, has only one per every 16 miles.

We've known for years that illegal immigration and drug smuggling are a problem, but now that the threat of terrorism has been added to the mix, some people are calling for massive crackdowns on border security. Increasing the current methods of border protection completely flies in the face of common sense when you consider that terrorists are well funded and ideologically motivated, whereas illegal immigrants are usually poor and are looking for work.

A terrorist's border-crossing techniques will be completely different from an illegal immigrant's. The illegal immigrant knows that he or she can take a chance running across the border, get caught, and try again in another week. The terrorist knows that getting caught is a serious problem and might remove him or her from play permanently. A migrant worker in Mexico who has no money will not travel to Canada where the borders are lightly patrolled. A terrorist will, assuming he or she doesn't walk in the front door, arriving on a plane in New York City and strolling down a red carpet.

THE MYTH OF THE BORDER IN AN OPEN SOCIETY

It's ridiculously easy for terrorists to operate with impunity inside the United States. If you think about it for a second, it's surprising that anyone is surprised.

KEEPING THE BAD GUYS OUT

Consider our track record with keeping undesirables out of the country. Drug dealers have operated with relative impunity for decades, and their illicit activities cause them to come into contact with the population at large with far more frequency than terrorists. It's harder for drug dealers to hide because they are engaging in commerce, but other than that, their problems are similar to those of terrorists: They need to acquire chemicals and materials that have a distinct "fingerprint" for law enforcement, and they need to keep their activities hidden. If you try to bulk-order 1,000 tablets of pseudephedrine (antihistamine), the feds don't need to be rocket scientists to figure you're making crystal methamphetamine. If you try to bulk-order concentrated hydrogen peroxide or fuming nitric acid, you're not planning on using it in your backyard to kill those pesky weeds.

you should know

When you hear about drug busts involving hundreds of pounds of substances, you can easily assume that hundreds of pounds represents a "normal-sized" shipment. And there are many more shipments flying around than the few that are caught. Now imagine that the terrorists have similar capabilities for shipping goods. A few hundred pounds of Semtex, the plastic explosive of choice for terrorists, can ruin your entire day, along with whatever city block you're in at the time.

Border protection assumes we'll try first to keep the bad guys out of the country and second to keep their equipment out of their hands once they are in. These are separate problems, because terrorists (like drug dealers) like the plausible deniability of not getting caught sneaking across the border with their tools. It's better to sneak across first and arrange to get the tools later.

Physical security also involves the protection of actual targets within the country. So, we have to worry about our terrorists loading explosives into a rented truck and parking it under the World Trade Center building as they did several years ago, or sneaking a bomb into a stadium where the Super Bowl is being played and detonating it at halftime.

If you think about it for just a second, you'll realize that there are an infinity of prime targets for attack within any country. Will we be able to adequately protect them all? If you think about it one second longer, you'll begin to wonder, how can a country that can't prevent destitute illegal immigrants from entering by the thousands prevent well-funded terrorists from entering by the dozens?

> " *How can a country that can't prevent destitute illegal immigrants from entering by the thousands prevent well-funded terrorists from entering by the dozens?* "

THE PAPER TRAIL

U.S. visas are big business abroad and a political football at home. Most U.S. citizens believe that the border patrols and immigration police actually *do* something. But in terms of their ability to protect the country from terrorist infiltration, they are primarily window dressing — money spent to make us *feel* more secure.

For example, in 1998, a group of people was indicted for their role in falsifying naturalization examinations of nearly *13,000* immigrants over a two-year period. Testers simply handed out passing grades to applicants who had not even taken the tests, and made over $12 million perpetrating the scam. The INS has never taken action to reexamine the citizenship status of the individuals who took advantage of the scammers' services. Unfortunately, even if the INS tried to, it couldn't take away citizenship once wrongly granted; that power lies with the Justice Department. Consequently, it is rare that there is a coordinated effort to act against people who bought their way into the country illegally.

you should know

A year ago I was on the program committee for a national conference. We got a number of applications to attend from individuals in China and Africa. For a while the program committee was puzzled: Why were these individuals, with no apparent background in computer security, so eager to attend a conference in a major U.S. city? The mystery came clear when one member of the program committee learned that this is a well-known trick for getting a visa into the United States. Once the "conference attendee" gets through U.S. Customs, he or she disappears into the population, finds a place to stay, and looks for work. Of course, it is a federal offense to overstay one's visa, but such immigrants virtually never get caught and are almost never deported when they are.

Why bother worrying about people trying to sneak in illegally when the U.S. government is busy ushering in thousands of criminals? In 1996, the Clinton/Gore administration offered the $96 million-plus "Citizenship USA Program," under which Vice President Al Gore pushed the INS to reduce the time between application and naturalization down from two years to a maximum of six months. This program was, presumably, an attempt to bring in a large body of new citizens who would return the favor by voting for the party and presidential candidate that had accelerated their citizenship bid. In order to meet the aggressive new schedule of processing applications, the INS was allowed to rush through and forego criminal background checks on *180,000* of the million new citizens that were created. Over *80,000* of the new citizens' fingerprints generated criminal records, but it was too late — they were already naturalized.

you should know

Six thousand of the worst offenders were finally denaturalized by the Justice Department. Could any of them be terrorist sleeper cells? Realistically, yes. Most likely, however, they were just ordinary criminals. Terrorists, so far, have not found it necessary to engage in prolonged preparation for citizenship before they attack.

WE'D LIKE TO DEPORT YOU — PLEASE

In December 2001, the INS admitted that there were over 300,000 "fugitive deportees" within U.S. borders who could not be located. What's a "fugitive deportee"? Behind the bureaucrat-speak, that's someone who was ordered to be deported, but who didn't show up to board the airplane. Generally, the INS has relied on the honor of thieves to enforce its deportation orders by mailing deportation notices to deportees asking them to turn themselves in. We can rest assured that, while terrorists might be ideologically motivated enough to fly an airplane into a skyscraper, they won't dare scoff at a deportation letter from a federal agency.

In January 2002, the Justice Department announced its Absconder Apprehension Initiative, by means of which the government was finally going to begin ejecting fugitive deportees, beginning with a group of 6,000 Middle Easterners from "Al Qaeda harboring countries" who had been convicted of felonies within the United States. It was claimed that this process could locate as many as 10 percent of the fugitives. After announcing the program, however, the Justice Department admitted it would take nearly a year to put the program in place, because the names and identities needed to be added to one of the FBI's criminal databases.

By June of 2002, the Justice Department admitted that only about 500 of the 300,000 fugitive deportees had been caught and ejected. These are the people that are supposed to be guarding our borders and making the terrorists run for cover? I don't think that any of us wants to live in a police state, but the expectation of a competent police force is not unreasonable, especially if you're paying top dollar.

REFUSING VISAS WHILE WELCOMING TERRORISTS

One thing that gets conveniently forgotten when the FBI talks about tightening up border security is that the 9/11 terrorists had visas at the time of the attacks. With visas in hand, tighter borders would have just ensured that there were more guards to escort the terrorists into the country.

Consistently, we've granted visas to dangerous terrorists. In 1992 Ramsi Yousef, believed to be one of the brains behind the 9/11 attack and the 1993 World Trade Center bombing, landed at New York's JFK airport. At that time he was traveling with an Iraqi passport that had no visa. After being detained briefly, he claimed political asylum and was allowed to remain in the country. The INS released him because there was no room in its detention facilities.

Three of the 9/11 terrorists were on overstayed or expired visas, but the rest had business or tourist visas. The individual thought to be the ringleader, Mohammed Atta, was allowed in despite having overstayed his visa on a previous visit. Richard Reid, the "shoe bomber," took advantage of a visa waiver program that allows free entry for up to 90 days to individuals with passports from one of 28 countries, including his native United Kingdom. Of course, Reid apparently never planned to arrive in the United States at all.

The visa waiver program is essential to a multibillion-dollar tourism industry. The House Immigration and Claims Subcommittee held meetings to review the visa waiver program following 9/11, but did not make any changes and merely discussed minor cosmetic options. One cosmetic option that was apparently considered was to request that participating nations in the visa waiver program be asked to inform U.S. customs when passports or blank passports are stolen, so that they can be flagged in the immigration computer system. But when stacked up against the billions of dollars tourism represents, you can rest assured there will be no substantive change, only a few acts of window dressing.

IMMIGRATION GRANDSTANDING

Immigration policies are a political football and are more strongly influenced by special interests than by national security interests. If homeland security involves securing the country's borders, we need to be willing to forgo some of those special interests.

CATERING TO THOSE VERY SPECIAL INTERESTS

Al Gore's citizenship-for-votes deal was the tip of the iceberg. Whenever people talk about tightening the borders, they have entered into a dangerous dance of special interests. Not only does each ethnic minority have its own backers who are willing to file a flurry of lawsuits, there are huge financial interests and organizations that have built industries around getting people U.S. and Canadian visas. As with everything else, it boils down to money.

> " Whenever people talk about tightening the borders, they have entered into a dangerous dance of special interests. "

For example, there's a program called the E-2 "investor visa" in which an officer of a company that is investing in U.S. businesses can stay indefinitely in the United States. Candidates must be from a list of countries with reciprocal investment treaties and must be investing "substantial" dollar amounts: $150,000 or more. Armenia, Bangladesh, Egypt, Ethiopia, and Iran are a few of the dozens of countries to whom we offer E-2 visas. Obviously, if someone tried to do away with E-2 visas, there would be an outcry from the well-heeled, followed doubtless by the opening of a new loophole elsewhere.

There's also a religious worker visa program that allows religious workers to get visas to fill needs (assumedly religious needs) within the United States. This allows religious organizations within the United States to sponsor non-minister religious workers to stay within the country as long as they want. In 1998, 11,000 visas were issued under the religious worker program. In June 2000 the House Immigration Subcommittee held hearings on the program. During the hearings, the State Department admitted that it performed no investigations of fraud in the program because of a lack of available data on fraud to investigate. In other words, "We didn't see any problem, because our eyes were tightly shut."

The Catholic Church is one group that takes advantage of the religious worker program and would doubtless apply pressure if someone tried to reform immigration controls in this area. How would the INS respond if some of the more radical Islamic churches began requesting visas for members of their flock who were considered potential troublemakers?

Meanwhile, in an attempt to make U.S. citizens feel that something is being done following 9/11, there have been some obvious grandstanding attempts by law enforcement. Student visas were an obvious target, and several jurisdictions have launched crackdowns on students who entered the United States on a student visa but are not carrying the required number of course hours, or who are no longer attending classes at all.

TOO LITTLE, TOO LATE

Several students have been jailed noisily, and there has been the usual right-wing chest thumping and left-wing hand flapping. But does any of it help? Of course it doesn't! There are so many ways to get into the country that it seems like pointing at any one aspect of immigration law or border control is just a fruitless exercise in trying to oversimplify a huge, complex problem. With over *8 million* illegal immigrants in the United States at the present time, blocking just one avenue of entrance is like plugging a single hole in a large sieve.

Terrorists Among Us: Imported Fruitcakes and Domestic Nut Bars

Even if we were able to solve the problem of foreigners coming to the United States to do mischief, we still have to handle our local "terrorists." Just consider:

- In the 1920s we had Bonnie Parker and Clyde Barrow.
- In the 1970s, we had the Symbionese Liberation Army (and we never found out where Symbion even *was*).
- In the 1980s a large part of Philadelphia was destroyed by police attempting to oust a politico-military group named MOVE from a row house they had turned into a fortress.
- Branch Davidians in Waco, Texas, were burned alive by incompetent federal agents, and apparently caused Timothy McVeigh to decide to take arms against the federal government.
- Timothy McVeigh blew up a federal office building in Oklahoma City.
- The Unabomber was possibly a "terrorist," or maybe just an ordinary madman.
- John Mohammed and John Malvo apparently went on a nonideological sniping spree that terrorized the Washington, D.C. suburbs.
- Someone, still unknown as of this writing, mailed "weaponized" anthrax to several offices in Washington, D.C., and in Florida. As of this writing we're not sure the perpetrator was an American, but the refinement methods used for the preparation were straight out of U.S. bioweapons labs.

What did all of these terrorists have in common? They were all "Americans." Keeping hostile foreigners out of the country wouldn't have helped protect us against them.

Countries around the world that deal with terrorism as a part of their national consciousness no longer make the kind of artificial separation between foreign and domestic terrorists that we try to make. The French have long dealt with their local Basque problem. The United Kingdom has the Irish troubles. The Germans had their Baader-Mienhof, and the Italians the Red Brigades. None of these terrorist groups was visually different from the populations they were attacking, yet they were all dangerous, dedicated, and ideologically motivated.

> " We have met the enemy and he's the quiet but slightly strange guy next door. "

So, what's really going on? Sealing our borders, even it that were possible, isn't going to eliminate the problem. Indeed, as we saw with the

Branch Davidian/McVeigh connection, there's every chance that a crackdown might be just the thing that sets off the next wave of dangerous nutcases. In this case, we have met the enemy and he's the quiet but slightly strange guy next door.

IN A PERFECT WORLD

The INS has been renamed and dissolved within DHS, but the same people run it and it still has the same problems. If there has ever been a government agency in need of being bulldozed, buried, and rebuilt from scratch, the INS is it.

Years of incompetence in use of information technology, and a lack of ability to enforce, imprison, and deport, have created a situation where there is an unknown number of illegal aliens within the country and nothing that can be done about them. Indeed, there are now so many illegal aliens within our borders that they are a political force to be reckoned with.

Reinventing the INS would be best approached by starting from scratch with a team that understands how to build large databases, authentication systems, and how to use computers to track people. I have no problem with requiring tourists and immigrants to update their locations every month while they are within the United States: This could be done via automated telephone systems using caller ID and a visa number/PIN code.

Implementing an automated entry/exit visa system may be rocket science to the current

> **" We have to stop accepting the current level of incompetence and find people who can do the job, because the people who are currently supposed to be doing it manifestly can't. "**

INS, but the wunderkinder who built eBay and Amazon.com can build systems to handle that many transactions in their sleep. We have to stop accepting the current level of incompetence and find people who can do the job, because the people who are currently supposed to be doing it manifestly can't.

6

Airline Insecurity

"The Department of Homeland Security has raised the current threat level to **Orange**. For security reasons, please do not leave any baggage unattended. Unattended baggage will be seized by the Chicago Police and may be damaged or destroyed." The message plays every five minutes in Chicago's O'Hare Airport. The part about "unattended baggage" has been around for two years now. The "threat level orange" bit is a recent addition. Are we somehow supposed to be more vigilant about unattended baggage because of the higher threat level? Are we expecting people to be more vigilant about unattended baggage after 9/11? No; we will continue to be unconcerned about unattended baggage until something happens that makes us worry about it.

If we all stayed put at home, it would be a heck of a lot easier to guarantee our security. Our government wouldn't have to watch people as they move from country to country, or even from one airline flight to another. But with the world in constant motion, homeland security necessarily involves keeping a close watch on our skies, our borders, and our boots.

AIRLINE SECURITY: ENEMY AT THE GATES

Many security procedures are based on well-thought-out responses to attacks. Other security procedures are knee-jerk responses that are intended primarily for cosmetic and psychological effect. Unfortunately, it's usually pretty obvious which is which.

It's demoralizing to be subjected to things "for your own good" that are obviously a waste of time. Perhaps the one area in which knee-jerk security procedures are most obvious is in the area of airline security.

Gentlemen, Start Your Laptops

In 1988 Pan Am Flight #103 was destroyed with total loss of life over Lockerbie, Scotland. The deadly device that caused the crash was a bomb concealed in a portable radio, a simple piece of commercial electronics. The radio was loaded onto the plane in a piece of unattended luggage that was checked and then abandoned.

Those who were frequent travelers right after the Lockerbie attack will recall that shortly thereafter airport security agents began asking travelers to turn on pieces of electronic equipment to make sure they worked properly. Laptop-carrying businessmen — frequent fliers with hundreds of thousands of flight miles — had to take their laptops out of their cases and turn them on so the security screeners could watch as they booted up and actually appeared to do something computerlike. Cell phone users had to turn their phones on to show that the LCD panel lit up if you pushed a button. Anyone who knew his or her way around a computer would eventually mutter something like, "As if you couldn't make a laptop-bomb that would light up the screen when you hit the on button."

> " Anyone who knew his or her way around a computer would eventually mutter something like, '...as if you couldn't make a laptop-bomb that would light up the screen when you hit the on button...' "

After 9/11, the security screeners stopped asking about laptops. Then, it was knives. Anything pointed, in fact: Fingernail clippers, knitting needles, tweezers, even pencils in some cases. Nobody cared about laptop or radio bombs; there was a newer and more pressing threat.

LOOK OUT: I'VE GOT A FINGERNAIL FILE!

My wife and I were married on October 27, 2001, and went on our honeymoon the 28th. Before boarding the plane we surrendered any object that could be construed as being sharp. After we boarded the plane and took our seats, the stewardess asked us if we were newlyweds. When we said yes, she came back and presented us with a bottle of champagne as a way of saying "congratulations." A broken champagne bottle would have made a vastly superior weapon to the fingernail file that security had broken from my nail clippers 20 minutes before.

YOU WOULDN'T WANT TO BE IN HIS SHOES

On December 22, 2001, Richard Reid, a British convert to Islam, attempted to detonate his shoes, which had been stuffed with an explosive known as triacetone triperoxide (TATP) or peroxyacetone. There have been various reports about the explosives Reid supposedly used, ranging from home-brewed chemicals to military-grade plastic explosives. But law enforcement may just be interested in making him seem smarter and better trained than he was: Do a Google search for "acetone peroxide" and you'll find almost 3,000 hits, many of which are recipes for how to make the stuff with hair bleach, acetone from the hardware store, and battery acid.

you should know

TATP is an extremely sensitive mixture. The fact that Reid was able to walk onto the airplane at all is an indicator that he probably got the recipe wrong or allowed the mixture to decay. Otherwise, he would have exploded before he got down the jetway.

Following this incident, passengers were subjected to a regimen of random shoe inspections at airport security stations. (We can all be grateful that Reid didn't place his explosives in his underpants, or the experience of travel would have been changed dramatically for the worse for many of us.)

Terrorists sometimes follow fads in their attacks. But so, apparently, do airport security regulators. What's so disappointing about this knee-jerk approach to security is that virtually nobody is fooled by it. So far, there

> **" The security establishment has grasped at the method, rather than search for the root cause and try to establish an effective response to it. "**

has only been one shoe bomber. There has only been one day of attacks with box-cutters, and there has only been one radio-bomb. In each case, the security establishment has grasped at the method, rather than search for the root cause and try to establish an effective response to it.

CAN DETECTION EVER PREVENT DISASTER?

One thing that's interesting to note about Reid's shoe bomb is that, at present, there are no suitable mechanical methods for detecting trace quantities of peroxide-based explosives. Sniffer dogs, apparently, cannot be trained to detect peroxide traces, either. Not only that, but the bomb as it was constructed did not contain metal parts that would have set off an airport metal detector.

Most of the current generation of airport explosive detectors are doing gas diffusion detection of nitrogen compounds and little more. They may also be looking for traces of drugs, but that's got nothing to do with homeland security. Why look only for explosives? What about sarin gas, chlorine and chlorine compounds, incendiaries, or even bio-hazards? Even black powder, kerosene, or flour dust can produce an explosion capable of destroying an aircraft.

It's really important to understand that a lot of the checks done at airports can never amount to much more than window dressing: The number of possible compounds and weapons that could be taken on a plane is simply too large.

BAGGAGE MISHANDLING

The bomb that destroyed Pan Am Flight #103 was in a piece of luggage that belonged to someone who did not board the plane. Now, years later, baggage-handling procedures are finally able to identify and remove luggage that boards a plane when the passenger has not. That's a far more practical response than forcing everybody to turn on their laptop, but not to turn on their vibrator or shaver, or to open and taste their food. (Food is now being barred from entry at some airport security checkpoints.)

Of course, a still more effective response would be to x-ray *every-thing* going onto a plane — checked luggage, carry-ons, postal freight, and so on. The search for weapons has always been an ongoing battle and probably always will be. What about the fine bottle of scotch whiskey purchased at the duty-free store prior to boarding? It is presented to me in a wrapped package once I get on the plane. What about my briefcase, which is metal, has a shoulder strap, and weighs something close to 20 pounds? I'd gladly pit my briefcase in a gladiatorial contest against a short-bladed box-cutter any day.

Fundamentally, the problem is keeping weapons out of peoples' hands on airplanes, and explosives, incendiaries, and chemical weapons off airplanes in general. The only way to do this is to stop looking at what the last terrorist tried, and establish consistent and well-thought-out procedures that cover all the bases.

LEARNING BY EXAMPLE: HOW EL AL DOES IT

El Al is an airline that understands security. Carrying 3 million passengers annually, it has the highest-possible level of security. "If you're a passenger on El Al, most likely you will be observed from the minute that you left your car or you have been dropped off ... and then you will have met the security agent before you go to check in to your flight," according to Issy Boim, president of Air Security International.

Not only are passengers carefully scrutinized, the planes themselves are guarded when on the ground during cleaning or maintenance. Aircrews are not armed, but the doors to the cockpit are bulletproofed and can be opened only from the inside. El Al's approach shows an admirable consistency, especially in guarding the aircraft when they are grounded or undergoing maintenance.

There were some scary early indications that some of the 9/11 hijackers may have had accomplices in the flight support staff at European airports. These rumors didn't pan out, but they raise a question: Who needs to sneak a bomb past security if he or she can get a job as a maintenance worker

> **" Who needs to sneak a bomb past security if he or she can get a job as a maintenance worker or a caterer? "**

or a caterer? In many airports, all that is necessary to get behind security is a magnetic-coded badge and a PIN code that allows a would-be terrorist into the baggage-handling area. You can get your hands on such a badge by getting a job as a baggage handler, or by taking a badge from a baggage handler and beating or tricking the PIN code out of him or her.

Successful defensive strategies all involve preparedness, rather than knee-jerk responses. Rather than examining people's shoes, we should be establishing a consistent perimeter around aircraft and ensuring that *everyone* with access to the aircraft or *anything* that goes on board is properly examined.

THE GOVERNMENT'S PANACEA: MAKING YOU FEEL BETTER, AT A PRICE

Immediately after 9/11, travelers were subjected to a confused and senseless mishmash of security practices. Worse yet, the media had begun to dig into the status of airport security prior to 9/11, and horrifying revelations surfaced regarding the training and qualifications of airport security screeners and their efficiency, or lack thereof.

HOW MUCH WILL THIS COST?

One of the first actions for improving air travel security was to federalize the airport security screeners, establish new standard security practices, and slap a 9/11 security surcharge tax on all airplane tickets. The 9/11 security surcharge of $3 per ticket raises approximately $3 billion to fund new government-mandated standards. This is in addition to an existing 7.5 percent excise tax and $6 in flight segment charges, as well as airport passenger facility charges that add as much as an additional $9 per ticket. With over 10 percent of most ticket costs going to existing fees and taxes, it's amazing that security has managed to remain unfunded for so long.

Industry officials were quick to claim that $3 billion was not enough money to implement the necessary changes. The mind boggles at such an assertion — you would think we could get something out of a $3 billion expenditure. The fact is that changes to security should have been implemented and paid for over a longer time with lower surcharges following Pan Am 103's destruction way back in 1988.

Did air travelers get better security in return for their extra billions of dollars in surcharges? Almost certainly not. But we did get a shiny new bureaucracy.

Probably the one ray of sunshine in the whole effort to reassess how we do airline security screening was the formation of the Transportation Security Administration (TSA), a centralized federal agency charged with overseeing airport security. (TSA is also responsible for security of buses and trains, but because there have been no terrorist incidents involving buses or trains, we'll just conveniently forget about that avenue of attack for now.)

TSA IN PLAY

Clearly, federalizing security screening at airports was a good idea; this is not a situation where you want to "go with the lowest bidder." But almost immediately after its formation, the Transportation Safety Administration became a political football. Congressional partisans began wrangling over whether or not the new body of approximately 27,000 federal employees would be allowed to join the government workers' union. Meanwhile, most citizens were wondering "and *how* exactly is this relevant?" As a result of partisan politics, the security screener issue dragged along for nearly a year.

you should know

The Aviation and Transportation Security Act, enacted in November 2002, required what it referred to as "security screening personnel" to pass a civil service exam, have a high school diploma or equivalent experience, pass a background check for a criminal record, undergo training, and show competency in written and spoken English. Apparently none of these was required for screeners until 9/11!

What the situation boils down to is *trust*. Security screeners, baggage handlers, and airport workers need to be trustworthy and competent. It is apparent that going with untrained minimum-wage workers has not been effective. In 2000, starting salaries for screeners at 19 of the nations' largest airports were $5.15 per hour to $6 per hour — some restroom attendants make $10 per hour. Now we're going to pay a premium for a new bureaucracy that provides no more in the way of security. TSA screeners' starting salaries range from $23,600 to $35,400 ($13 per hour to $19 per hour, assuming a standard government full-time employment conversion of 1,776 hours/year without adding benefits). Still, with that price tag it's just as possible for a mole to get a job with TSA as it would be with any of the private security firms that used to provide airport screening.

What we're getting with TSA is the feeling of comfort that comes with paying top dollar for something. The annals of great marketing triumphs are filled with cases where products managed to soar ahead of their competitors by charging more and letting customers assume that they were therefore somehow better. That's what we're getting ready to do with our airport security. It's hard to quantify how much the government has already spent to make people feel that they are more secure. It's harder still to quantify any material benefits from the effort.

TRUSTING CITIZENS

One aspect of the Aviation and Transportation Security Act that has come under considerable fire has been a requirement for U.S. citizenship — a requirement that disqualified nearly one quarter of the existing security screeners. As the ACLU points out, it is unreasonable to require citizenship of security screeners when baggage handlers and other crucial airport workers are not required to be citizens.

It's certainly easy for an illegal immigrant to get work as an airport screener employed by TSA. Never mind the usual argument as to whether or not illegal immigrants should be barred from working security; screeners are people who need to be trustworthy. The Department of Transportation (www.oig.dot.gov) lists 796 indictments and 402 convictions for felonious falsification of security badge applications on its Web site.

" Airport security is a sieve. "

Falsification of information on job applications doesn't suggest a high level of trustworthiness in my book.

Look at some examples of the current situation:

- In 2003, 42 foreign nationals pleaded guilty to charges of gaining access to secure areas of the Charlotte-Douglas International Airport under false pretenses. The investigation resulted in 66 indictments and the arrest of 51 individuals on charges of use of false immigration documents, fraudulent social security numbers, and falsified badge applications. A total of 49 of the defendants have pleaded guilty and are being processed for deportation; an additional 15 are fugitives.
- In another case in 2003, 28 airport employees were arrested at Bush Intercontinental Airport in Houston, Texas. A total of 143 people *including 5 TSA contract screeners* were indicted with various violations of federal law during the process of applying for airport security badges.

The list goes on and on. Airport security is a sieve.

THE TSA AT WORK

For a time there was a fad in which the press eagerly reported each case where someone was able to sneak something past the screeners. Clearly, something had to be done, if only to keep up appearances. The first big piece of window dressing took place almost immediately, with the appearance of soldiers carrying automatic weapons to back up the security screeners. These soldiers showed that the government was serious, at least, and probably also served to help remind people to stay polite in the face of city-block-long lines at security screening stations in most major airports.

Did having men in military uniforms carrying empty rifles improve security? Of course not. The armed soldiers did not apprehend a single terrorist. Neither, by the way, did the security screeners. But it was an important step because it tested the waters of the federal government taking a direct hand in airport security.

CENTRALIZING SECURITY

One role the federal government can play is in establishing consistency of procedures and training. In terms of preparedness, it is *absolutely crucial that airport security screeners be centralized* and undergo consistent training. Centralization that replaces the kind of random security rules that reigned during the weeks following the 9/11 attack is the key to being able to adapt quickly to new threat models as they evolve.

> " *Under the old system, each airport had its own security services, usually contracted out to the lowest bidder.* "

Centralizing airport security is also crucial because it builds the necessary management structures and communication practices that allow information to be shared among airports. Under the old system, each airport had its own security services, usually contracted out to the lowest bidder. Imagine if you discovered, through a counterintelligence source, that a group of terrorists was going to attempt to pass through security carrying devices matching a certain description. With no centralized communication system, whom would you tell? And how would you ensure that the information was propagated to those who need it in time?

ENTER THE FEDS

The federal government's involvement in airport security, as embodied in TSA, has already made great strides toward regularizing practices. In the years since Pan Am 103 was destroyed, domestic checked luggage was *still* not subjected to X-ray examination. In December 2002, new policies implementing X-ray screening of all checked and carry-on luggage went into place. It seems to be a fairly obvious thing to have done, but it required a high-level mandate backed up by money in order to get it done.

As a frequent traveler, my impression of the new security screening practices is favorable, overall. A lot of the "random" checks have been phased out in preference to simply applying the same searches to every-one. That's the most conservative and evenhanded approach.

TRAINING IS KEY

TSA employees, in their new white uniform shirts, seem to be more professional, more experienced with their equipment, and more moti-vated on the whole than their predecessors. Training is key, and money is being spent on training. Baggage screeners actually have to pass pro-ficiency tests now, rather than simply be warm bodies.

So, has TSA made us more secure? Probably, a little bit. The real place where TSA could pay off is in the future. If terrorist attacks continue or increase, TSA could provide a critical organizational structure at a crucial time. Failing that, it's an obvious sign of change in practices following

---

BACK TO SCHOOL

Recently, there was a report on CNN that during training for new screeners, the screeners were "given the test answers in advance of the test." The report described in a shocked tone how testers were coached on the answers for the tests as part of review prior to taking the exam. For anyone who has been through military enlisted training, that should sound familiar. Most nonacademic testing programs tell the student "Here is what you will be tested on. Here is the precise answer you are supposed to give." This is actually extremely effective because it ensures that everyone has a common baseline of knowledge at a minimum. There is no quicker and better way to achieve this core knowledge — baggage screeners don't need a master's degree in psychology; they need expertise on a narrower, less creative intellectual front.

9/11. Nobody would expect things to stay the same; therefore, change must be visible, even if it means putting all your security screeners in matching white shirts with the same patches on their shoulders.

WHAT'S IN IT FOR SECURITY VENDORS?

A few short months after the 9/11 attack, I was commuting home, listening to a popular news radio station, when they played an ad (the first of many I was to hear in the next few months) by a company touting products that could help to secure the government's systems to defend against terrorism. The particular product being advertised was a customer relations management software product intended to make it easier for sales representatives to manage customer contacts and the sales process. Amazingly, it was now a premier tool for helping government agencies be responsive in the event of emergencies.

At my previous company, we had actually purchased the product (at enormous cost). We had a small army of consultants (at enormous cost) work to make it actually useful for its intended purpose. I can only imagine an emergency response organization trying to use something that took so long for a private company to install and train users to use.

Everyone was rushing to cash in on 9/11. Everyone was trying to figure out how to repurpose their products to somehow be useful or important in national security.

PUT YOUR THUMB THERE . . .

A few days after the 9/11 attacks, some biometric products vendors began floating the idea that airport security could be dramatically improved if thumbprint readers were used to help ensure the identity of travelers. Some airports have even followed the buzz and announced that they have deployed biometric systems. Generally, these devices are used for access to baggage or other restricted areas. Access to restricted areas usually requires authenticating hundreds of people per hour; compare and contrast that to a passenger-screening checkpoint that deals with hundreds of people per minute.

Let's examine this for a minute, because it's a perfect case study of how the hype bandwagon operates. Biometric systems require that the user be "introduced" to the system beforehand, in order to work. After all, because the biometric system is going to somehow "read" the passengers, it has to get a chance to make the first reading so that it can recognize them next time they want to come through. In other words, for a thumbprint reader to function, the user's thumb must first be placed on the reader and his or her identity added to the system. Usually, this takes more than one thumbprint; it may take several attempts so that the computer has a better chance of recognizing the person again.

How is this going to work for hundreds of thousands of travelers? It's not. Nobody — not even the biometrics vendors — was crazy enough to think that it would. But if you listened to the marketing after 9/11, the biometrics vendors were trying to sell it as a solution to airline security, nevertheless. The implication was that it would be useful for travelers and that, if only the airports had been using biometrics, 9/11 might not have happened. Is that intellectual dishonesty? In order to thumbprint-authenticate *every* traveler, some kind of centralized computer database of thumbprints would be necessary, which would be a humongous technical undertaking.

But there are even more fundamental flaws with the concept: How could the fingerprints be entered into the database in the first place? For *any* authentication system to work, some kind of strong association needs to be made between the person being identified and the means of that identification. In other words, a thumbprint might be entered into a database, but somehow it's got to be guaranteed to belong to the person it's purported to belong to. A photo may be entered into a database, but someone has to make sure that it's the right photo in the first place. How would this be done? All travelers would have to get their biometric information entered into the database, but how would they prove their identity? With their driver's license and a credit card?

> **" The terrorists were able to obtain their driver's licenses by taking advantage of a Virginia rule that allowed them to get a license based on a local resident vouching for them. "**

When the 9/11 terrorists boarded their fateful flights, they were carrying government-issued ID cards in the form of driver's licenses that had been obtained under false pretenses. The terrorists were able to obtain their driver's licenses by taking advantage of a Virginia rule that allowed them to get a license based on a local resident vouching for them. The terrorists paid local migrant workers who had already obtained driver's licenses to shepherd them through the process. In a sense, they were *authorized* individuals who were validated to the system. Biometrics, had they been deployed, would have identified them based on whatever had been installed in the biometrics database.

you should know

Needless to say, now that that particular horse has left the barn, Virginia has changed its rules regarding driver licensing. No effort is being made to look at the large number of licenses already issued under the previous scheme. Within the United States, state-issued driver's licenses are not standardized and resemble everything ranging from cheap plastic-covered paper to holographically "tamper-proof" ID cards. Most of them could easily be faked using a desktop scanner and a $200 inkjet printer.

AUTHENTICATION CHALLENGES

In fairness, biometrics vendors weren't claiming that everyone traveling should be identified biometrically. I think they just thought that there was a good opportunity to hype awareness of their products and what they could do in a more controlled environment than a public airport. The reality of the situation is that authentication is a hard problem. It's an *extremely* hard problem.

The actual mechanisms of authentication are irrelevant to the larger problems of making sure that the binding between the authentication mechanism and the individual is strong enough. Also, authentication doesn't address an important problem: Once they are authenticated, authorized users may do unauthorized things. Basically, it's hard to prevent abuse of authority once the authority is granted. For example, there have been several cases where INS agents have given visas to immigrants in return for money or sexual favors. These individuals were *doing what they were empowered to do, even though it was not what they were supposed to do*. Abuse of authority becomes an extremely severe problem in computerized environments because a computer doesn't exercise judgment; it just follows orders blindly.

AN ENEMY IN OUR MIDST

Many intelligence organizations are constantly worried about enemy infiltrators and spies. Such infiltrators can be extremely damaging, since they have inside knowledge, inside access, and are extremely hard to discern from legitimate members of the organization. So far, we have been spared (as far as we know) terrorists getting jobs as baggage handlers, chandlers, or pilots.

But the threat exists. American spies Aldrich Ames and Robert Hanssen greatly damaged CIA and the FBI, respectively, effectively making years of work moot, doing billions of dollars in damage, and costing dozens of lives. Some intelligence analysts believe that the damage done by Ames and Hanssen *nearly completely invalidated* CIA and the FBI's anti-Soviet efforts for a period of 10 years.

In the 1950s Russian intelligence forces scored massive successes against British intelligence by infiltrating them with a set of deep-cover mole agents. Kim Philby, Guy Burgess, and Donald McLean were moles who worked to positions of considerable responsibility; in fact, Philby was head of MI-6 counterintelligence. Philby, Burgess, and McLean were, at various times, in positions of authority within the British intelligence apparatus, and were able to support each other and even help advance each others' careers. Philby was actually recruited into the intelligence service by Burgess, with whom he had gone to college.

Several of the moles had long careers (nearly 20 years) and were promoted and respected until they finally were discovered and fled to the Soviet Union. The Kim Philby story is a perfect case in point for why intelligence organizations must do background checks on individuals before they grant them access and authority.

So what's the point of having biometrics at an airport at all? It makes the customers feel better, but only if the customers don't really

---

MOLE PEOPLE

There are some interesting differences between Kim Philby and Aldrich Ames. Philby claimed until his death that he was never a traitor, and that he was always loyal to the ideals of Marxism and the Soviet Union. Ames was a bitter little bureaucrat who loved money, and who was "turned" by skilled handlers. The difference between these characters was *ideology*. This is the same kind of ideology that makes Palestinian teenagers strap bombs to their bodies and detonate themselves in public places, or that makes young men fly airplanes into buildings. It's a hard thing to dedicate your life to being a mole within an enemy organization, but it's probably easier than losing your life. Anyone who has the dedication to be a suicidal terrorist certainly can serve as a mole.

GIVE UP? THE ANSWERS ARE NO AND NO

For over 16 years, ticket agents have been required to ask passengers the ritual questions: "Has anyone unknown to you asked you to carry an item on this flight?" and "Have any of the items you have been traveling with been out of your immediate control since the time you packed them?" Both of these questions are no longer necessary, according to the Transportation Safety Administration. Apparently, asking those questions has never successfully prevented a bombing or hijacking.

---

understand the issues. Prior to 9/11 you needed an ID card and a PIN code to gain access to most baggage areas at major airports. Today, in a handful of airports, you might need a thumbprint that matches an authorized ID in a database. Are we more secure? Probably not. But a lot of money has been spent, and the biometric product vendors would be happy if we continued to buy their products. Would biometrics help protect airport security against a terrorist mole? Of course not; they can't even weed out the illegal aliens and luggage thieves — let alone an ideological mole or saboteur who keeps a low profile.

PROFILING MEETS SECURITY

One topic that comes up in the media is the question of "profiling." Profiling is the practice of identifying primary characteristics of the enemy, and more closely scrutinizing individuals who have those characteristics. For example, all of the 9/11 terrorists had swarthy complexions: Naïve profiling would tell us that individuals with similar complexions should be more carefully searched at airport security. Of course, profiles can be refined to be fairly precise and more useful: Facial features, skin colors, types of clothes, frequency of flights, or one-way versus round-trip itineraries are all possible criteria for a profiler to examine.

REARING ITS UGLY HEAD

Profiling is a controversial topic when it comes to airline security. Many people have pointed out that it's silly to deep-search a 70-year-old nun when the problem we're facing is terrorist violence from Islamic fundamentalists. The argument goes "We know who is causing the problem; let's look there, not elsewhere."

Following that logic will only prepare us against the next attack from people who look the part; in fact, it explicitly opens the door to anyone with a modicum of skill at disguising him- or herself. How hard would it be for a dark-haired, dark-skinned man with a beard to become a sun-bleached beach bum? It would take only a few hours or days.

Someone who is willing to give his or her life in a suicide attack will be willing to give up his hair or her color and wear a Hawaiian shirt.

> " *Most mileage-plus platinum members didn't get their 500,000-mile flier status by blowing up the airplanes they are on.* "

Fundamentalist terror organizations may also be able to recruit misguided Americans and convince them to take arms against their country. The shoe bomber Richard Reid was not a Saudi Arabian or Palestinian; he was a British citizen. John Walker Lindh, the "American Taliban," was a white suburban California boy. If Walker Lindh had chosen to show his devotion to Islam by getting on a plane with a bomb, no amount of racial profiling would have detected him.

Relying on racial appearance is probably a terrible metric for profiling. Relying on frequent flier miles would probably work better. Most mileage-plus platinum members didn't get their 500,000-mile flier status by blowing up the airplanes they are on. Ironically, some airlines appear to be using frequent flier status as a discriminator for whom to search. I've noticed that when I fly first class, I am much less likely to get screened. That's not a scientific study, of course, but it makes you wonder if terrorists would be willing to buy first-class seats.

Sarcasm aside, it is dangerous to rely on shortcuts like profiling because shortcuts are really a way to reduce preparedness. In the event of an emergency alert, security needs to be looking at everyone — even the people who look like 70-year-old nuns.

THE PROFILING CONTROVERSY

Experts are divided on the issue of racial profiling; they always have been and probably always will be. 9/11 certainly hasn't helped. If you look at the pictures of the 9/11 terrorists, they were all male, dark-eyed, dark-haired, swarthy-skinned individuals. If security on 9/11 had been carefully searching everyone matching that profile, the attack *might* have been thwarted. It's not likely, though. Even if they had been searched, the worst-case scenario for the terrorists would be that they would apologetically give up their knives and apologize for not leaving them home.

It's easy for the pundits to wail "Why don't we do something?" However, during 2002, when you boarded an airplane, you were subject to random search regardless of whether or not you fit a particular profile. We've all heard stories of 10-year-old kids being asked to take off their shoes so that they could be searched, while tall young men behind them were waved through security and onto a plane. Does this make sense? No; it's patently stupid. In fact, the whole profiling question is patently stupid.

Profiling works in some places and times, but rarely. Setting racial insensitivity aside, profiling assumes that your enemy is visibly distinguishable from your friend, and that you have a single distinct enemy. In countries that are very racially homogenous, for example, profiling may work if you're dealing with a relatively homogenous enemy. If Japan were having problems with Arabic extremists, it might be sensible to try to profile the population. In the United States, we have loyal citizens who fit every ethnic description you can imagine, which reduces the effectiveness of profiling to the point where it's most effective only in 20/20 hindsight.

POLITICS AND PROFILING

Unfortunately, profiling is a topic that also runs afoul of political correctness. The United States is still trying to deal with the cognitive dissonance of having our own domestic version of apartheid and all of the cultural and moral aftershocks of how that policy conflicted with the American dream.

During WWII we interned Japanese-American citizens in prison camps, thereby dealing a gross insult to a large number of loyal citizens, while simultaneously denying ourselves access to a valuable intelligence asset. We've done profiling in the past, and it hasn't worked particularly well. Would it work any better today?

FLYING UNDER PROFILING'S RADAR

If you establish a profile, it's a safe assumption that sooner or later the enemy will study that profile and exploit that knowledge to his or her own ends. If profiling were in use, it would take about a day for an intelligent person, sitting at an airport departure lounge near the security screening area, to figure out the criteria that were in use. Drug runners have understood this for years, and they have learned to effectively "decorate" their "mules" with children, tourist costumes, and so on. In other words, a strict profiling regime works, but only for a short time and mostly in hindsight.

Remember, if we had been monitoring Arab-Americans, Timothy McVeigh, a domestic white male nutcase, would have easily evaded the profile. When the Washington, D.C.-area sniper suspects were at large, there was considerable public discussion of profiles, and many pundits pointed out that the sniper was almost certainly a white male because most mass murders of that type were committed by white males. This teaches us a fundamental lesson about profiling: The profiles must be updated constantly, and the events that trigger the updates are the kind you don't want to occur. Next time there's a mass murderer sniper on the loose, will African-Americans be on the potential suspect profile until we have sufficient ethnic diversity in our murderers to abandon that paradigm?

So If Not Profiling, What?

If airport security was completely based on profiling, we could expect it to lurch from threat to threat, always one step behind the current actions of the enemy.

In fact, U.S. federal law prohibits profiling based on race or religion. So what's the alternative? The alternative is a fail-closed security approach that turns a blind eye to race or religion by searching everyone equally. Would American passengers tolerate a three-hour wait to clear through security? Probably not. Remember, we're the same culture that resents being asked, "Has anyone unknown to you asked you to carry an item on this flight?"

El Al Airlines privately interviews each passenger before anyone is allowed to board an airplane, as well as performs a close examination of passports and past visas, carries on a discussion of trip plans, and so on. When a ticket is issued, the passengers' names are checked against appropriate watch-lists for possible connections. Of course, with only about 40 flights per day, it is possible to provide such a level of scrutiny.

FAIL CLOSED OR FAIL OPEN?

As mentioned briefly in Chapter 2, there are two fundamental approaches to security: Fail closed and fail open. The *fail-closed approach* assumes that everything is potentially threatening and tries to apply security at every appropriate level. The *fail-open* approach tries to build a list of everything that is known to be threatening and to apply security against the known threats.

Obviously, fail closed is a much more expensive and intrusive approach, since it involves designing security into all aspects of a problem, while fail open usually relies on applying fixes whenever a new problem is identified.

Take a look at some relevant examples. In a fail-closed approach to aircraft security, *everyone* getting within 50 feet of an aircraft would have to submit to a consistent and detailed search protocol, whereas in a fail-open approach, a subset of the population would be searched based on rules that change over time depending on the current threat model.

The recent aircraft security focus on checking passengers' shoes is based on a single attack that has caused our threat model to be updated. This is an example of fail-open security, because it ignores other items of clothing that could contain explosives just as easily as shoes.

In a fail-closed security system, all passengers would be searched, along with all their clothing and possessions. No security system is entirely fail closed, because defensive techniques change and evolve over time, usually in response to changes in the threat model or defensive technologies.

In the United States, with hundreds of flights out of a single airport in a day, a thumbprint reader or a check for photo ID offers the appearance of security without any of the annoying headaches associated with actually having it.

IN A PERFECT WORLD

In a world where crowded airports and frequent border crossings aren't going to go away, what can our government and security professionals do to protect us? Though they probably can't make travel completely secure or borders completely inviolable, they can do a lot more than they're doing today.

MAKING PLANES SECURE

While I was researching this book, I tried desperately to find even *one* example where U.S. airport passenger screening had actually prevented a terrorist incident. We have this gigantic, expensive bureaucracy and infrastructure that has no actual history of serving a purpose other than keeping up appearances. Of course, if it wasn't there, the terrorists *would* have a field day, so the question is this: How *can* we get as much mileage as possible out of the billions of dollars we are spending on it?

The TSA is obviously a huge improvement over the old way of doing things. But that's not much of an accomplishment. The value I see in TSA is that *finally* some of the screening rules and processes are being established and enforced consistently. This gives us two crucial pieces of leverage: consistency and a single place from which to update rules. In theory if the FBI sent out an alert to be on the lookout for cellular phones packed with explosives, there is a single central organization that could react efficiently as a unit. In theory if the FBI sent out such an alert, *all* airport security would adjust their security posture to take into account the new information. In reality I think that's probably just wishful thinking.

So what can we do? Let's demand more of TSA: Develop and drill screeners to be on the lookout for new threats as threat models are updated. Make certain that communications between TSA headquarters and the screeners in the field are fast and efficient. Do some war games — send out a flash alert to look for a particular object and have a group of testers try to carry that object through security at a variety of airports.

> " *The connection has to go far above and beyond 'Hey, it's a code orange day, so be on the lookout. OK, guys?'* "

And last but far from least, establish tight connections between TSA and the FBI and CIA's counterterror offices so that if they believe that something is in the offing, the baggage and security screeners can be on the alert for it. The connection has to go far above and beyond "Hey, it's a code orange day, so be on the lookout. OK, guys?"

FORGET PROFILING

Profiling is the bad idea that won't go away. Let's *just forget about profiling completely* and make sure that *everyone* goes through the *same level* of screening regardless of how they look, act, or dress. That way nobody can complain that they are being singled out for persecution. I think we're already heading down this path. Gone are the days of random searches; now everyone's baggage goes through the X ray. How much more democratic can you get?

BIOMETRICS? I DON'T THINK SO...

Forget biometrics; they are too expensive and unreliable. If we want to go the route of authenticating everyone, then let's implement a national ID card. That card should come with attached digital storage that includes a digitally signed photograph, read/write-once memory to contain information about when you've entered and exited the country, and a transponder system like EZPass that allows the data to be accessed remotely. Include on the card an ID number that ties to a database of DNA samples and fingerprints. Don't let anyone drive a car, get a job, open a bank account, or make a purchase larger than $100 without showing his or her ID. Let's take it a step further and give immigrants and visitors visas only after they submit a DNA sample, and give them a similar ID card with a code that expires with their visa. Make it illegal for anyone to be out and about without his or her ID.

None of this is by any means technologically far-fetched. In fact, I'm pretty sure that some of our smart uber-geeks in California could whip it up pretty quickly for a whole lot less than the INS has wasted on its fingerprint database. Big Brother would love it. But it'd work.

Of course I didn't think you'd like any of these suggestions. They remind us that we have to choose what kind of society we want to live in. The issue is not a technological one — it's a question of what we're willing to give up in return for security.

7

Irresistible Force versus Inscrutable Object

Last week a friend forwarded me one of those "quotable quotes" emails that circle endlessly on the Internet. At the bottom, it read: "You read about all these terrorists — most of them came here legally, but they hung around on these expired visas, some for as long as 10 to 15 years. Now, compare that to Blockbuster; you are two days late with a video and those people are all over you. Let's put Blockbuster in charge of immigration."

Post-9/11, the pundits were asking "What kind of failures led to 9/11?" as if something *existed* and then *failed*. Asking "What went wrong with homeland security" brings the implicit assumption that there actually was any in the first place. Why do we believe that? Whatever justified that belief?

Without delving too deeply into the history of security, please ask yourself "Has the U.S. homeland ever been secure?" The answer may surprise you. We've been most secure when we've been on the *offensive*. We've been secure between wars because, in general, most of the world has seen what happens when the United States goes on the offensive and wants no part of being on the receiving end. Have we, as a nation, ever shown particular expertise at antiterrorism? Perhaps the "failures" that led to 9/11 were fundamentally no more difficult to understand than *we never learned how to do that stuff.* Looking at where we've been might tell you a bit about where we're going.

THE SABER AND THE SCALPEL

The security of the U.S. homeland is implemented by four main components of force:

- The military: the guys and gals with guns (Army, Navy, Air Force, and so on)
- The border watchers: INS, Customs, Coast Guard
- The intelligence community: the spies and counterspies (CIA, NSA, NRO, and so on)
- The FBI and other law enforcement agencies

The behaviors of these particular organizations, and their organizational missions, make them variously successful at offense or defense.

A MILITARY APPROACH

The military, because our national existence is at stake, is programmed to align itself toward the greatest threat currently existing to our survival as a free nation. This has been consistent and is exactly what they are supposed to do; and they do it well.

Still, the fact remains that the forces that crushed Imperial Japan and Hitler's Germany don't work well against our own citizens or domestic population: Armies make mediocre police forces unless their purpose is ruthless pacification.

The modern U.S. Army has actually done a very good job of coping with irregular actions and police duties in trouble spots around the globe, but generally it is still dealing with police duties that would make the LAPD SWAT team blanch in terror. Soldiers understand how to arrest a perpetrator who is shooting at you with a machine gun; the trick is being able to find pieces of him afterwards to put on trial. In Afghanistan and Iraq, U.S. forces were quick to try to coordinate with local police to get them back on their feet; I think our military has a good grasp of this problem: Soldiers are not cops.

If 9/11 can teach us anything, it's that instability in global crisis points can directly hurt us at home. We haven't internalized that lesson, yet, but once (or if) we do, I predict we will see a new focus on global stabilization as part of our foreign policy. In a sense, it would be a continuation of Cold War foreign policy — instead of trying to halt the spread of global communism, let's halt the spread of exporters of ideological violence and those who arm them. The Bush administration appears to understand this connection between global stabilization and homeland security at a gut level, and I applaud that understanding.

Soldiers exist to clean up the mistakes of politicians and diplomats, and it's good to have them on the team. The U.S. military spent a lot of time and blood cleaning up the mistakes of politicians in the twentieth century. If we had security at home between 1918 and 1997, it was mostly because the most egregious of those mistakes happened in Europe and the Pacific Rim, not in North America.

> " *Soldiers exist to clean up the mistakes of politicians and diplomats.* "

However, sabers are not an effective tool when what you really need is a scalpel: In an antiterrorism environment there is no opportunity to prosecute the kind of total warfare that Western armies have been built to wage since WWI. In total war, the best defense really *is* a strong offense. 9/11 was the crowning event that forced us to realize that you can be in a war that your army can't end single-handedly; something we *might* have learned in Vietnam if we'd been paying close attention. The Bush administration appears to have gotten this message, though, and is executing a new form of combined-arms attack: military force, diplomacy, financial incentives, and reconstructive assistance. In a very real sense, the military is being used to tackle terrorism on the broad scale— the national level — while CIA and U.S. aid organizations are working at the detail level. The Bush administration appears to be effectively using both the sword and the scalpel, and the rate at which Al Qaeda members continue to be rounded up shows it.

BORDER PATROL

The border watchers are an important part of the homeland security picture as well, but unfortunately ours are incompetent at keeping bad guys out of our borders. They always have been.

It's not their fault — the border watchers' mission has always been overshadowed by drug smuggling, booze running, and trying to keep out would-be immigrants. (Keep in mind that the latter group is so weak they don't have the financial wherewithal, patience, or savvy to get into the country without doing something as obvious as getting caught sneaking across the border with all their worldly goods on their backs.)

you should know

Nobody has a reliable estimate, but experts guess that between 100,000 and 400,000 (depending on the political agenda of the expert, I suppose) illegals enter the border every year.

The reason our border watchers never developed serious skills at protecting against people invasions is because they have been focused on drug interdiction, other forms of smuggling, and illegal immigration, not terrorism. Drugs and smuggled goods are pretty easy to identify when they are found. Terrorists with real passports and visas look just like every other legitimate visitor to the country: A completely different and much higher level of scrutiny would be required to catch them. Drug runners drop their goods into the Florida Everglades from silent airplanes at night, or transport them in false-bottomed oil drums — when you catch someone doing that, it's pretty obvious what is going on. Terrorists entering a country are not obvious.

We've used incredibly advanced technology like military Airborne Warning and Control System (AWACS) planes to track drug aircraft from Colombia, and military satellite reconnaissance systems to vector Coast Guard ships to catch drug runners. But we haven't used the same level of good old American technical know-how and ingenuity to address the issue of border controls. We certainly have the technology; it's just not being employed.

During the first and second World Wars, enemy spies were able to enter the country pretty much at will. Crossing the border was never a problem for spies; the border is too long. It's also difficult to detect someone's intentions at the border of a country. During the Cold War, Russian agents entered the country at will through Canada. Many KGB agents were utterly innocuous as they entered the country; some of them even carried diplomatic passports.

Like the army, the border watchers have never really been an effective force for homeland security because they've never been asked to be. The military and the border police are powerful tools, but they do not offer the kind of scalpel-like precision that is necessary to deal with terrorists. Whether we like it or not, that can only come from intelligence backed by law enforcement.

THE MIND OF A COP, THE MIND OF A SPY

There are fundamental differences in the agendas and thought processes of law enforcement agents and spies. It is probably *impossible* for them to fully cooperate unless they exist within a relationship that is carefully structured to encourage it — and to keep them apart until it is necessary to bring them together. This dynamic tension is incredibly apparent in the problem of getting the U.S. FBI (cops) to work effectively with the U.S. intelligence community (spies).

Consider the emotional, organizational, and cultural differences between these two groups:

- Police officers produce arrests and catch bad guys. Spies produce intrigues and often work with, deceive, and manage relationships with the same kind of bad guys police officers exist to catch and put away.
- Police officers wear badges and give evidence. Spies blend in, collect information, and only rarely disgorge carefully processed intelligence.
- Police officers are proud to divulge the methods they use to catch the bad guys. Spies collect the secret tricks of tradecraft, double cross, and disinformation, and hoard them for reuse whenever possible.
- Police officers are most effective against lone gunmen, because these bad guys represent a loose end that can be neatly tied up. Spies always assume that an individual enemy is the tip of a much more deeply sunken iceberg of operations and plotting.
- Police officers are often driven by a desire for justice. Spies are often driven by a sense of expediency.

It is this tension between justice and expediency that is the oil-and-water nature of the relationship between law enforcement and espionage and forms the interface boundary where they either fight most ferociously or cooperate most efficiently.

Cops and Robbers

There is one area where police officers and spies share a common agenda: They always want to know what the enemy is doing, but they go about that differently.

Police officers revere good old-fashioned detective work, collecting facts and making observations to build a complete picture of events. When necessary, facts and observations come from people, but the mind of a police officer is usually happiest when dealing with something that, unlike a human, can't lie.

When police officers get to the point where they are ready to start interviewing people regarding a suspect, they are either close to a solution, or they are fishing for some kind of trigger that will cause the suspect to react and give him- or herself away. This doesn't require secrecy; it requires a kind of mechanically precise discipline of leaving no stone unturned and no avenue unexplored. In virtually every police case where there's not an outright confession, the police officer's process involves sorting through a mountain of lies and comparing them with the evidence.

We're all familiar with the stereotypical police movie: The police detective confronts the wrongdoer with enough evidence that he finally confesses or pulls a gun and dies. The media myth of the police officer is one in which crime does not pay and the police officer makes sure everyone knows it. In a sense, it's a very American idea and pervades not only our media but our foreign policy.

> " The media myth of the police officer is one in which crime does not pay and the police officer makes sure everyone knows it. In a sense, it's a very American idea. "

In the semiotics of a police officer's mind, bad people do bad things, and good people do good things, and it's their job to sort the two out and provide evidence as to which is which. Nothing makes a police officer more uncomfortable than the "stool pigeon" or turncoat who appears to be so divorced from a clear morality that his or her allegiance is purely a matter of convenience. Intelligence agents *love* to find people like that— especially in the enemy camp — because they are the primary source of human intelligence. What a police officer holds in deepest contempt is a spy's greatest asset: a traitor.

Bond, James Bond

A spy is a different kind of creature entirely. They don't get the public reinforcement of seeing a criminal undone in the defendant's box. They get the quiet whispered congratulations of their peers and the knowledge that they accomplished things in the vast grey area below the public's ken. Intelligence professionals know that their stories may never be told, and if they are told, it won't be during their lifetimes. Having your exploits publicized is a sign of failure for a spy, the sign of a blown operation, a defeat. For a police officer, it is vindication.

The G-man wants to see Bonnie and Clyde either tearfully repent and be put safely away or be unrepentant — caught in the act — and gunned down in a hail of bullets. Where "case closed" is music to the police officer's ear, spies don't close cases, they just wrap them in deeper layers of code word secrecy and bury them. When spies get their hands on a bad guy, they wonder if they are seeing just the tip of a larger iceberg. When dealing with enemy agents, you don't put them away, you try to see if the agent can be turned, or somehow tagged and used as a lure to identify who supplied them with weapons, fenced their stolen goods, and carried their information back to their bosses.

> " *Mixing cops and spooks results in conflict, a police state, or a surveillance state.* "

The collision between cops and spooks is not just a cultural conflict; it is a fundamental difference in function and purpose. Mixing cops and spooks results in conflict, a police state, or a surveillance state.

THE 62-YEAR-LONG PISSING CONTEST

If the FBI and CIA were as effective against their enemies as they are against each other, the United States would have the best intelligence and enforcement in the world. Unfortunately, the relationship between the cops and the spooks has been a case of "one step forward, two steps back" since the very beginning.

NATURAL ENEMIES

As the United States was about to enter the Second World War, it had no effective foreign intelligence organization to speak of, and the president, with prompting from the British military intelligence apparatus, was encouraged to establish an office of intelligence and appointed William Donovan to head it. And so the pissing began.

> " J. Edgar Hoover, the man who created the myth of the 'G-man,' was a pillar of stubbornness, a master of bureaucratic skill, and a marketing genius. "

J. Edgar Hoover, the man who created the myth of the "G-man," was a pillar of stubbornness, a master of bureaucratic skill, and a marketing genius. The FBI that he created in his image is probably the finest law enforcement agency that has ever existed. William "Wild Bill" Donovan, the head of the newly formed intelligence organization, was almost the anti-Hoover. Where Donovan was Ivy League, well traveled, and well read, Hoover was anti-intellectual, stubbornly smart, xenophobic, and mistrustful of "culture."

Every aspect of Hoover's FBI seemed to be the very antithesis of espionage culture. Agents were expected to never hold back the truth, to dress the same, to speak the same, and to show intense loyalty to their teammates. Unlike the head of the highly secretive intelligence organization, Hoover was deeply concerned with the public image of the G-man as the white knight of the American experiment. He was relentless in promoting solved cases and ensuring that when the FBI did something smart, everyone heard about it.

you should know

Conversely, the FBI's occasional failures were quietly chalked up to experience and not discussed. Even early in the FBI's institutional history, there was a strong culture of "circling the wagons" when the Bureau was under attack or criticism.

Both men, however, were skilled bureaucrats and immediately began fighting for territory. The methods Donovan and Hoover used against each other became the weapons that today's FBI and CIA are still using against each other, even following 9/11: leaking internal memos, uncovering each other's operations, and launching periodic witch-hunts against foreign-intelligence moles in each other's organizations. The behavior of these two agencies would be a laughable Keystone Cops-quality performance if it wasn't coming from two organizations so vital to homeland security.

you should know

Readers who are interested in learning in detail how dysfunctional the FBI/CIA relationship has been should read Mark Reibling's *Wedge: From Pearl Harbor to 9/11 — How the Secret War between the FBI and CIA Has Endangered National Security*, a meticulously researched, fascinating, and depressing book.

TRYING TO FIX IT

Throughout the history of the FBI and CIA, "cooperation" has been mandated by a literal stream of executive orders, presidential directives, memoranda of understanding, and agreements intended to enhance and improve relations between the organizations. Virtually every president has made some attempt to establish liaison and improved coordination. None of these efforts has worked.

The only thing that has improved coordination has been national "wake-up calls" such as Pearl Harbor and 9/11. The coordination that results from these events usually lasts only a month or two before the relationship breaks down into bickering again.

So what's the problem? Unfortunately, there are three causes of conflict that make it impossible to enforce a rapprochement:

- First and foremost is the basic tension between the goals of police officers and spies. I believe that the other causes are more apparent but less intractable, so government tends to focus on them for a quick fix.
- The second cause was the personality conflict between Hoover and Donovan, both strong-minded leaders who were extremely jealous and protective of their "territory." In order to accomplish the goal of having a foreign intelligence service, without entering into open warfare with J. Edgar Hoover, the president tried to avoid conflict by dividing intelligence down an artificial line between "internal" and "international." In an attempt to avoid a huge battle, we got a prolonged low-level conflict that has seriously impaired the United States' ability to do intelligence since just prior to WWII.
- This personality conflict between Hoover and Donovan resulted in the third cause of conflict between the agencies: an artificial division between domestic and foreign intelligence objectives.

IT STARTS AT THE TOP

J. Edgar Hoover was a marketing whiz kid. When he took over the FBI, it was a corrupt organization that was bumbling and inefficient. By turning its agents into clean-cut, well-trained, nearly robotic copies of himself, he formed it into the finest police force the world has ever seen. He also marketed the FBI to the American public as an unstoppable force: During the 1940s and 1950s, the FBI was highly regarded and the myth of the G-man reigned supreme.

Wild Bill Donovan realized that two could play that game, and following the end of WWII, began promoting CIA in a similar manner. Hush-hush "never before told" tales leaked into the popular press, including tales of daring-do against the Nazis. These tales evolved into a mainstream genre of "spy novel" that reached its height with the writings of Ian Fleming's James Bond.

It's hard not to recognize such self-serving marketing as bureaucratic empire building, but unfortunately it also served as a weapon during the protracted CIA/FBI war. To this day, the FBI is notorious for trumpeting its big kills to the press.

you should know

It's widely known in the computer security community where I work that many of the big hacker cases the FBI "solved" were in reality solved by contractors, outsiders, or sometimes the victim. But the FBI has stood ready to claim the credit, when it looks like the credit is worth claiming. CIA is a bit more low-key as a general rule, but many of the bits of embarrassing information regarding the FBI screwups appear to have originated from sources close to CIA.

> **" After 60 years, the FBI/CIA war has continued despite presidents, real-world wars, and wake-up calls. It's a war to the death. "**

Where do we stand today? In February 2003, George W. Bush announced that there had been past coordination problems between the FBI and CIA, but that they had all been worked out. Don't believe it! After 60 years, the FBI/CIA war has continued despite presidents, real-world wars, and wake-up calls. It's a war to the death, and the only way it will end is when one (or both) agencies disband.

WATCHING INSIDE, BLIND TO THE OUTSIDE

The division between domestic intelligence and international intelligence is an artificial concept that is utterly nonsensical in today's geopolitical climate. It didn't even make sense in 1940, and it certainly doesn't make sense now.

Consider that, under the CIA/FBI rules of engagement, the CIA's counterterrorism analysts had to stop surveillance of foreign nationals once they had entered the United States. Indeed, this is exactly what happened with several of the 9/11 terrorists. CIA memos regarding their entry into the country were passed to the FBI months after the terrorists had entered the country; this gave them plenty of time to go to ground. Even if the FBI had been notified in a timely manner, of course, the INS had no means of tracking foreign visitors once they were in the United States, and there would have been no chance of actually finding them.

On January 15, 2000, CIA's Counterterrorism Center (CTC) learned that Khalid Almihdhar and Nawaf Alhazmi, listed as suspected Al Qaeda terrorists, arrived in Los Angeles. CIA waited over a year before notifying the FBI. Now it gets complicated: Because of the FBI's requirements to prove that suspects are breaking the law before the agency can get telephone taps or engage in surveillance, the terrorists were actually safer in the United States than abroad. Ironically, had they been in another country, they could have legally been watched by CIA and also monitored by foreign intelligence services.

KEEPING SECRETS FROM EACH OTHER

Foreign intelligence services appear to share information with CIA regarding terrorists and possible terrorists. This information goes into CIA databases where it, apparently, sits.

After the first attack on the World Trade Center, FBI investigators found out that Egyptian intelligence had already provided CIA fairly detailed information about Sheikh Omar Abdel Rahman. Rahman was the leader of the Egyptian Jihad, the extremist group responsible for the assassination of Egyptian president Anwar Sadat in 1981. He was allowed to enter the United States in 1990 and establish mosques in Brooklyn and New Jersey, where he was safe from detailed investigation until two of his followers were indicted in the World Trade Center bombing.

At the same time this was going on, civil liberties activists were using congressional pressure to help block sharing of CIA intelligence to be used in processing visa requests. Rahman had already come to the attention of the FBI when he was apparently involved financially in supporting the assassination of Rabbi Meir Kahane, in 1990. It was during this investigation that the FBI learned that Rahman was on CIA's international terrorist list.

In 1990, the FBI gathered evidence that Rahman's followers were studying bomb design and collecting pictures of the World Trade Center, but since it was tied to the murder investigation of Rabbi Kahane, the information was not used. Both CIA and the FBI were at pains to interpret events as indicating noncooperation on the part of the other, but as a taxpayer, I have to say I am extremely unimpressed with both agencies.

In 1993, Ayatollah Khomeini, Muammar Ghaddafi, and Saddam Hussein issued a call for holy war against the United States and enemies of Islam. At that time, Egyptian intelligence informed CIA that there were Muslim extremist terrorist attacks being planned. CIA took the tip seriously enough to notify all U.S. embassies of a possible threat, but not the FBI. Or, perhaps CIA "forgot" to notify their counterparts at the FBI. In any case, deliberate or accidental, it was an egregious example of what passes for interagency "cooperation."

Civil libertarians are concerned that membership in or support of terrorist groups is difficult to define and determine, and that conferring of this status might be abused to unfairly deny visas.

JUST HOW DID YOU GET THIS INFORMATION?

One of the issues that concerns members of Congress is that some foreign intelligence may be collected by use of torture and shouldn't be usable by U.S. agencies. While this is a very well meaning and moral position to adopt, it ignores the reality of intelligence: Information is information, and in order to gather it, you sometimes resort to unsavory methods. That's a completely different approach, of course, from the standards we hold the FBI to: They're cops; they collect evidence. Basically, it seems as if all the forces of the U.S. government are working to make sure that the other forces are ineffective, underinformed, or otherwise hampered.

SHOOTING CIA IN THE FOOT

In 1995, CIA's foreign intelligence capability was almost completely demolished. Because of the Aldrich Ames case, and CIA Director John Deutch's charter to overcome barriers between CIA and the FBI, CIA's practices were altered to become more "consistent with American values." The Justice Department began making legal rulings on the appropriateness of sources and methods. At the same time, a huge investigation was being launched to determine the impact of Ames and whether there were other moles in CIA. Dozens of senior officers retired or resigned as the agency was raked over the coals by ham-fisted FBI counterintelligence teams, huge numbers of sources or informers were dropped, and attempts to penetrate terrorist or suspect organizations were stopped. Temporarily, the FBI had won the war, and it was a dark period for CIA.

In 1995, the FBI was given the lead role in antiterrorist activities, as well as counterespionage. By 1996, The FBI's Counterterrorism Center employed over 2,500 full-time staff. Once again, the FBI and CIA were collecting information and failing to share it.

After 9/11, former FBI Director Louis Freeh complained that the FBI was underfunded and had been unable to provide adequate intelligence, in spite of massive increases in budget year after year. In 1996, the FBI's counterterrorism budget was about $100 million; by 1999 it was $300 million. The FBI was not underfunded; it was too busy chasing after the popular threat models of the day: right wing militias and the Unabomber. Only in Washington is lack of funding an excuse used for failure on the part of agencies that are growing rapidly. "We had our heads up our asses" would probably hold more water as an excuse.

> **" The FBI was not underfunded; it was too busy chasing after the popular threat models of the day: right-wing militias and the Unabomber. "**

DHS, FBI, CIA: NOPE

How is merging this mess under DHS going to help? The answer is, it isn't.

Under DHS, the FBI and CIA are still two separate organizations, one of which is chartered with internal law enforcement and counterintelligence, the other of which is chartered with external intelligence and counterintelligence. DHS is supposed to "coordinate" and "facilitate" between the two. Coordinating and facilitating between CIA and the FBI has been tried before, and in the absence of fundamental change, it's going to fail again.

At least the administration managed to resist the temptation to give DHS its own counterintelligence and counterterrorist responsibility so that there could be a third organization collecting information that they wouldn't share with anyone else.

IN A PERFECT WORLD

Is there a way to resolve the historical competitiveness and mistrust that exists among our intelligence and law enforcement agencies in the age of homeland security? Yes...and no.

SHARPENING THE SABER AND THE SCALPEL

Since 9/11 the Bush administration has done a tremendous job in effectively orchestrating its use of the saber and the scalpel. We probably don't know enough, yet, about what happened in Afghanistan and Iraq to fully understand his methods, but I believe that one of the things we saw in Afghanistan was a new and extremely effective synthesis of combined arms operation. CIA intelligence teams were on the ground in Afghanistan, working hand in hand with military Special Forces teams and tribal leaders. Stories have already emerged of how money was used to grease the skids of war, as well as those of the ensuing peace. Operations in Afghanistan also resembled WWII in some of the ways in which interservice rivalry was shelved in the interest of getting the job done right and quickly.

you should know

My guess is that once we're done goofing around with this Department of Homeland Security nonsense, we'll take a few quick lessons in antiterrorism, and then the heartless bastards who made us realize we need to enroll in that particular school will really regret it. Indeed, the way in which international terrorists have been vacuumed up since 9/11 is thought-provoking. Observing the rate at which Al Qaeda members have been reeled in and gaffed shows that CIA has been on a very steep and positive learning curve.

The post-action reconstruction of Afghanistan is noteworthy also for not being particularly noteworthy. The media was all in a flutter about how Afghanistan had the potential to become a man-eating quagmire, or to explode in tribal or sectarian violence. Instead, it seems things are going about as well as could be expected. Once again, the pundits who predicted disaster have vanished back into the woodwork. In Iraq, the pundits who predict chaos and disaster every time someone takes a shot at a U.S. soldier are ignoring the fact that there would probably be more shootings and trouble if the troops were stationed in any major U.S. city.

In short, I think this is one place where we're pretty much doing it right. The military has a place in homeland security, but it is mostly from a standpoint of providing massive muscle where necessary to ensure that homeland security is not threatened by instability abroad. As cynical as it may seem, the way in which the U.S. forces elegantly toppled Afghanistan and then crushed Iraq will probably do more to improve our homeland security than any other single thing that we have done. Consider the number of tin-pot dictatorships around the world that are suddenly moving with blinding speed to eschew terrorism and render up Al Qaeda operatives. They're not doing it because they've seen the light — they're doing it because they've felt the heat.

> " *The way in which the United States forces elegantly toppled Afghanistan and then crushed Iraq will probably do more to improve our homeland security than any other single thing that we have done.* "

ENDING THE 62-YEAR PISSING CONTEST

Of all of the reorganizations that could have happened under the Department of Homeland Security, the big one that would have made the greatest difference — working out the issues between the FBI and CIA — simply didn't happen because some changes are too big for most bureaucrats to contemplate.

Shooting the Beast

The lack of cooperation between the FBI and CIA is not going to end just because another president asked them to play nicely. They will only end when serious, major efforts at restructuring our intelligence and national police force are undertaken. Some of these efforts would entail changes to laws, executive orders, and presidential directives. But half-measures won't cut it no matter how much wishful thinking you engage in. If you have two animals in a cage that won't stop fighting, sooner or later you need to remove or shoot one of them. It doesn't matter which, really, because you can then negotiate and train the survivor much more effectively.

Going Out of Business

The FBI needs to be taken out of the counterterror business entirely. In fact, the FBI needs to be taken out of the counterespionage business as well. It's only got a toehold in those fields as an historical artifact of a president who was scared to cross J. Edgar Hoover and whatever dirt he had on him in his legendary files.

The FBI, as one of the world's best police forces, should be refocused on crime fighting at a national level. They are, after all, our national police force — and that's the job they should be doing. Sure, let the FBI build cases, arrest spies, and use their awesome investigative capabilities — but only after the intelligence agencies have decided that a particular spy or terrorist is a job for the police.

Performing this refocusing would address one of the big unasked questions left over after 9/11: If the FBI is spending all this time now on counterterrorism, who is looking after the drug smugglers and child pornographers? We absolutely need a top-notch law enforcement and investigational organization. But get them out of the espionage and counterterror business and keep them out.

Redefining Intelligence

The intelligence community is more than just CIA. Indeed, the intelligence community is a fractured set of fiefdoms that grew up as the result of various small bureaucratic turf wars.

For example, the National Reconnaissance Office (NRO) — the supersecret organization that controls our spy satellites — evolved because

CIA and Army Intelligence each appeared to be preparing *its own* satellite reconnaissance programs in the 1950s and 1960s. NRO was an early attempt to prevent duplication of effort and was mostly successful in that regard.

you should know

The National Security Agency (NSA) is a completely separate "turf" that focuses on cryptography, communications security, and signals intelligence.

As always, when there are many fiefdoms, there is much duplication of effort and considerable inefficiency. I believe it is time to recentralize intelligence into two distinct organizations: strategic intelligence and tactical intelligence. The strategic intelligence agency would subsume virtually all of the disparate components of the intelligence community except for the military's intelligence organizations, which are optimized for handling tactical real-time battlefield intelligence. It would be this strategic intelligence organization that would be responsible for espionage and counterterror analysis and operations, both foreign and domestic.

Such a recasting of our intelligence organization brings up several issues. As a privacy-minded individual, the idea of creating a super-spy organization worries me. As a citizen of a global superpower that has foreign enemies, I am amazed that our intelligence agencies are allowed to operate as a group of autonomous entities that might or might not cooperate. And as an amateur student of the history of bureaucracies, I know that it's dangerous to suggest we combine CIA, NSA, NRO, and so on into a single organization — not because it wouldn't work, but because the usual bureaucratic response to combining multiple dysfunctional bureaucracies is to add another layer of dysfunctional bureaucracy on top of the existing mess.

> " *The usual bureacratic response to combining multiple dysfunctional bureacracies is to add another layer of dysfunctional bureaucracy on top of the existing mess.* "

Since this section is entitled "In a Perfect World," I get to be fanciful. Let's imagine a corporate-style merger, not a bureaucrat-style one.

Let's imagine that the best and brightest executive managers from those organizations are selected to make up the executive management of the new agency. The rest get pink slips or are offered the opportunity to find a place to contribute someplace lower in the ranks. Let's imagine that redundant capabilities are ruthlessly eliminated, to save money and increase efficiency. Let's imagine that the FBI agents who've been playing spy and counterterror are given a chance to switch agencies.

You see, in a perfect world, I'm not suggesting that we simply shake the tree: It's time to chop the tree down and plant a whole new one.

8

The Media: Disaster du Jour

The media is having a field day with Severe Acute Respiratory Syndrome (SARS) and was headlining it every hour during the height of the outbreak. So far, about 200 people worldwide have died of SARS. That is 100 times fewer than die of the flu every year and about twice the number that choke to death on ballpoint pens. If you add the number of people who die annually by falling down stairs with the annual ballpoint mortality rate, SARS no longer appears to be the scourge that the media tries to make it out to be. How did we engender a media that exaggerates and takes license with the truth whenever it likes, from reporting on so-called epidemics to inflating the terrorist threat?

America's love affair with the media is notorious. We're the country that invented "real-time" news channels like CNN, and multimedia fire hoses like MTV. We're a society that is conditioned simultaneously to listen to a constant stream of noise coming from a television and to tune it out so it becomes part of the background.

In creating the greatest flood of media the world has ever known, American society created the greatest imaginable demand for content. Whether it makes sense or not, whether it's intelligent and reasoned or not, whether it's harmful or not — someone is going to say it on television.

THE ROLE OF THE MEDIA

Media-bashing is all the rage, especially if you're a member of the media. The most egregious example I ever saw was during the Washington, D.C.-area sniper case. Journalists were constantly leaking information about how the case was going, and the police chief in charge of the investigation castigated "the press" for interfering with law enforcement. That night, when I turned on a television, I was bitterly amused to see a round table of journalists debating whether the media was acting responsibly by hyping the case and whether it was hindering the investigation. The irony of a bunch of talking heads debating whether or not other talking heads talked too much was simply overwhelming.

> *" The irony of a bunch of talking heads debating whether or not other talking heads talked too much was simply overwhelming. "*

I'm not particularly interested in media-bashing, but in order to understand the myth of homeland security, it's crucial to understand the feedback loop that exists between terrorists, the media, the people that the terrorists are trying to scare, and the politicians who are trying to win votes.

The issues are complicated by the fact that there is no obvious "right answer" and the parties involved need to exercise judgment — something politicians and the media are not particularly adept at doing.

> *" The parties involved need to exercise judgment — something politicians and the media are not particularly adept at doing. "*

WATCH OUT: THIS MEDIA IS LOADED

Terrorism is the attempt to manipulate the political process and public opinion through acts of violence and mass terror — and the members of the media are the greatest weapon in a terrorist's arsenal because they are the gateway to public opinion. How terrorist attacks and terrorism are covered in the media will have a greater impact on the target population than the acts of terror themselves.

Think for a moment about the mechanism of terrorism — how it actually *works*. Just killing people doesn't accomplish a terrorist's political agenda; usually that's only an option if you have sufficiently overwhelming firepower to start a war of genocide. The terrorist is, practically by definition, attacking society from a position of weakness: under-armed, undermanned, and going up against the might of a nation-state. So it's crucial for the terrorist to be able to *erode the population's trust in the nation's ability to protect them.*

When terrorists pull off spectacular acts of violence, they are trying to show the people that the government is helpless to protect them. Second, they are trying to drive a wedge between the government and the people by forcing the government to overreact and become oppressive itself in order to detect and defuse the terrorists among the population. If the government is unable to protect its people, it will suffer loss of confidence, and eventually

> *" Terrorism is a horribly effective tool because it places the government in a no-win situation wherein the terrorists control the agenda, the timing, and the location of the battlefield. "*

the people will get sick of the attacks and push the government to a political rapprochement with the terrorists.

If the government responds with door-to-door searches, militia with guns on street corners, and an effective police state, the terrorists have again caused a loss of confidence and achieved their goals. Terrorism is a horribly effective tool because it places the government in a no-win situation wherein the terrorists control the agenda, the timing, and the location of the battlefield. The media is a critical component for the success of the terrorist because it acts to magnify the terrorists' message. Every time CNN shows a blown-up bus with bloody people being carried away, the terrorists have won a major battle.

THE STOIC MEDIA

Every time some talking head intones, "But, really, there is very little we can do to stop this," the terrorists have made another convincing argument for why it's better to accede to their demands than to continue to suffer random horrifying attacks. Whether or not they want to admit it, the media become the unofficial spokespeople for terrorists every time they cover a terrorist incident.

The emotional passivity of modern media coverage further plays into the hands of terrorists. Indeed, the modern journalistic philosophy is to be as detached as possible when covering an event and not to editorialize. It'd be one thing if the reporter showed that he or she felt outrage, disgust, and anger at the terrorist attacks, but instead we are treated to a dispassionate and stoic reportage of a horrifying event. It's as if the media wants to help convince the terrorists' victims that such attacks are as inevitable as thunderstorms and earthquakes. "Just sit there and take it" seems to be the message.

Polarizing the Masses

Eventually, terrorism can polarize a society to the point where it's nearly impossible to make steps in a positive direction. The political conservatives in the victim society will entrench and become increasingly reluctant to even consider the terrorist political agenda, while the more liberal members of the victim society will begin to question whether the terrorist agenda might be, in fact, valid. The media, of course, helps add fuel to the fire by presenting the extremes of both perspectives rather than a centrist view, which serves to increase the level of cognitive dissonance in the victim society.

On the average, most Americans know two or three people who have been killed in automobile accidents — relatively few people know someone who has been killed in a terrorist incident. This is not to belittle the seriousness of terrorism, but it's important to understand that people place a disproportionate value on some risks. If you're more likely to be injured in an automotive accident than a terrorist bombing, you should be more worried about drunk drivers and making sure that your seatbelt is fastened than you should be about terrorists.

When we act disproportionately in response to a threat, it's almost always because we misperceive the level of risk that the threat poses to us — which is where media come into play. Drunk driving, for example, was not considered a separate threat from just plain "car accidents" until several public policy organizations began raising awareness of the problem as a *separate* issue that needed to be addressed. As soon as people started seeing statistics in magazines and ads on television from

---

DIRTY BOMBS

Consider, for example, the media's coverage of the threat of terrorist attacks using "dirty bombs" or radiological dispersion weapons. The FBI arrested one Jose Padilla, a U.S. citizen who had apparently traveled to Pakistan to train with Al Qaeda, and who was purportedly researching how to build dirty bombs. Suddenly, there were experts on the television talking about how plutonium particles kill, what civilians could do to protect themselves (basically: nothing), and so forth. Bear in mind that there is *no* evidence that Padilla had access to radiologic materials at all, let alone plutonium. The government has so little evidence, apparently, that Padilla actually *did anything* that they had to transfer his case to a military jurisdiction instead of seeking a criminal indictment. In fact, I've probably done as much research on radiologic dispersion weapons as Padilla did, as part of background research for this book. Don't tell the media, though, or they'll have experts on the television tomorrow talking about how easy it is to build your own radiological dispersion device, and generally helping to terrorize you in the guise of helping to inform you. Then it'll be time for everyone to run to the hardware store again and buy up all their supplies of duct tape and plastic sheeting.

Mothers Against Drunk Driving, and began hearing about the number of deaths that could be avoided, they had a new issue to think about.

Once awareness was raised through media exposure, people began to understand the level of risk posed by drunk drivers and to demand changes to public policy; then lawmakers got into the fray. My using this example should not be construed as condoning drunk driving! In fact, drunk driving represents a significant threat to many people's health and welfare — it's not a *disproportionate* threat. When the media crosses into hype and manipulation is when a relatively insignificant problem is magnified all out of proportion.

SCARE TACTICS

In the mid-1990s there was a report that some bottles of a particular batch of expensive mineral water had been tested as showing slight traces of benzene. Immediately, the press took up the story, and there was a hue and cry about how benzene is carcinogenic and toxic. Many bottled water drinkers swore off the stuff until the "crisis" was over. Some lawmakers loudly pondered regulation of the bottled water industry.

Nobody during the entire crisis mentioned the fact that smoking a cigarette exposed you to 10,000 times as many toxins, or that commuting to work for one-half hour exposed to you 100 times as much benzene as was in the water. What's wrong with this picture?

The media triggered a public response by presenting the public with just enough information to be dangerous, to provoke fear, and to fill the intellectual desert between advertisements. If the story had been reported responsibly, it wouldn't have even been news, let alone newsworthy.

Did the media later run a series of stories saying, basically, "Don't worry about it, we screwed up"? Of course not! But the benzene non-event happened in the mid-1990s — today, we'd have probably been treated to a congressional investigation, ads from the orange juice growers promoting their products as more healthy than benzene-toxified bottled water, and, finally, a bunch of talking heads on TV debating whether the media had acted responsibly in how they broke the story.

TERRORISM: THIS JUST IN...

When it comes to terrorism, irresponsible reporting that blows the threat out of proportion plays into the hands of the terrorists, by helping them in their mission of sowing fear, uncertainty, and doubt. Unlike the benzene story, terrorism, at least, is legitimately newsworthy. But what is the right amount of fear? I believe the media has acted irresponsibly by encouraging exactly the kind of panicked overreaction that results in people doing stupid things. Overreaction is the perfect fodder for cynical politicians who see an opportunity to seize an "issue" and show leadership by enacting stupid legislation or doing stupid things like spending billions of dollars establishing the Department of Homeland Security.

LATE-BREAKING GUESSWORK

The media collectively form one of the greatest institutions on Earth because they can be a watchdog for freedoms and a voice for the people, as well as a source of valuable information. Unfortunately, the 24-hour news channels and MTV have created an environment in which the viewing public expects to be able to get "late-breaking news" at any time. As a result, the big players such as CNN, MSNBC, FOX, the Drudge Report, and so forth are rewarded by their viewers if they present half-baked conjectures as quickly as they can be pulled out of the oven. In fact, some news junkies have become addicted to the "evolving story" — they want a real-time feed of half-baked conjectures as fast as they can be served up.

These half-baked conjectures make it increasingly hard for common sense to be heard. When the Space Shuttle Columbia broke up on reentry, some idiot immediately said, "At this time, there is no indication it was an act of terrorism." No sooner were the words spoken into a live microphone when everyone had to tumble in a rush to explain how it couldn't (or could) have been an act of terrorism. My hat is off to the scientists at NASA who said, "That's the stupidest thing I've ever heard — it was going 12,000 miles per hour and was at an altitude of 200,000 feet."

> **" The first thing they think of when they hear of a disaster is 'How can we link that to another disaster and make it into a bigger Earth-shattering disaster?' "**

Of course, the news stations didn't carry the real scientist's quotes; they waited until interest in the terrorism angle waned and then started showing pictures of the mangled pieces that were being recovered. What on Earth is going on in the minds of the people at the news studios if the first thing they think of when they hear of a disaster is "How can we link that to *another* disaster and make it into a *bigger Earth-shattering disaster?*"

WHEN THE GOVERNMENT USES THE MEDIA

The media's rush to identify new disasters makes it nearly impossible to sort the real disaster from the disaster du jour. Worse still is how the problem gets magnified when politicians and government agencies decide to use the media to garner attention for their own agendas.

The FBI is notorious for using the media to promote itself, or to generate scares about issues that play into its legislative or funding agenda. Prior to 9/11, the FBI was pursuing a course of promoting "right-wing militias" as the next big threat that needed to be stopped. There were news reports about these amorphous bands of well-armed citizens who wanted to hole up in private estates in Montana, evade taxes, and drink beer. The implication was that they were some kind of threat that might eventually materialize in the form of an attempted beer-sodden, tax-evading, counterrevolution. Again, the media was trying to link one or two small disasters (the Branch Davidians at Waco and the Weaver family at Ruby Ridge) into one bigger better scarier disaster: armed nutcases that want to be left alone.

Unfortunately for us all, Osama bin Laden's marketing was more effective. The real issue — the issue everyone seems to want to forget — is that there are *enough* problems out there without having to create more just to have something to report at 6 o'clock every day.

A BLUEPRINT FOR THE BAD GUYS

When the media has no information about a topic, they reach for prognosticators, self-proclaimed experts, and media whores who are happy to provide information that is even remotely related to the topic. In fact, the more tangential the information, the better, because that just adds fuel for more uninformed speculation. This further fuels media hysteria.

> " Free speech is one of the greatest political concepts of the current age, but it's not an invitation to blather inanities into a live microphone. "

In a bizarre form of self-aggrandizement, many of these experts feel compelled to show that they could think of attack methods that would be much easier or deadlier than those used by the terrorists. Or, the experts cheerfully pontificate about how useless it is

---

THE MANLESS MANHUNT

In February 2003, the FBI started a national manhunt (with help from the media) for five Pakistani "potential terrorists" who had supposedly infiltrated the country via Canada. The media was frustrated because they had no pictures of the infiltrators and no other information regarding them or their possible plans. Conjectures were made and aired on television, but the whole hype bubble collapsed several days later when the FBI admitted that the whole thing was a story made up by an informer who had lied to them. What was interesting about this sequence of events was not that it happened, but just how *much* television airtime was devoted to the topic, considering the fact that there was nearly *zero* actual information for the media to impart to the public.

LOOK OUT: IT'S A PIPER CUB!

When the attacks happened on 9/11, someone mentioned that small private planes might also be used in similar attacks — resulting in the immediate closure of a number of private airfields in the Washington, D.C., area. This was based on pure, uninformed speculation, but once the issue had been raised in a public forum, *something* had to be done. Never mind the fact that a small private plane full of explosives would do less damage to a building than a big jetliner loaded with fuel. If some idiot on TV on 9/11 had speculated that "if terrorists really wanted to destroy our cities, they would combine the aircraft attacks with coordinated use of truck bombs," then we'd have probably had all the major roads in most cities shut down. Be afraid! Why worry about one thing when you can worry about two! The sky is falling! Oh, and don't we need a department of homeland security?

---

to try to defend against certain forms of attack. This amounts to drawing up a blueprint for the bad guys. It's irresponsible and stupid to air that kind of thing on national television, regardless of how you feel about free speech. Free speech is one of the greatest political concepts of the current age, but it's not an invitation to blather inanities into a live microphone.

When 9/11 happened, I went home that evening and suddenly the thought hit me, "How horrible. But thank *goodness* they didn't think to fly those planes into a nuclear reactor!" The idea was so horrifying I didn't even mention it to my wife — ideas like that are best buried and, one hopes, become the special problem for those who are responsible for protecting us against them.

These kinds of dark thoughts are certainly not acceptable as a side dish with your breakfast, but that's exactly what I was treated to several days later when some expert on terrorism said, "It could have been worse! They could have targeted a nuclear reactor and made most of the eastern coast of the United States uninhabitable!" This guy even had a nifty chart with reactors and wind patterns. The only thing he didn't provide was a flight plan for any terrorists who wanted to try it.

The next day, an expert pointed out that U.S. reactors are designed to withstand serious impacts and that the containment systems are intended to hold against the impact of an aircraft. I breathed a big sigh of relief as I realized that engineers — real engineers, not the idiots on television — had been thinking things through while they designed such critical systems. You can imagine my horror when, the next day, the expert on terrorism was back, explaining that *two* aircraft, hitting nearly simultaneously, ought to be enough to breach a reactor's containment. Thanks a lot! (I sincerely hope this guy enjoyed his 15 minutes of fame before he crawled back under whatever rock he came out from.)

What's going on here? The media wants us to be scared. They don't want us to be thinking about what's going on; they want us to be terrified and glued to our chairs so that we'll watch more advertisements. 9/11, after all, was bigger than the Superbowl.

A BAD THING: TOO MUCH INFORMATION

The anthrax attacks through the U.S. mail were another interesting case. We got to listen to experts on television announce that "anyone with basic knowledge of biology can grow anthrax." At least they stopped short of giving the directions. But we were all educated as to the various types of anthrax: which strain was worst, what was "weaponized" anthrax, and how it's processed into a fine powder with special chemicals so it'll float into our lungs more easily.

My favorite "anthrax in the media" moment was when some expert was describing how terrorists might spray anthrax spores over a town using a crop-dusting airplane. He even brought an example of a sprayer nozzle to the TV studio with him, as if that somehow helped bolster his argument. When the talking head asked him what the nozzle was and where he got it, he explained something to the effect that it was an ordinary sprayer nozzle and that they'd be perfect for disseminating bioweapons! Neat-o! Maybe as an encore he'd like to suggest the proper dosage to use per city block in case I ever need to try to wipe out a city?

Did we need to know all that? Most of us shouldn't be growing any anthrax — sometimes there is such a thing as giving too much information.

you should know

Following the Oklahoma City bombing, I saw a couple of experts on television who explained how easy it was for anyone to make fuel-oil ammonium nitrate explosives, and how you could buy explosives in Arizona with just a driver's license. Thanks, guys!

MEDIA IN WARTIME

When the United States launched attacks against the Taliban and Al Qaeda forces in Afghanistan, the media was quick to begin reporting as much information as they could gather regarding U.S. plans, troop dispositions, tactics, and techniques. In case anyone wanted it, information about the Predator unmanned aerial vehicle and its weapons systems was posted on CNN.com. It's probably valuable for psychological effect to reveal to one's enemies that you can stalk them day or night, in silence and with impunity, but is it really a good idea to tell tactical details?

At least the media didn't have experts explaining how easy it would be to avoid hellfire missiles — but if they refrained, it was most likely only because they didn't know.

Most disturbing was the questioning from the media, in which they kept asking the Secretary of Defense whether Afghanistan might turn into "a quagmire" or a military disaster like the Vietnam War. Whose side are these people on? The classic response to that question is "the side of truth" — the ideology of the reporter — but "truth" does not always need to be front-page news, especially if it affects military strategy and may cost lives by either accelerating timetables or revealing plans.

SECRET WEAPONS?

Back when the open military question of the day was whether or not United States-led coalition forces were going to attack Iraq in an

---

WE SAW IT ON TV . . .

During the Iraq war, I believe the media were a consideration in the allies' timetables of operations. It's interesting that immediately after Peter Arnett's famous interview in which he declared that the war was not going well, the allies began aggressive maneuvers within Baghdad itself. Were lives risked in order to show Peter Arnett for a fool? It'd be a shame if that were the case; catering to media hysteria is not worth a single soldier's life.

Memo to Peter, wherever you are. Repeat after me: "I was wrong. I overstepped myself. I'm sorry." It's not hard to say it. We'd all respect you more.

attempt to change its political leadership, several national magazines and newspapers ran articles outlining, based on "insider sources," how such a war might be fought. They outlined what new advanced weapons systems might be seen for the first time during such an engagement.

One report that particularly surprised me was the description of an "E-bomb" — an advanced electromagnetic impulse weapon designed to disrupt communications. I'd never heard of such a thing before, but now there are articles about how they work, including one in *Popular Mechanics* (September 2001) with the helpful come-on, "In the blink of an eye, electromagnetic bombs could throw civilization back 200 years. And terrorists can build them for $400." The article goes on to give a practical explanation of how they might work — enough to shave months or even years off of such weapons development.

Another article in *The Weekly Standard* went on to describe where in the United States research is being performed on directed energy weapons, and it names a few of the projects that are under way, as well as some of the projected capabilities of such systems. The article concludes by observing that "if you ask the folks at the Air Force Research Laboratory, they'll tell you they 'regret that there is very little that is releasable on the subject.'" Well, I wish the journalist who wrote the article would just sit and think for maybe a minute and ask, "Why?" If the folks who are working on weapons systems aren't releasing information to the press, they might have a *good reason*.

It turns out, as far as we know, that a lot of the advanced experimental weapons weren't used, or were used without a lot of publicity. In some cases, it's clear that the military used the press as their patsies: When the Massive Ordnance Air Burst (MOAB) bomb was tested, it got a lot of press coverage. Doubtless this was a heavy-handed threat to the Iraqi military: "See what we have?" and it apparently worked. Later during the war, the press was leaked information that an MOAB had been sent to the Iraq region, presumably to drop on holdout Republican Guard troops. Perhaps this time the deliberate leaks saved a few Iraqi lives. Clearly the war fighters are factoring the media into their plans both as a positive and as a negative.

MEDIA IN THE TRENCHES

If the media had its way, our military would go to war with reporters tagging along, broadcasting complete details of their deployment so that the enemy wouldn't have to bother trying to locate them.

Of course, the media is practically riding on the coattails of the troops right now, but at least the military has made the press follow (in theory) some strict rules about not revealing operational details. Without these rules soldiers would be carrying weapons systems that were completely understood by the enemy, and the enemy would know how to protect themselves against them because of helpful hints on news Web sites. Reporters would sit in on mission briefings and announce the plans for tomorrow on the evening news. "Here I am, outside of Normandy, where it looks like the big invasion is scheduled to begin tomorrow morning! Just look at all those landing ships!" We'd lose the war, and the media would cheerfully cover the debacle — including the weeping spouses and parents — and then the talking heads would sit around and hold lengthy debates about what went wrong.

Of course, the military understands the media mind-set and is taking steps to channel it and control it. During the Iraq war, the so-called embedded media were a fairly effective propaganda device. I think most people felt that the media would certainly dwell extensively on any U.S. screw-ups or abuses, so they were acting in the role of de facto watchdogs. It was a very powerful message to have attached journalists describing some of the irregular warfare that was being fought, without this information being filtered through military spokespeople.

I, for one, find it ironic that people are more inclined to believe a camera crew than a U.S. Marine corps officer — which do *you* think is likely to have a better understanding of what's taking place on a battlefield? Unfortunately, the media's cluelessness makes them unreliable patsies at best.

During the incident when U.S. troops came under sniper fire from a hotel inhabited by journalists, there was a hue and cry when the fire was

SENSATIONALIST CLAP TRAP

Remember how we were treated to the spectacle of Geraldo Rivera, one of the embedded journalists, giving a description of his unit's location and the overall objectives for the next day on live television? Honestly, I can't believe anyone could be so stupid; perhaps it was a deliberate gesture to get some attention and to revitalize a flagging career. For once, it was such an egregious act that even other journalists didn't stick up for him. I respect and admire the military's attempt to let Geraldo save face by choosing to leave. I'd have thrown him out of a Humvee in the desert and let him walk home.

returned, the hotel was damaged, and people were injured. Excuse me? Did anyone pause to ask "What kind of 'soldier' snipes from a building full of noncombatants?" Did anyone pause to be impressed by the fact that the sniper was taken out of action and the hotel was still *standing* afterward? Today's military are infinitely more respectful of noncombatant lives and property than any other army in recorded history. Did the media once — just once — say "Gee, thanks, guys, you were pretty darn gentle, considering you were invading a country with a professional standing army that had plenty of advance opportunity to dig itself in for a fight"?

It's almost as if the media *want* a humanitarian disaster, because somehow they think a disaster is eminently newsworthy. I don't think that's actually the case — I think that what's going on is that *bad news trumps good news*, so there's a constant search for worse news — even to the point of unconsciously helping to create it.

> **" I think that what's going on is that bad news trumps good news, so there's a constant search for worse news — even to the point of unconsciously helping to create it. "**

THEN AND NOW

During the first and second World Wars, the press was more tightly controlled and exercised some common sense in how things were reported. What has changed since then? It's not just the difference between wartime mind-sets and peacetime mind-sets; it's got more to do with *not being sure we'll win*.

The main reason for the difference we're seeing in reporting style is that the "younger generation" has never felt the icy hand of doubt on the back of their neck as they wondered, "Are we going to *lose* this one?" Most Americans in the 1940s understood that losing World War II would mean the eventual end of the United States of America. That is a completely different state of mind than worrying about a "quagmire." Nobody asked if Iwo Jima was a "quagmire"; the entire world had been plunged into horror that would have made a mere "quagmire" a big relief.

Once WWII was over, and the Korean War was over, Americans wanted to treat war as something neat and contained that happened someplace else. The media went along with it — in popular perception, *war became optional* — which is a nice idea in line with the 1960s peace ideology, but which isn't realistic when you're dealing with an opponent that is willing to *come to you* and who won't take "no thanks" for an answer.

Our media, in other words, has confused an important message. On one hand, they are telling us we are at war, while on the other hand, they aren't acting like it. For the media, it's business as usual.

WARTIME MIND, PEACETIME MIND

What are the differences between a wartime media and a peacetime media? First and foremost is the acceptance that the media has a responsibility to consider the impact of its information. I'm not advocating "self-censorship" (such a negatively value-laden term), but I do think there is a place for being responsible. The media cannot hold itself aloof from society and refuse to acknowledge that it may, in fact, hold sensitive information that should not be divulged. This applies to military plans, civil defense, technological information, and operational information.

Indeed, many nations, such as the United Kingdom, have an Official Secrets Act, which holds the media accountable for overstepping those boundaries of reasonableness. The viewing public also needs to hold the media accountable for its actions. We're the ones who fund the whole media circus, after all, and it's our responses that make up the Nielsen ratings.

Legislating media responsibility goes a long way toward helping to prevent the kind of playing-to-the-camera we often see, in which members of Congress deliberately "leak" sensitive or even secret information in order to manipulate events in their favor. The fact that the media greedily sucks up such leaks and broadcasts them only helps to ensure that there will be more leaks. A little bit of personal accountability would help bring the reality of the situation home to the various parties involved in the leak game.

you should know

The FBI recently proposed using a polygraph test to determine which members of Congress had leaked sensitive information pertaining to 9/11 — a proposal that, not surprisingly, was shot down pretty quickly by a majority of Congress members.

The culture of leaks and media-whoring has done more to damage the effectiveness of government than many realize. It has certainly done more damage than the media is ready to admit. During the Gulf War in the early 1990s, the media complained that the military tightly controlled their access to information and restricted their movements. Some complained that the media's reportage was being censored implicitly through such tight controls. Others felt that it was necessary to control the media's view of events because the media couldn't exercise judgment.

I suspect the truth lies, as it often does, between the two extremes of opinion. The media's access to information was restricted because the military was convinced that the media would not act responsibly if given more. Yes, it was a form of censorship, but one that resulted from a violation of trust.

WHO'S GOT A BIGGER MOUTH THAN THE MEDIA?

We have seen similar patterns play themselves out with Congress and the intelligence community where CIA or the FBI are reluctant to disclose anything worthwhile to lawmakers because they know that it'll be leaked to the press virtually instantaneously. So, as a result, we are left with the FBI and Department of Homeland Security issuing vague warnings about "credible threats" that are completely unspecific — and the media and lawmakers rumbling about how they can't take such threats seriously without more information.

The perfect example of this dynamic came while the United States was trying to make a case for the war on Iraq because of its weapons of mass destruction. Crucial intelligence information that might have been convincing could not be presented because it would have been all over the news the next day. Regardless of the truth of what the Iraqis did or didn't have, the problem of sharing sensitive information with lawmakers and the media is at a severe impasse because of distrust. The information won't be forthcoming until the media and lawmakers can convince the intelligence community that they know how to be good custodians of such information. In other words, it'll be a cold day in hell.

THE AMERICAN PEOPLE: PARTNERS IN DECEPTION?

Would we rather *feel* safe than *be* safe? Probably. The overwhelming message from the media is that safety is impossible to achieve. No matter what defenses are attempted, some expert will get on the late-night news and explain how they could be bypassed by a sufficiently motivated attacker. We get a contradictory signal from the press: Something must be done! Nothing will work!

Worse still, we hold our elected leaders accountable for delivering on the mixed message we get from the media. Something *must* be done, so it's the government's job to do it. Of course, it shouldn't have any impact on social programs, interfere with our personal liberties, make us wait in long lines at airport security, or cause any perceptible change in our day-to-day lives. We want it all, but we don't want to face the real cost of what we're asking for. Don't give us real security; we'll settle for the illusion.

If we're not careful, we're going to wind up with low-fat antiterrorism: a huge amount of money being spent in order to accomplish very little except the expenditure of a huge amount of money. The media will be happy with that, because they'll be able to amuse us for years by reporting on government waste and incompetence in our antiterrorism efforts.

> " *If we're not careful, we're going to wind up with low-fat antiterrorism: a huge amount of money being spent in order to accomplish very little except the expenditure of a huge amount of money.* "

EURO-WIMPS AT THE OK CORRAL

Americans, even at the highest level of government, are perplexed by European and global reactions to the war on terrorism and foreign perceptions of security issues within the United States. The gap in perception is continually widening, and it was especially apparent regarding the

United States' attempts to get international support for a military-led regime change in Iraq.

The issues are complex and have much more to do with international finance, national pride, and international desires to form balancing power-blocs to curb what is increasingly viewed as the world's first military hyperpower. The Iraq war and the international political jockeying leading up to it had nothing to do with terrorism or weapons of mass destruction. Yet that was all that was discussed. I wish that all the parties involved had just cut the nonsense and dealt with their real agendas openly.

On one hand, we have an American President who talks about "God" and "a crusade against terrorism," and on the other, we have an international community that is dumbfounded that Americans don't see why the worldwide Muslim population doesn't trust his motives. Americans are infuriated by the fact that some Europeans can't seem to clean their own dirty laundry and are incensed at the fact that what is fundamentally an Arab/Israeli issue has resulted in damaging attacks against U.S. citizens. Of course, the Arabs point out that the U.S. relationship with Israel *makes* us part and party to conflict in that region regardless, and so it goes on, endlessly.

There's a cycle of misperception, and it has grown larger as the media seeks the maximum "zing" in stories that help highlight the growing divisions between long-term partners. When criticisms are offered, it's front-page news. When partnerships are formed and international commonalities are discovered, the media reports on celebrity murders in Los Angeles.

At the same time, most of the rest of the world is puzzled by the American reaction to our security being breached. Most Israelis find U.S. airport security to be either humorous or unsettlingly bad. Most Europeans are not uncomfortable about seeing uniformed military police in airports with automatic weapons. Yet many Americans worried about "jackbooted Gestapo" when uniformed military with empty M-16s were deployed to stand around airports looking impressive. Europeans don't understand why American libertarians complain about the very forces arrayed to protect them.

The French find American squeamishness about racial profiling to be hypocritical and silly, while the Israelis think it's stupid to even worry about it. Never mind racial profiling; they're into walling off entire towns with barbed wire and machine guns. The Israelis, remember, are living in the wartime mind-set and consequently are a lot less inclined to worry about the niceties.

you should know

Post-9/11 I've had conversations with friends in the United Kingdom, one of whom pointed out that we're silly to worry about terrorism when we have so many handgun deaths every year. Yet he had to fall silent when I pointed out that they kill more of their citizens with tobacco than we do with handguns. The bottom line is that you can't stack one form of pointless death up against another and come up with any kind of useful comparison.

All of these misunderstandings between countries are perception issues more than they are grounded in any kind of reality. Media reality is crucial in creating or destroying these perceptions. Does the media have a responsibility to adjust perception, or merely to report it? This, fundamentally, is the question underlying the entire issue of the media and its relationship to terror and foreign policy: Do the media stand outside of the arena, or is it a player in the game? The media want to have it both ways; they want the privilege of being a player without the responsibility. That simply doesn't work.

> **" Does the media stand outside of the arena, or is it a player in the game? "**

IN A PERFECT WORLD

There's an old saying that you shouldn't shoot the messenger. If the messenger is not only bringing bad news but slanting or sensationalizing it, or is just simply getting it wrong, what can we do besides pull out a handgun and fire away?

SOLVING THE MEDIA DILEMMA

The media has been guilty of gross intellectual dishonesty regarding its role in the modern world. There's a theoretical and largely false separation between reporting and editorial: In theory the news is reported with as little "spin" as possible, whereas editorials represent only the opinion of the individual presenting them. In reality, news is selected for newsworthiness, and facts and sources are selected based on how reliable they are. Both of those selections may have a critical impact on the story.

Frequently, "both sides" are aired, but the choice of who presents which "side" has a lot to do with how that reporting comes off. News outlets also pretend to be trying to make the other side's views heard, but in reality they're looking for sensationalism, a scoop, or a freak show. Peter Arnett's famous interview on Iraqi television is a case in point: It wasn't an attempt to air both sides of the news; it was a blatantly sensationalistic grab at the limelight. Of course I'm not the first person to feel that there's sensationalism or bias in the media. I'm sure I won't be the last, either.

What can we do about it? Honestly, I don't think there's much we *can* or *should* do about it, other than to make sure everyone understands that they can't believe everything they see on television. It used to scare me that I knew people who'd believe anything they saw in a newspaper — after all, it was in print! What scares me is that now I am seeing the beginning of a generation that believes everything they read on the Internet.

In that respect, P.T. Barnum was right: There *is* a sucker born every minute. The most important thing we can do to counter media misreporting is to make sure children are exposed to the concepts of media bias, propaganda, and slanted perspectives before they lose their ability to judge the things they are told critically.

THE AMERICAN PEOPLE: PARTNERS IN DECEPTION

In a perfect world, people wouldn't lie to themselves. Of course, then they wouldn't be human; it's just the nature of the beast to want to believe in some things so completely that you overlook the obvious problems.

It's one thing for me to write this book and complain about politicians jockeying for attention and pork-barrel points, incompetent government workers, and wacky media hysterics — it's another to actually *do* something about it. The only person on earth, dear reader, who can *do* anything about the nonsense I'm describing in this book is you.

Politicians pander to us for our votes — either by telling us what we want to hear (and we believe it) or by trying to make us happy by bringing home the bacon for our home districts. Those reporters tell stories of doom and gloom and talking heads babble endlessly in order to keep us glued to our television sets. Those squabbling, turf-hungry bureaucrats worry more about their organizational charts than getting the job done because we let them.

As depressing as it seems, I think we need to be a bit more cynical and reflect on our own role in the homeland security scam. A disastrous attack scared us badly, and we wanted an immediate solution. We were told that the solution was to stand in line to take our shoes off for airport security, open our wallets, and spend a ton of money and it'd all be okay — and we fell for it.

> " *We were told that the solution was to stand in line to take our shoes off for airport security, open our wallets, and spend a ton of money and it'd all be okay — and we fell for it.* "

We've got to stop falling for the appeal of the "get rich quick" "lose weight without exercising or dieting" "improve your homeland security overnight" solutions that won't actually accomplish anything.

9

The Electronic
Pearl Harbor

Whenever you're dealing with new technology, be on the lookout for hype. Hype and new technology go together because when something's new, it's not fully understood by most people, which makes it an ideal vehicle for the hypesters and their overinflated claims.

For years now we've been hearing about the threat of an electronic Pearl Harbor attack launched against the United States. How real is the threat? How much would it hurt us if someone did get the e-drop on us? As usual, the answer depends on whom you ask, what they are trying to sell you, and whether or not they know what they are talking about.

THE MYTH OF CYBER WAR

All wars, whether real or cyber, depend on the balance of five things:

- Command
- Techniques and technologies of offense
- Techniques and technologies of defense
- Logistics
- Manpower

If you have the best troops, and state-of-the-art gear, and there are only 10 of them, you're going to lose to the guy who has a million less-well-trained troops with gear that's half as good. If you have loads of troops and they're led by incompetent commanders, you will lose to the smaller force that is expertly handled. If you have a terrific offense but no defense, you'll lose to a surprise attack; and if you have terrific defenses but no offense, you'll never be able to accomplish more than tiring your enemy out by letting them rage against your impenetrable defenses. If you have terrific troops, great commanders, and no supply organization, you'll fight one brilliant battle, then lose the rest of the war.

> " If you have terrific troops, great commanders, and no supply organization, you'll fight one brilliant battle, then lose the rest of the war. "

This same set of dynamics applies just as aptly to cyber war — but most of the proponents of cyber war prefer not to see it that way, for their own reasons.

In Command

Right now, we have a lot of people talking about cyber war as if it exists to a significant degree, but very few of the ingredients for fighting a successful cyber war actually exist.

For example: command — how many people in the world know how to fight an offensive and defensive war online? To date, the topic simply has not been studied, except by a tiny handful of hacker collectives. So who are the players out there who could even participate in a cyber war?

Are the hackers a threat? The hacker groups are just worrying about which Web sites to deface or how to steal credit card data — they aren't thinking in terms of military-style combined operations. I think they're mostly a pain in the ass; more like fleas and cockroaches than anything else. Like cockroaches, they tend to vanish when the lights come on. Because they're badly socialized, dress funny, and talk cryptically, the media love hackers. In fact, it's pathetic to watch the way the media get excited to rub shoulders with the hackers at hacker conventions like DEFCON.

What the journalists don't understand is that, given a slightly different set of childhood influences, hackers would be wearing rubber forehead prostheses and talking Klingon at Star Trek conventions. They're just immature, poorly socialized punks; they are not a military or social threat to the world order.

What about the terrorists? Are they preparing for cyber war? Our scare- and hype-mongers tell us repeatedly that someone could launch crippling electronic attacks against our infrastructure. Could Al Qaeda?

I'd have to answer with an unqualified "no." From the tiny amounts that have leaked into the media regarding computers that were seized during the war in Afghanistan and against terrorist cells in Pakistan and elsewhere, it appears that Al Qaeda's use of information technology is extremely primitive and unsophisticated. These, after all, are the same guys who apparently had laptops containing operational research, unencrypted, just sitting on the hard disk. There was no attempt to destroy computer equipment in the event of capture; compare that to the way in which U.S. embassy computers are wired with high-temperature thermite grenades so they can be melted into a puddle of slag at a moment's notice.

Richard Reid and Zacharias Moussaoui (who, I should note, has not been found guilty of terrorist acts as of this writing) both used email from public computers where it is easy to retrieve from backup tapes. In terms of computer security sophistication, your typical 12-year-old beginner hacker is far ahead of Al Qaeda. So, could Al Qaeda launch a crippling cyber strike against the United States? Not unless they bring in

> " *Hackers are just immature, poorly socialized punks; they are not a military or social threat to the world order.* "

outside talent. Can you imagine Al Qaeda rubbing shoulders with the aforementioned hackers from DEFCON? I don't think so. I can picture a bunch of teeny-punk hackers in the presence of truly dangerous terrorists such as the Islamic Jihad or Hamas; frankly, they'd pee themselves.

ON THE OFFENSIVE

There hasn't been much sign that coordinated operations techniques are evolving, either. In fact, the state of the art for hacker-offensive techniques appears to rely on massive-scale, brute-force attacks.

Hacker tools known as "mass rooters" attempt to break into literally thousands of machines automatically. By their nature they are obvious when they are in use, and undirected — they are usually used to attack wide ranges of undefended targets virtually simultaneously. A mass rooter in operation is about as subtle as a column of armored vehicles crossing your lawn: You know they're coming, you know where they're going, and you damn sure know they've been there after they've left.

Militarily, mass rooters would be limited in their usefulness because they don't work well against individual, high-value, well-defended targets. They *might* have nuisance value if used as the electronic equivalent of "harassment fire" — simply a way of keeping network administrators burning the midnight oil and getting ulcers from drinking too much coffee.

There *have* been rumors of Chinese and U.S. government research into developing new forms of cyber weapons for offensive purposes. That is one area where the myth of cyber war seems to verge on reality. Sadly, when the military develop new weapons, they will eventually find an excuse to use them, if only to see if they work. There, I believe, lies the greatest potential danger for cyber war.

Of course, that begs the question, "What *is* a cyber weapon, anyhow?" The short answer is I don't know, because they may not even exist. I can imagine a cyber weapon might be an attack program designed with the specific purpose of penetrating an organization's Internet firewall and crashing its internal infrastructure. But no such thing exists, because it would have to know how to break through any possible configuration of any possible firewall. There are over 400 firewall products on the market, and each firewall is configured in a highly site-specific manner — you do the math. On top of that, every organization's infrastructure network is uniquely constructed and might use a variety of equipment from multiple vendors. So our mythical cyber weapon would have to know how to penetrate or crash any of 20 different router manufacturer's products, dozens of different releases of Windows, UNIX, IBM mainframes, and so on. And, it'd have to be able to do it all perfectly and so fast that nobody would have a chance to react.

> " *In the meantime our networks and computer systems are so complicated and redundant, it's hard to understand or maintain them, let alone attack them.* "

Basically, cyber weapons are such a scary threat because, like any other boogeyman, they are imaginary. Therefore it's possible to ascribe awesome powers to them. *Perhaps* if we ever develop truly functional machine–intelligences, we'll see cyber war evolve into a real battlefield, but in the meantime, our networks and computer systems are so complicated and redundant, it's hard to understand or maintain them, let alone attack them. Bottom line: It's extremely difficult to build a cyber weapon that has the general-purpose usefulness of a rifle bullet or a bayonet. It would be expensive and time-consuming to design a cyber weapon, because it would have to be very specific to each target. In fact, the cost and complexity of launching a massively scaled attack would be gigantic.

CIRCLING THE WAGONS

Defensive technology for cyber war is fairly well understood. Most corporate entities on the Internet have been holding a defensive position against thousands of hacking attempts for years. With the advent of new self-propagating worms and email Trojan horses, buffer-overrun tools, and mass rooters (see the sidebar for more about how these work), the world's computer security practitioners have come to understand the need to react to new attack techniques in order to neutralize them rapidly.

> " When worse comes to worst, many of those organizations are prepared to simply unplug from the Internet. "

Most commercial organizations of significant size have incident response and preparedness capabilities that are intended to allow them to quickly repair holes in the walls of the software that is supposed to insulate them from attackers. When worse comes to worst, many of those organizations are prepared to simply unplug from the Internet or reduce their access level to a safe baseline until the storm blows over.

you should know

Here's an example of how reducing access levels can help in the event of an attack. When the recent "bugbear.b" worm infected a friend's company, they responded effectively and quickly by shutting down some of the key services the worm uses to replicate itself. Shutting those services down resulted in a temporary delay in message transmission for some email users, but no messages were lost and the pesky worm was squashed.

CYBER ARSENAL FOR HACKER KIDS

There is a large variety of types of attack tools currently in use or autonomously roaming the Internet. Here are a few of them:

- Worms: A worm is a self-propagating program that breaks into a computer using some kind of hole in that system's defenses; it then establishes itself on that computer as a base of operations to launch attacks against other computers. Worms breaking into multiple systems can generate so much traffic that they degrade the networks they infest or crash the systems they are penetrating.
- Viruses: Viruses are self-replicating code fragments that copy themselves into other pieces of software and reproduce when those pieces of software are executed. Antiviral software is available that can prevent successful infection for most major platforms that suffer from virus infection.
- Mass rooters: Mass rooters are similar to worms but don't self-replicate. A mass rooter performs analysis of thousands of computers and identifies vulnerabilities in the software they are running. Where it finds vulnerability it exploits it, then installs remote control software and back doors so the hacker can access the machine later. A hacker can penetrate thousands of machines during a good night's sleep if his or her Internet connection is fast enough.
- Root kit: A root kit is a set of remote-control programs and back doors that a hacker installs on a system once he or she has compromised it. Many root kits are fully automated and take care of removing many traces of a hacker's activities to make it harder for the victims to discover they have been hacked.
- Buffer overruns, CGI bin exploits, and other exploits: An "exploit" is hacker-ese for a hole in a system's software that can be used to compromise the system's protection. Buffer overruns are one of the most popular forms of exploits and work by taking advantage of sloppy programming practices when software is written.
- Scanning tools: There are a variety of scanning tools that allow a hacker to quickly map a victim's network and try to identify the kind of systems and software they are running. Many of these scanning tools are quite stealthy and try to hide their activities by pretending to be normal traffic. They're actually fairly easy to detect if you're looking for them. Most sites that are Internet-connected at T-1 or higher speeds are scanned several times a day, without them being any the wiser.

Organizations without organic incident response teams can rely on responses (albeit slower responses) from their corporate counterparts elsewhere, numerous computer-security oriented online forums, and product signature updates from antivirus and intrusion prevention product manufacturers.

LACKING EVEN THE BASICS

The public at large hears a great deal about Internet security problems, most frequently about worms such as CodeRed or Slapper, which cause considerable damage and disruption. What the public at large may not realize is that these attacks usually only disrupt organizations that have failed to take even basic precautions to protect themselves. Imagine if a new "attack" was launched against a residential neighborhood. In this attack, the burglars try every basement door of every house to see if it is unlocked. Odds are, a few houses will be vulnerable, but none of the residences where the people take security at all seriously will be at serious risk. Once that "attack" has gone through a neighborhood and the neighbors hear about who got broken into and who didn't, the ones with any brains at all will check their basement doors.

It's the same way with Internet security — once an attack has been fielded, the good guys who are on the ball are quick to react and block it, though it will continue to cause vast damage against the congenitally unprepared or those who don't care about security.

you should know

When CodeRed broke out, my company's system administrator knew about it within an hour, had verified that our systems weren't vulnerable to it, and had gone on to doing something else. We weren't vulnerable to CodeRed because CodeRed relied on a vulnerability that the security community had known about for the past three months, and that had been fixed by most diligent system administrators.

"AN ARMY MARCHES ON ITS STOMACH"

Logistics, as Napoleon Bonaparte knew, are everything. It doesn't matter how many soldiers and guns you have, if they have no food, ammunition, or shoes. But cyber war brings a completely new set of logistical problems that nobody has ever encountered before. Pundits and hypesters who promote the fear of cyber war have never paused to consider the logistical problems inherent in a protracted (or even short-term) cyber offensive.

The logistics of cyber warfare are entirely in favor of the defender because the defensive technology community has already established information-sharing, incident response, and security update practices. This, I believe, will create a hellish logistical problem for making *offensive* cyber warfare a reality.

> " *The logistics of cyber warfare are entirely in favor of the defender because the defensive technology community has already established information-sharing, incident response, and security update practices.* "

Imagine you're a cyber weapons developer at a top-secret government facility, developing new attacks. You develop a new attack that is capable of taking down a particular version of Windows' software and add that to your nation's arsenal. Now, as soon as that attack is fielded against an enemy, there's a good chance that they will be able to figure out what happened. Within 24 hours your attack will be published and everyone who cares about security will be rushing to update their systems to resist the attack.

Consider the effect on conventional warfare if, each time a particular kind of bullet was used on an enemy, its effectiveness was reduced by one-half. Conventional warfare would take on a horribly expensive logistical dimension as countries had to constantly reevolve, reissue, and update their weapons. Because many security flaws are operating system-dependent, a cyber warfare armorer would need to develop attacks targeted against a wide variety of platforms and would have to keep modifying and updating the weapons whenever a vendor issues a new release or patch that might fix the security hole. To make matters worse, there are a large number of amateur weapons-builders (the hackers) that periodically discover and publish new weapons, rendering stockpiled weapons instantly obsolete.

WHERE'S THE ARMY?

The last missing component of cyber war is manpower. To make cyber warfare effective, one would need more than just a couple of retrained hackers; one would need cyber armorers to build new weapons and defenses, and one would need commanders capable of evolving a military doctrine for combined-arms cyber attacks that would work. No country, not even the United States, has that many skilled security experts with the requisite maturity to be able to engage in such an activity in secret.

you should know

The secrecy necessary for cyber war would be dramatically different than for normal warfare, since the weapons can only be used once and have to be closely guarded secrets during development and deployment. How do you train a soldier to use a new rifle in secret? During the Cold War we saw how difficult it was to keep secrets in the field of weapons development — why do we think we could do it now with cyber weapons development?

At this time, the cost/benefit equation for cyber warfare just doesn't work out. Perhaps in the future, there will be cyber warfare that is as effective and deadly as the pundits are predicting today. But for the time being, the technological advantage and logistical factors are overwhelmingly on the side of the defender. The whole idea of cyber war is really just a bunch of marketing malarkey cooked up by computer security product salesmen, Cold War-era info security practitioners who

> *" The whole idea of cyber war is really just a bunch of marketing malarkey cooked up by computer security product salespeople, Cold War-era info security practitioners who are trying to modernize their mission, and media whores. "*

PRACTICAL MATTERS

The logistics of keeping a cyber warfare facility ready for offensive operations will be prohibitively expensive. The popular myth of cyber warfare is that critical infrastructure systems will be taken out in large numbers to cause a panic — but that ignores the reality that critical systems are generally not very vulnerable to well-known attacks and an adversary would have to develop broad-spectrum weapons to use against a wide variety of systems. Certainly such an attack is feasible, but is it practical? It would be much more practical to just send some head cases with guns and plastic explosives to shoot their way into critical facilities and blow them up the old-fashioned way.

are trying to modernize their mission, and media whores who are trying to create a modern technology boogeyman.

THE EFFECTIVENESS OF CYBER WEAPONS

For the sake of argument, let's look at the type of cyber attacks that the pundits claim could be launched. The most typical scenarios involve coordinated attacks against infrastructure — attacks designed to interfere, demoralize, and disorganize.

SORRY, THIS ATM IS CLOSED...

Imagine the chaos that would result if the ATM networks went down, the Internet went down, and some cellular telephone systems went off the air at the same time. Frankly, worse things have happened and chaos has not resulted.

When cyber warfare proponents first started hyping the "threat," they painted pictures of disaster not unlike the Y2K scenario: the U.S. economy in a tailspin because of electronic interference with the stock market, rioting in urban areas because ATMs and banks are offline, aircraft falling out of the sky because flight control systems had been tampered with, and so on.

What is the reality? Last time I was in the cockpit of a Piper Cheyenne, the pilot showed me all the neat triply redundant navigation systems he had on board in addition to his eyeballs. Most planes carry everything from a magnetic compass to paper maps and air-pressure altimeters. I'm absolutely certain he could operate the plane if every air traffic system on Earth went down. Any pilot could.

As far as rioting in urban areas because ATMs went down — give me a break! The news media would gleefully carry the news about the e-banking collapse and whichever bank's ATM network remained up would make a fortune and everyone else would use credit cards or cash for a day while the computers were rebooted. It would be the same with the stock market. The cyber war fanatics make the same feverish claims as the Y2K survivalists — but if they're so scared, why aren't they running out and buying generators and guns?

If the Internet went offline for a week, telephone companies would increase their long-distance revenues, America Online (which is a private network) would gain another zillion subscribers, and overall productivity in the workplace would soar.

How can cyber warfare proponents so glibly pronounce the
death of civilization without sensible people laughing at them,
when their premises are so obvi-

> ## " The reality is that the system is resilient. "

ously out of touch with reality? The reality is that the system is resilient.

WHAT'S WRONG WITH THIS PICTURE?

How is it that people forget that we survived *just fine* without all the new-fangled technical toys, and that virtually every high-tech system we've come to enjoy has a low-tech fallback? Sure, telephones aren't as cool as instant messaging, but they would work fine during the hours or days until an attack was dissected and a means of blocking it was developed.

Did the country collapse into chaos when the entire U.S. air fleet was grounded for two days during 9/11? Of course not! I know people who were in various states of travel at the time; most of them improvised and overcame the situation with little difficulty. One friend who had an important meeting rented a car and drove from Arizona to California — a dramatic gesture that probably wasn't necessary, given modern teleconferencing.

you should know

Ironically, on 9/11, the cellular infrastructure in New York City was so over-loaded it was very difficult to get calls through, so the local FBI office used Internet instant messaging while the phone systems were clogged. When one of our high-tech toys is taken offline, people immediately start trying other options until something works — then a new ecosystem briefly springs up around that technology until the crisis is over.

I guess you could say I believe more in the resilience and creativity of humankind than I do in cyber warfare, at this time. If cyber terrorists took all of our whiz-bang communications offline for a year, the Morse code operators, ham radio fanatics, carrier-pigeon breeders, and bike messengers would have a great time.

Perhaps in another 20 years the fallback low-tech systems will have been dismantled, and then we'll have a greater level of inconvenience if something goes wrong. But if you look back at history, I suspect that the Victorians felt the same way about steam locomotives; they didn't want to go back to horse-drawn carriages, but the horses were still there, just in case.

E-BOMB POWER

The other day someone on CNN was talking about E-bombs and how they'd disable the electronics in cars and make us all pedestrians. I'd certainly miss my computer until I could buy another one, but in the meantime I'd be the guy riding the big bay gelding to the grocery store with a grin on my face.

I'm not a survivalist and we're not a society of survival freaks; I think Americans are a society of practical people who are accustomed to creature comforts but who don't fold up and run crying to mommy when those comforts break down for a time.

PRELUDE TO A CYBER WAR

Could cyber weapons be used to disrupt communications as a prelude to a more general military attack or invasion? Of course they could. But that invasion would somehow have to be kept secret enough to preserve the element of surprise, which is increasingly difficult with the type of surveillance systems available to national governments these days.

Indeed, the advantage of surprise is mostly going to be the special province of the terrorist or guerilla warrior for the foreseeable future. Terrorists and guerillas wouldn't launch cyber attacks as a prelude to an assault, because it would be more likely to alert the target that something was afoot.

> **" Terrorists and guerillas wouldn't launch cyber attacks as a prelude to an assault, because it would be more likely to alert the target that something was afoot. " "**

Until 20 or 30 years from now, when virtually everything has a networked computer in it, cyber war won't be a practical way of launching an attack that is more than an annoyance. Unless some nation-state decides to invest massive resources in developing a cyber war doctrine and logistical system, it simply won't be effective enough to justify the effort.

THE INSECURE REALITY

So, if cyber war isn't a threat, we don't need to worry about the electronic Pearl Harbor, right? Wrong. When pundits talk about the electronic Pearl

Harbor, they're usually thinking of the kind of massive surprise attack that made our entry into the World War II so sudden. When I think of the electronic Pearl Harbor, I think about the events *leading up to the attack on Pearl Harbor* that made the attack so successful.

WIDE OPEN TO ATTACK

Prior to the sneak attack, Japanese spies were able to easily observe battleship row, identify which ships were docked where, and determine what time of day would be best for the attack. A tremendous amount of information regarding the capabilities of the ships was available to the not-yet-declared enemy because, for all intents and purposes, the base was a wide-open facility.

While the ships themselves were guarded against people wandering around on them, there was no wartime mind-set and it would have been easy for a listener to pick up a tremendous amount of information in a short time by just paying attention. Does that sound familiar to you?

When I hear someone talking about the "Electronic Pearl Harbor" in our future, I think of pre-Pearl Harbor America: naively letting people wander around sensitive military installations because nobody was overtly hostile at

> *" It's not that we're vulnerable to cyber attack — we're vulnerable to cyber espionage. "*

that particular place and time. These days we put all the interesting sensitive stuff out there on the Internet on poorly protected Web sites. It's not that we're vulnerable to cyber attack — we're vulnerable to cyber espionage. One of the hottest topics in the intelligence community during the early 1990s was the notion of "open source collection" and "open source intelligence." The premise of open source is that you collect as much public information as possible regarding your target, collate and sort it, and weed out the contradictions. The resulting web of information often contains surprisingly useful information.

Consider, for an example, if one took the financial disclosures from publicly traded companies that did defense work, all the information from their Web sites, all the Web pages Google found in a search that contained the company's name and the word "resume," and threaded the information based on keywords in context. You might learn budget information for defense-related programs, information regarding projects employees were working on, and who the projects were for.

Try It Yourself

Go to Google.com and enter the following search: "employee locator" "search." You'll get back over 4,000 references. Of those 4,000 references I immediately recognized dozens of government agencies in the first few pages of search items. One of them, helpfully, offers wildcard matches on employee names. Searching for "a★", "b★", and so on will return a complete employee list. That particular government agency also identifies employees with a helpful "organization code," so one could, conceivably, infer the existence of various departments, their budgets, staffing levels, locations (using phone number prefixes) of facilities, and so on.

Imagine that some guy launched a social-engineering attack against that organization. He can quickly learn the phone number for the data center. Perhaps he can learn the name of a supervisor in a networking group. Then he could call, claiming to be a new employee having problems accessing his computer account, and probably get assistance logging in. If you sound like you belong someplace, it's amazingly easy to gain access.

Is this valuable information for legitimate users as well? Absolutely. But do we need to have this information just sitting out on the Internet for everyone to use or misuse? In truth, it's hard to say — we need information to do our jobs, but where do we draw the line?

OOPS . . .

A number of years ago, as an experiment, I performed an open source search on a certain large corporation's computer security systems. During the course of the search I learned a tremendous amount about the products they were relying on, who had run them, where services were outsourced, and in one case, how much key employees responsible for security were paid.

In a demonstration I performed for a government customer in the early 1990s, I located a number of documents regarding projects and budgets for weapons systems that were being researched on behalf of the military, as well as training manuals for military intelligence officers. All of this material was accessible using a browser, public search engines, and some patience.

OPEN SOURCE GOVERNMENT

I believe that a modest investment in technology for correlating key-words automatically and establishing relationships between documents with similar semantic content would dramatically enhance one's ability to sift through the information that is available. The open source collection organizations within the intelligence community have been building tools for doing exactly that for at least the last 10 years. It would be silly to assume that other nation's intelligence agencies have not also developed similar capabilities.

If technically collected intelligence (intercepts, satellite images, and so on) and human intelligence (espionage) were combined, an attacker would have a very accurate window on the next Pearl Harbor.

If that's not bad enough, there are a number of Web sites that specialize in collecting information related to specific topics, and correlating or publishing it. Sites such as the Federation of American Scientists (www.fas.org) or John Young's site (www.cryptome.org) collect and publish data on the activities of intelligence organizations or the military. All of this information is public, but gathering it into a single location only makes it easier to use.

you should know

Can't afford your own spy satellite? You can always use Terraserver (www. terraserver.com) to build an overview image of your target — including a special hot link for "famous places" so you can jump right to them. Because the imagery is from old declassified satellite imagery and LANDSAT databases, it's not "real time." But it's still potentially useful. I was able to locate my farm and build a 1-meter resolution composite image of the place in under an hour. The imagery was from 1966, but you could see where the cars were parked in the driveway. It's not state-of-the-art imagery, but it's pretty cool to have Terraserver show you pictures of Groom Lake, the Air Force's secret testing facility at Area 51 (www.terraserver.com/a51.asp).

THAT'S CLASSIFIED

Electronically, we're the most open country on Earth. We've paid as little attention to our electronic borders as we have to our physical borders — or less, if that's possible. I think the situation has gone so far it's probably too late to fix it. There's an electronic Pearl Harbor waiting to happen.

As mentioned in a previous chapter, one of the greatest myths in computer security is that there's a difference between "classified" and "unclassified" information. Technically, a tremendous amount of information is "sensitive but unclassified" (SBU), which means, basically, the information is important enough that it should be guarded but it's not going to be.

Most government computer systems are either unclassified or SBU; a decision that is largely left to the discretion of the agency generating and managing the data. Maintaining classified material is a painful, expensive, time-consuming process that involves clearances, special facilities, and access logs to certain materials. Given the discretion between classifying materials and leaving them SBU, what do you think most agencies will choose?

In fact, it's very difficult for one branch of the government to tell another, "You ought to classify your stuff." Things like military logistics systems, military purchasing systems, and so on remain unclassified. Many White House documents that are extremely sensitive remain unclassified because classifying them would make them harder to share when they need to be shared.

you should know

Classifying information as secret is *not* a panacea. As we saw with KGB moles Aldrich Ames and Robert Hanssen, traitors can still leak information out of an organization. However, allowing agencies to decide what to classify based on what's convenient to them is just a step short of telling them it's okay to put it on their Web sites for public download.

The problem, fundamentally, is about keeping secrets when you have a gigantic logistical system with thousands of suppliers and consumers needing to share information, about all that you can do is make it *harder* for the other guys to learn what you're doing. It's extremely difficult to even understand how exposed our systems are, electronically, because of the potential for open-source-style correlation attempts. SBU information gleaned by journalists or hackers might be combined with public information to provide an extremely detailed view of the inner workings of sensitive operations.

For example, imagine that someone takes the public Securities and Exchange Commission filings from a group of defense contractors and sifts through them to gain an approximate picture of the budgets of certain weapons research projects. That picture might be further refined by searching online conference attendee lists to get information about staffing levels, both at government agencies and at the contractor level. Purchase orders for innocuous component parts might be found online with a little bit of hacking. Orders for consumable supplies might fluctuate depending on whether the project was in a testing cycle or a development cycle. All of this information could be combined to form a surprisingly accurate picture of what is going on within a classified project.

> **❝ When you have a gigantic logistical system with thousands of suppliers and consumers needing to share information, about all that you can do is make it harder for the other guys to learn what you're doing. ❞**

you should know

There's an interesting story (which, unfortunately, I can't confirm) that during the first Gulf War, journalists were able to tell when the fighting was about to start because the pizza joints near the Pentagon were swamped with delivery orders around the clock. Couldn't the equivalent of pizza order spying be done with military online ordering activity?

Just as Japanese spies were monitoring what ships went in and out of Pearl Harbor in order to improve the effectiveness of their strike, our electronic Pearl Harbor could come as a result of our pell-mell rush to put everything online where it's convenient — for everyone.

WHO'S LEAVING THE DOOR OPEN?

Why is information security such a huge problem? It's largely complicated by the sheer size and complexity of the organizations involved. Imagine trying to understand how information is used throughout the entire Department of Homeland Security, and then extend that to wondering about how that information could be shared securely with contractors and companies providing goods and services. The problem is

> " *Imagine trying to understand how information is used throughout the entire Department of Homeland Security, and then extend that to wondering about how that information could be shared securely with contractors and companies providing goods and services.* "

literally too big to understand, let alone fix. Even so, we could be doing a better job than we are today.

THE DESIRE TO BE CUTTING EDGE

The desire to be cutting edge is not something to underestimate. Many government agencies suffer from the same image problems as corporate IT departments: If you're using old computers, software, and techniques, it is taken as an indicator that you don't know what you're doing. Still, I have to admit that the times I've worked with government computers, I've been amazed at the disparate mix in equipment that is available. Some agencies have state-of-the-art stuff, while others appear to be scraping by on machines that wouldn't fetch a $1 bid on eBay.

More importantly, if you're not constantly upgrading, buying newer, more state-of-the-art systems, then you're likely to have trouble getting the budget you request next year. Anyone who has ever worked with government contracts will have, at some point or another, gotten the "we have to spend this money by October or it'll go away" phone call. Artifacts of the budgeting process that have nothing to do with the merit of budget requests frequently take precedence.

There's also the sheer gratification of working with newer cutting-edge stuff. For federal IT workers, being close to the cutting edge represents an opportunity to get training in the latest thing, improved job security, and career mobility.

Unfortunately, the latest thing usually is the least secure thing. Computer systems and software that have been in fielded use for a longer time are often more mature and have been time-tested. This was especially the case in the early 1990s when the uber-new-thing — the Internet — exploded on the scene. Early versions of Web servers and browsers completely lacked security features, were rife with vulnerabilities, and were poorly understood even by experts at that time. Yet many government agencies, eager to show they were part of the new wave, rushed to connect their mission-critical assets and networks to the Internet. Most (but far from all) did it behind firewalls and attempted to provide basic security, but the litany of federal systems that have been compromised by hackers grew and grew. Remember: Keeping up with the Joneses is a bad idea, when the Joneses are dousing themselves with hi-tech gasoline and playing with cyber matches.

OFF-THE-SHELF INSECURITY

When the microcomputer revolution happened in the mid-1980s, suddenly a department could accomplish new things faster because they no longer had to cooperate with other departments — they could just buy a few computers and do their own thing. When this was happening, I was working as a systems manager at a large hospital, so I saw it all take place firsthand. Someone who had an application he or she wanted to get running quickly no longer had to go, hat in hand, to the mainframe operators in the basement and suffer interminable wrangling over schedules and features. Now, people could go buy a PC, an off-the-shelf software package, and do it on their own terms.

In intensely competitive bureaucracies the ability to buy your own technology has a profound effect, because information technology is a great tool for empire-building and achieving dominance in departmental budget appropriations. From a technology strategy standpoint, unfortunately, this is a disaster because it exacerbates the tendency for government agencies to purchase incompatible systems and to "do their own thing."

A TALENT FOR LOSING TALENT

Federal IT workers have consistently lagged behind their commercial counterparts in expertise and training. Until the early 1990s it was primarily because of differences in pay scales and the perception that government service wasn't particularly exciting. From the 1990s until the dot-com bubble burst in the 2000s, there was a tremendous hemorrhage of talent from federal IT departments to the private sector. Why work a boring government job full of bureaucracy and office politics when you can go to a startup, double your salary, and get stock options and a neat-sounding title?

Some high-tech government agencies' staffs were literally gutted as recruiters for new companies looked for people with Internet, software, and networking experience. Those federal employees who did jump on the bandwagon early and got involved with cutting-edge technology virtually all took pay raises and left for greener private-sector pastures.

Nowadays, of course, it's the other way around — with the dot-com collapse a lot of former government workers want their old jobs back, and huge numbers of recent graduates are applying for these positions as well. This represents a terrific opportunity for the government to breathe some new life into its high-tech staff.

WIRELESS NIGHTMARE

Wireless networking is the latest cutting-edge horror that is going to affect government (as well as corporate) computer security. Access points are inexpensive devices, under $100, that virtually anyone can afford to deploy. Unfortunately, they are also a security disaster waiting to happen.

> " Access points are inexpensive devices, under $100, that virtually anyone can afford to deploy. Unfortunately, they are also a security disaster waiting to happen. "

Many organizations have no idea how many wireless access points have been installed, or where they are, since they're cheap enough that many departments just install them on their own initiative. These self-installed access points are the worst, because often the people installing them don't bother to turn on the security features that prevent unauthorized users from accessing the network remotely.

you should know

Even if the security features are turned on, the encryption in first-generation access points was fairly easy to break; there are tools and directions for how to do it on the Web. Consequently, many government and commercial networks are now easy to hack into, simply by driving around the building and parking nearby with a directional antenna, a laptop, and wireless hacking software.

When wireless systems were first being developed, security was left disabled because it made it easier to set them up. Meanwhile, the makers of wireless products were relentlessly hyping the convenience of

WAR DRIVING: JUST A CRUISE
AROUND THE BLOCK

"War driving" is the term many hackers use for a fun new hobby they've invented in response to wireless computer network technology. The hackers drive around technology office parks with laptops and antennas that have been tuned to boost their transmit/receive capabilities, and look for unsecured network access points. Once they find them, they either use them to send spam, to surf the Web, or to search for interesting data on the wireless network.

Some war drivers have reported dozens of unsecured wireless access points within a single block in high-tech dense areas such as San Francisco. These unsecured access points represent not only a weakness in their owner's network; they represent a jumping-off point from which the hackers can attack other networks.

wireless and omitting to mention any of the security risks it presented. In fact, one of the reasons it's so convenient is because it's so insecure.

This is a pattern that has played itself out over and over in recent years as new technologies with security loopholes built in get installed without many organizations effectively analyzing the risks they pose: Internet, wireless, always-on cable modems, Microsoft Windows, and on and on.

CONFUSION: CORPORATE COMPUTING
VERSUS GOVERNMENT COMPUTING

In corporate America, when companies grow past a certain size, they tend to realize the importance of using their buying power to get better pricing, demand better support, and establish standard software platforms, operating environments, and applications. If a FORTUNE 500 firm goes to a vendor and expresses interest in purchasing products for enterprise-wide use, they get *much* better service and pricing than if each separate business unit went and negotiated its own deal.

Most large corporations follow a process in which they determine the type of software products they need, then standardize on it across the enterprise. It's not unheard of for an IT manager to get in serious trouble for purchasing products that were not "supported" or part of the "strategic product line" — because corporate America recognizes that adopting and upgrading software and training users in its use are a major expense.

For example, FORTUNE 100 firms typically select a standard antivirus product and mandate its use and implement a standard firewall product, a standard desktop operating system, a standard database, a standard Web server, and so on. Does the government also do this? No. In fact, government computer systems are the greatest hodgepodge of incompatible software imaginable. Every department makes its own decisions and spends its own IT budget, and nobody makes any attempt to coordinate anything. When attempts are made to coordinate, they are often sidetracked into turf wars and office politics.

> " Every department makes its own decisions and spends its own IT budget, and nobody makes any attempt to coordinate anything. "

Small wonder that we taxpayers hear about hundreds of millions of dollars being spent on massive database conversion projects, or projects

---

THE FBI IT CHAOS

Within the FBI alone there are over 12 major databases that contain information regarding possible terrorists and other criminal information. On the rare occasion when someone from INS actually would try to check to see if a visa request was from a suspected bad guy, he or she had to log in to at least six different computer systems, query them separately, and then make sense of the results manually. What is wrong with this picture? It's as if Amazon.com had six different Web sites, and to find a book, you had to search each of them separately because you weren't sure which one had the book. Is this a hard problem to solve? No, not in corporate America. In the government, however, it appears to be a nearly impossible problem to solve. Indeed, each time the FBI or INS tries to link databases to automate sharing, it costs tens of millions of dollars and results in another incompatible database. In corporate America it would result in a heavy rain of pink slips from the CIO on down.

to interconnect incompatible systems. Why have the federal government's IT professionals failed to learn from how corporate IT professionals do things? Are the government's current cyber security initiatives going to somehow turn around years of neglect? With computer infrastructure security as part of its bailiwick, how on Earth is the Department of Homeland Security going to coordinate securing this mess?

Hint: It won't.

IN THE PROVERBIAL LURCH

So where does that leave us? We're left with a government IT infrastructure that is a hodgepodge of systems with no planning, no standards, and very little security. There is no real understanding of where sensitive information is kept, or how much of it is exposed to the public, either through Internet security holes or because information is just sitting on Web sites for the taking.

you should know

Information that can be collated by enemies to produce useful live intelligence is completely uncontrolled and is a frequent target for joyriding hackers.

So far, we have been willfully blind to our *real* electronic Pearl Harbor: the fact that we've built an electronic ecosystem so permeable that enemy intelligence can search it practically at will, and we have very little chance of detecting anything. They won't attack us by taking our computers down — why should they?
Our computers are their best source of information.

> " They won't attack us by taking our computers down — why should they? Our computers are their best source of information. "

IN A PERFECT WORLD

Government IT is a disaster waiting to happen. How could things be improved to a point where we can all feel more secure? I have a few little suggestions...

WWW.E-PEARLHARBOR.GOV

What should we be doing about the huge amount of potentially sensitive information that is being made available to the public? Some good news is that post-9/11, federal agencies have been much more careful about what they publish. That's a favorable sign that indicates an awareness of the problem is starting to dawn. However, we could do better. Since DHS is chartered to deal with security for critical infrastructure, it sounds like this would be a terrific opportunity for them to show some leadership.

The current approach for handling security in government agencies is to provide broad directives and otherwise pretty much let the agencies do as they will. The agencies lack guidance because there is a profound vacuum of leadership. DHS has an opportunity to prove its usefulness by establishing sensible standards for how agencies should review what they publish and make accessible on the Internet, as well as standards for government firewall and network security controls. These should not be standards that recommend "pretty please, lock down your network" — they need to be strong, enforceable, easy to implement, and considerably more strict than the current state of affairs. That's bound to create a gigantic turf battle. Right now, there is a narrow window of time in which aggressive leadership could have an impact, but the opportunity is slipping away. In a few more years, there will be no secrets left to protect; everything will be on the Web.

"There are many computer systems and networks in the federal government that should *never* be connected to the Internet or to another network of any type." Every time I say this in the presence of federal IT workers, they look shocked: They are all horrified by the inconvenience that would cause, and complain that they wouldn't even be able to surf the Web or even get email.

> **" Simply put, the federal government is going to have to take computer security seriously — lip service is not, and never will be, enough. "**

Still, when you consider how many times government networks get hacked, it's kind of foolish to overlook such an obvious, effective solution. The government is way behind in understanding Internet technology and its impact on federal computing. By allowing each department or agency to do its own thing, the genie has been let out of the bottle and it's going to take incredible willpower to put it back. That, however, is what we must do. Simply put, the federal government is going to have to take computer security *seriously* — lip service is not, and never will be, enough.

GETTING OUT OF THE LURCH

Back in the days when I started working in the area of computer security, one of the things that amazed me most was the fact that computer users simply didn't appear to care that they were running insecure products full of gaping holes. It simply didn't bother them enough to get on their radar screen. But then I had an illuminating conversation with one of my consulting clients over a couple of beers. She observed that most customers of computer products are amazed to find out that the stuff they've bought is insecure and full of gaping holes! After all, most commercial products you buy are designed with safety in mind where appropriate. So a lot of computer consumers simply *assume* that the product vendors have worried about security and that, if it's on the market, it's probably okay. It took me years, literally, to internalize that observation, but now I am convinced she's right.

So, usually, when computer security people start philosophizing over beer, someone inevitably says, "You know, what we need to do is get a bunch of lawyers involved and start holding vendors that produce security software liable for the damage caused by their insecure products." That *would* be one approach to the problem, but mostly I think it's like shooting yourself in the foot to distract yourself from a headache: The cure is worse than the problem.

There are, basically, three things we can do to improve the state of computer products and software:

Hold vendors liable.   This option would mostly just feed lawyers and would probably have a stultifying effect on our entire technology industry.

Get the government to step in and regulate security.   This option would create another bureaucracy, and the government doesn't have a history of being particularly astute when it comes to regulating cutting-edge stuff.

Stop buying crap.   Let the forces of the free market do their thing, and eventually the problem will take care of itself. Of course, this assumes that the mythical *informed consumer* is the one who is making the purchasing decisions.

Last year Microsoft's Bill Gates announced a "secure computing initiative" in which Microsoft's engineering department would stop adding
features for six months and instead focus on fixing all the security holes
in their products. That effort has had exactly *zero* affect on the rate at
which holes are found in Microsoft's products, but it shows that Gates,
at least, recognizes that eventually security might become a consideration in a buy/don't buy decision.

So it's safe to say security is on the radar screen. But what can we all
do? It's simple: *If you're not an informed consumer, shop with consumers who
are.* This is a theme you may notice cropping up over and over throughout this book: The current approach of allowing federal agencies to
make their own product purchasing selections does not work. It doesn't
just apply to federal agencies. If all the banks in the United States
announced that they had decided they were going to standardize on a
single platform for e-banking and that stringent security design was a
feature they were going to judge as a selection criterion, how long do
you think it would take for the software product vendors to take notice?
In the case of the Microsoft secure computing initiative, the tail was
wagging the dog: A more effective approach would be for 50 percent of
the FORTUNE 500 to announce that they were not going to buy any
more Microsoft products until they met stringent security requirements.

In a perfect world the federal government could lead by assuming
its place as the ultimate informed consumer. After all, it is a *huge* and
very important consumer for virtually every vendor of software products. Of course, if the government started standardizing on products
based on whether they met reasonable requirements, the companies that
lost out would scream foul and would complain that they were being
put out of business.

You know what? That doesn't bother me at all. Think of it as evolution in action.

10

IT, American Style

My friend Nat Howard and I were chatting at a conference, and he had a pithy explanation of government bureaucracy: "The dynamic of government is to be just exactly as bad as it can be without getting voted out." The trick is that we need to figure out new reward structures for bureaucracies. The current reward structure rewards size, expense, and amount of office space required rather than competence, cost savings, or efficiency.

When it comes to cutting-edge technologies, Americans are the guys who actually *sharpen* the cutting edge. There's one important lesson when you're out there keeping the cutting edge sharp: Sometimes you bleed a little bit.

The United States has been the driving force behind most of the new technologies that support the global information infrastructure. The Internet, the desktop revolution, desktop publishing, email, online banking, and electronic supply chains are either direct results of United States-led research or United States-developed information technologies. This cutting-edge status has given us the "first-mover advantage" — as well as the *disadvantages inherent in* being the innovator.

THE DOWNSIDE OF LEADERSHIP

The first-mover advantage means that we're the first people to reap the benefits of new technologies and methods. But the disadvantage of being the first user of something new is that it's usually still a bit buggy and a lot more expensive.

That bugginess can make all the difference in the world when it comes to something like military or homeland security technology. Buggy early versions of technology are expensive to have in your infrastructure because you have to either fix them constantly (at a cost) or replace them entirely (at a greater cost). This dynamic works against building secure, damage-resistant systems because it's easier to cost-justify maintenance than replacement — which tends to further entrench those bug-ridden components. That's a big problem if those components are strategic to our national security and are full of gigantic, gaping security holes.

PATCHING IT UP

When it comes to security, we persist in compounding bad decisions by throwing more money at them. We do that because any alternative requires an admission that the first decision was irreparably bad.

Here's a scenario that I have seen play itself out over and over again during the last few years: Someone calls me to get my assistance to help secure an online application that has fundamental design flaws. The client inevitably asks for workarounds.

For example, a friend's company purchased an online banking application that they wanted to roll out so thousands of their customers can check and manage their bank accounts over the Internet. The online banking application was written by a company that used to write banking applications for mainframes and that is now moving into the Internet age. Of course, there are differences between those environments: Mainframe applications generally are designed to work over closed (presumably secure) private networks, whereas Internet applications need to function over a network infested with thousands of aggressive hackers.

So what did the authors of the banking application do? Because they knew how to write stuff for closed networks, they pretty much just left security out of the Internet version by ignoring the problem. All they would have needed was a few days of research and asking the right people a few questions and they'd have been fine, but they didn't bother. That, unfortunately, is typical of how most software is developed — especially security-critical software.

To make matters worse, the vendor that wrote the software made it rely on Microsoft's IIS Web server: a piece of software that is notorious for being rife with security flaws. I'd be surprised if a month has gone by in the last few years where there hasn't been a new security hole found in IIS. Using IIS as a core component for a security-critical online banking application is kind of like deciding to use sand wrapped in duct tape as the foundation for your new house. It's going to look OK and hold up long enough to impress the neighbors, but your whole house is likely to collapse before the ink is dry on the mortgage.

LAYERS OF MISTAKES

So what does the typical IT organization do when confronted with shoddy security in its systems? Simple: Add more duct tape. The computer security equivalent of more layers of duct tape is firewalls, application content scanners, Web security modules, and so forth. By the time my friend's company has secured an application that should have been secure in the first place, they will probably be paying a 20 percent additional markup for all the duct tape, not to mention the time they are wasting in meetings dealing with the problem.

The problem is most likely never going to get fixed, either. Because my friend's company has already paid for the software and spent months working with it, their project schedules and budgets are now irrevocably tied to the existing approach; changing horses in midstream is not an option. Besides, they've already proven that they're willing to throw huge amounts of additional money and time at the problem — why would the vendor care to fix their software if their customers are willing to go the extra mile to work around the problem for them?

I've seen this pattern play itself out over and over again, and it shows no sign of improving. It's part of the joy of being cutting edge: After a few years these details get worked out and embedded into the whole packaged solution so that there aren't any nasty surprises. Of course, usually that packaging means that you get the same crud the earlier customers got, but now it comes with a roll of duct tape included in every package.

The end result, of course, is systems that are more expensive, less reliable, more complicated, and less secure. Welcome to the critical infrastructure! Welcome to IT, American style, where the guys on the cutting edge bleed green!

Now consider this entire scenario applied to a critical homeland security system such as the one that tracks immigration or maintains records on terrorist activity at CIA or the FBI. Just how secure does that make you feel?

KEEPING UP WITH THE JONESES

In the high-tech industry the popular term *early adopter* is used to describe the intrepid souls who buy the latest technologies as soon as they come to market. Usually, early adopters can expect to reap immediate benefits if the technology works right, or considerable headaches, as they are the extended "field test" of often unproven new products.

BAD INVESTMENTS

The fate of early adopters is sometimes paradoxical — they wind up with orphaned products that were "almost good ideas" or early versions that lack an upgrade path.

I know a number of federal agencies that invested huge amounts of money to build early-generation fiber-optic campus and office networks using a system called Fiber Distributed Data Interface (FDDI). FDDI was extremely cutting-edge, very expensive, and very cool — five years ago. Now, you can buy similar capabilities that rely on copper cable for a fraction of the cost of FDDI, and there's no upgrade path for the FDDI networks except to rip them out and start over. Being on a dead-end upgrade path means you're going to eventually have to pay sticker-shock prices for a whole new infrastructure.

Sometimes all of the end users of a large system are put at risk by implementing new technology. During the late 1990s, when everyone was rushing to cash in on the Internet bubble before it burst, software was being shoveled out the door as fast as possible, with no attempt to test it to make sure it worked, other than in the most basic sense. Millions of users rushed to download the latest versions of Web browsers every time a new release came out, hoping that they'd find a version that was relatively stable and didn't crash as much as the previous version. And, at the same time as they were cheerfully downloading and running beta-test-quality code, people were using those same programs to do their online banking, network administration, and confidential communications. Most people just complacently assumed that someone was looking out for their security. They would have been horrified if they'd known that there was, in fact, no safety net underneath them.

you should know

I remember one of my old bosses was very proud to buy an Apple Newton when it came out. It cost an arm and a leg and was pretty much useless; but it was very cool. Ten years later, the technology was (arguably) ready for prime time, and everyone got excited about Palm computing. In the meantime, the Newton had come and gone and left all of its proponents hundreds of dollars poorer. Every so often, however, an early adopter gets to have the last laugh: For every Newton, there has been an ebay.com: the early adopter that was able to gain the high ground in a new area and leapfrog to incredible dominance.

WHEN GOVERNMENT PAYS THE EARLY-ADOPTER PRICE

The United States is a nation of early adopters, and our status as the world's preeminent technological superpower is a direct result of our willingness to spend huge amounts of energy pursuing technologies that aren't quite ready for prime time, because they stand us in good stead when they finally do become ready.

The recent war in Iraq demonstrated convincingly how good it is to be an early adopter when that technology delivers on its promise. The overwhelming speed and ease with which the Iraqi regime was toppled was due to a whole new set of battlefield tools and techniques that were beta-tested and debugged in the first Gulf War, the Balkans, and Afghanistan. Warfare is *the* place where the early adopter can shine.

When it comes to government IT, it's a complete crapshoot. Some agencies (mostly in the intelligence community or advanced science) *define* the state of the art, while others wallow in the Stone Age. Frequently, you'll find weird mixes, in which one part of an agency has state-of-the-art technology and another is struggling along with equipment so ancient that it qualifies as "quaint." Consequentially, securing it is a nightmare.

For one thing, systematic attempts at securing the government's critical infrastructure can immediately be transmuted into massive requests for funding; in order to secure the systems, they should be brought up to a reasonably state-of-the-art baseline, after all. Security gets blamed for a lot of expenses that are really just upgrades in disguise or attempts to recover from unwise purchasing decisions made long ago.

DHS is somehow supposed to coordinate getting federal systems' security out of the Dark Ages and into the sunlight. Given that DHS has no say in how federal IT purchases are made and no authority over how systems are deployed, how, exactly, are they going to do that? In fact, it's pretty safe to guess that it would take a gigantic effort to even *understand* federal IT purchases and get a handle on what's going on — let alone actually do something about it.

THE SECOND SYSTEM

The corollaries to the first-mover advantage are the *second-system* effect and *third-system* effect. The second-system effect is an observation among computer scientists and engineers that, usually, when a replacement is designed for an early prototype, it's often overdesigned, overengineered, over cost, late, and over budget. The third system is usually pretty good and usually incorporates the basic principles that made the first a success, without the baroque features of the second system: an ideal fusion between whatever excited the early adopters and the lessons learned from exploring the feature envelope in the second system.

Sometimes, the costs of the first system are so high that it's never even feasible to replace underlying technologies; it's necessary to search for an endless upgrade path. For example, the United States has a huge infrastructure of copper wire resulting from our early adoption of residential telephone technology. In the long run, that technology has proven extremely beneficial — yet many countries were able to deploy telephone technology using second-, third-, or fourth-generation technologies that are cheaper, more flexible, and more maintainable. Some late adopters have been able to buy telephone technology for a fraction of what it cost the early adopters, resulting in systems that are significantly better than those of the first generation.

There's one place where the U.S. government gets it right with respect to the flow of technological innovation: weaponry. When the military is satisfied with a particular weapons system, they are always designing the next version. This is perfectly understandable, since human societies have learned throughout history exactly what happens if you fall too far behind the weapons technology leading edge. Perhaps it's time for the federal government to believe a bit of its own rhetoric and act like knowledge, in the form of information technology, is power.

INSECURE SECURITY

The human tendency is to leave security out of systems until their use has become widespread enough that security becomes a problem. That's usually not until the second or third generations have been adopted.

Telephone systems, for example, had virtually no security until
the 1970s, when it was demonstrated conclusively that it was
easy for "phone phreaks" to
obtain free service. It turned out
that the mechanisms controlling
phone systems were childishly
simple and easy to interfere with:
Pay phones used auditory codes

> *" The human tendency is to leave security out of systems until their use has become widespread enough that security becomes a problem. "*

to let the central phone switches know they had received adequate coins
to place a call. Phone phreaks like the legendary John "Captain Crunch"
Draper quickly learned the right noises to make to steal "free" long-
distance calls. Draper's weapon of choice was a child's whistle from a
Captain Crunch Cereal box.

Today's networks and computers have important components that
are just as weakly designed as the early pay phones' payment systems —
and many of the hacking attacks we hear about on the news are just the
tip of a very huge iceberg. For every major Internet security flaw you
hear about, there are hundreds of security flaws that would apply to our
systems if we didn't have layers of firewalls and duct tape between them
and the Internet. Like my friends' online banking application, 95 percent of operating systems software is not designed with enough security
built into it to run over the open Internet.

Amazingly, this type of flawed security infrastructure is considered
perfectly normal. For example, most Microsoft Windows system users
on networks use Windows' file-sharing services to get data to and from
their local servers. The networking protocols used for this data exchange
are extremely easy for anyone on the network to break into. So organizations put a firewall between their network and the Internet or other
untrusted networks.

If you think about it, we've become completely accustomed to having to add layers of security software or workarounds as a matter of
course. Why is it that you have to install an operating system, then
antivirus software, a firewall, and a fistful of different patches downloaded off of vendor's sites via the Internet to piece together a secure
system? In what other industry are we so complacent about utterly horrible quality and lack of safety features in products? Imagine if you
bought a car and had to install seat belts and a parking brake before you
felt you could use it safely on the freeway!

We're in big trouble because, as a nation of early adopters, we have a high-tech infrastructure that is a misdesigned hodgepodge of new stuff, old stuff, insecure stuff, and the usual duct tape, spit, and baling wire that passes for "integration" or "backward compatibility" in the high-tech world.

Most corporations seem to understand this, intuitively. Regardless of the fact that it is painfully expensive, they periodically overhaul their IT infrastructure. These overhauls usually coincide with management fads; in fact, the fads often become the excuse for the overhaul. During the late 1980s, outsourcing was a popular corporate IT strategy: Instead of owning and managing millions of dollars of computer resources, make it someone else's problem and pay a flat monthly fee for service. Many companies dumped a lot of obsolete equipment in favor of outsourced services, and then brought everything back in-house during the 1990s when the Web phenomenon and the Internet bubble put our entire high-tech sector into warp speed. Suddenly, instead of having an integrator or outsourcer do an organization's project work, you had entrepreneurial groups taking advantage of Web technologies that allowed rapid development with a very low skill threshold. Anyone who could write HTML and set up a Web server could build a corporate "intranet portal" and completely bypass the traditional IT function.

The Y2K "crisis" also justified replacing whole categories of systems with more recent Y2K-compliant implementations. The end result was an across-the-board upgrade for many corporate IT departments. Unfortunately, a lot of this work was done on the quick, taking advantage of newfangled Web technologies and rapid development techniques: techniques that gave short shrift to security and technologies that often lacked security features entirely.

Federal IT departments appear to be outside of this cycle; they are budgeted on a schedule that is tied to annual review and inflation. Many federal IT departments face the end-of-the-year crunch as they run low on money — or a use-it-or-lose-it spending spree as they have to get rid of extra cash. No government bureaucrat ever "gives back extra budget dollars" because if they did, their budget would be "cut" the next year. In this case "cut" means it would be put back to where it should have been in the first place, considering how much actual money was expended. Thus, the entire budgetary process used by government agencies conspires to encourage waste by failing to reward efficiency.

BUILDING EMPIRES: GOVERNMENT IT

What does all of this have to do with procuring sensible technology for the U.S. taxpayers? Nothing. It's all about empire building and making sure there's enough cash in the drawer for bureaucrats. The bureaucrats feel safe in pulling such shenanigans because they know that there's not a snowball's chance in hell they'll ever be fired for incompetence.

Recently at a conference, I attended a special session titled "How to Sell Security to the Government." The presentation featured a speaker who had spent the last six years working in federal systems sales. One of the pieces of advice he gave was to understand that outsourcing and managed security services were always going to be a tough sell to government managers because more

> " *The bureaucrats feel safe in pulling such shenanigans because they know that there's not a snowball's chance in hell they'll ever be fired for incompetence.* "

SECURITY AT A PRICE

There are also the "discretionary funds." Back in the late 1990s the administration raised a hue and cry about computer security, and many federal agencies were given extra budget dollars to spend on improving their overall security posture. At that time, I was working for a security products vendor, and we had a large opportunity that we and other firms were pursuing with a certain government agency. To our surprise and consternation, the agency didn't actually buy any security products — they spent their entire $400,000 security budget on upgrading all of their PCs with enough processor speed and memory to run Windows NT. The rationale? Windows NT was more secure than Windows 95, so the upgrade was a "security upgrade." This same agency, of course, didn't have antivirus software or even a firewall, because they were too expensive. (Lest the reader think this is sour grapes on my part, I should state that I was selling neither firewalls nor antivirus products.)

In corporate America, it's possible that mid-level managers would get away with a maneuver like that for a year or two, but they'd lose their job the first time there was a major viral outbreak or an intrusion.

efficient systems deployments meant a cut in head count or budget for the manager in question. He went on to explain how to propose such projects by working through system integrators that would require "project managers" in the government IT department — justifying more hires at higher pay grades and, potentially, internal promotion for the IT manager's buddies. We can see the results of this approach to building a computer infrastructure: a management-heavy bureaucracy of technological illiterates managing an army of system integrators and consultants.

CONNECTING THE DOTS

One of the great things about the data age is its potential for transfer of information. The Internet is just the tip of the iceberg, really, since its mechanisms are largely ad hoc and the format of data beyond HTML is arbitrary. It's still impressive: You can put a link on your Web page that allows a friend to search a completely different Web site for a book of your choosing. Imagine the potential advantages for an electronic government. The CIA and FBI might even be able to share information usefully, assuming that the nontechnical bureaucratic impediments to information sharing could be worked out, that is.

Most "computer people" will tell you that, aside from cases where pure computation is key, the value of computers is in the *information* they manage and how the information can be processed. For modern computing, this boils down to *compatibility* — data needs to be securely exchangeable between machines that talk the same networking and file-sharing protocols. Good compatibility is when the stakeholders managing a particular type of data agree on a common database layout so they can easily link their databases. Bad compatibility is when one department does one thing and another does something completely different.

The key ingredient in ensuring compatibility is coordination between organizations that are trying to solve similar technological problems. That's why, in most large corporations, there's an office of the chief technology officer or chief information officer that is the primary coordinator of technology strategy. It's the CIO's office that decides what standards will be applied across the enterprise.

Most federal agencies have a CIO responsible for overall technology strategy — for that agency. Is there any effort to standardize with other federal agencies? Usually this happens only when absolutely necessary, or when it's already too late. On the occasions that standardization and interoperation actually do happen, it's never a simple process: It involves some serious politics and a huge amount of negotiation. That's how the federal government's computer systems became an incompatible mess: Each agency does its own product selection, and no effort is made to coordinate. The times when interagency working groups are formed to standardize on implementations are rare compared to the number of interagency working groups that are formed to figure out how to connect incompatible systems.

you should know

I've seen this process in action when I was involved in a communications security system between CIA and NSA. We had a huge, complex problem to solve — a problem that would have been a small, easy problem if even a tiny bit of thought had been put into designing systems with the eventual goal of CIA/NSA cooperation. Of course, why would anyone have planned for that? When bureaucracies find themselves with compatible overlapping systems, they get *scared* because it might result in someone saying, "Maybe these two agencies should be merged into one!" which is akin to bureaucratic death.

INCOMPATIBILITY IN ACTION

Government technology strategies are not just a theoretical exercise in systems design. On 9/11 it was discovered that police and firefighters had radio technology that couldn't be made to communicate effectively between their central dispatch systems. Not only that, but their radios couldn't work effectively with out-of-state law enforcement agencies on the scene, or with the military.

you should know

At least firefighters have been smart enough to standardize hydrant and hose diameters and threads; imagine how pathetic it would be if your local fire department showed up and had to scrounge around with an adapter while your house burned to the ground! You'd think that it would be glaringly obvious that fire and police radios should be able to interoperate in an emergency. And, you'd think that if they teamed up and bought their radio gear from the same company on the same purchase order, they'd save a lot of money, too, right?

[Handwritten note in margin: What mythological planet does he live on where all large companies are efficient and perfect?]

ng compatibility between such crucial infrastruc-
nt to be obvious. The CEO of a FORTUNE 500
olerate such lack of professionalism from IT pro-
ncompatible police and fire radios issue came to
sponse from the affected agencies, predictably, was
n money to buy new equipment." As if not having
ow somehow excuses the fact that they bought
with the money they *did* have, when they had it.

I   work administrators of a FORTUNE 500 company   g kind of networking hardware, and when the
CTO   t it and questioned them, they responded, "Give
us mo   on't have enough money to buy new equipment
to rep   ff we incorrectly bought." They'd never get the
chance   g for that company again before they were given
the co   lesk in a box and escorted out of the facility.

CHA   HE OIL

Buying the right software and hardware is only the beginning of the
game. Keeping it working correctly is equally critical. Today's computerized environments are ridiculously high-maintenance. Most desktop
users will spend a significant amount of their time performing Windows
system administration tasks, installing software, or downloading and
installing patches. It's necessary to do these things because the software
environments we have gotten used to are simply not reliable enough to
be ignored and allowed to run: They don't just keep working.

> " Hackers can cause hundreds of thousands of dollars of damage in a matter of hours, simply in lost productivity and cleanup costs. "

Add to the mix the hackers,
spy ware, viruses, and self-
replicating worms that rampage
rapidly through networks, infecting as many machines as they can
in the shortest-possible time.
These represent not only a huge
ongoing expense to protect
against, but a gigantic mainte-
nance expense. Ignored, however, the potential expense is even greater;
hackers can cause hundreds of thousands of dollars of damage in a matter of hours, simply in lost productivity and cleanup costs.

ONLINE DAMAGE CONTROL

Organizations, particularly in the federal computing area, have shown a tendency to make bad decisions when assessing the likelihood of a particular type of online damage. Many Internet-connected government or civilian networks have installed some kind of firewall technology to help keep hackers out of their networks. This is a good start. But viruses and worms are a hugely expensive threat that often migrates through firewalls in the form of email attachments.

With most antivirus products in the $20 to $40 range, it's unbelievable that people still see them as an extra expense they're unwilling to pay. When you're paying between $800 and $1,200 for a computer, $200 and $1,000 for the software on it, and you're skimping on $40 for antivirus software, you're not making an effective cost/benefit analysis.

Shockingly, few organizations have global antivirus software deployments. Even organizations that have brokered site licenses with antivirus product vendors seldom mandate that all users install the software.

Right now, spy ware is the big problem that everyone is sweeping under the rug. Spy ware (or "sneak ware") programs are small programs that lurk on your computer and periodically send off reports to their owners regarding the Web sites you like to visit, what programs you have installed, what kind of Internet connection you have, and so on. Most spy ware programs transmit their reports to their owners periodically in the form of traffic that is nearly indistinguishable from normal Web traffic — which is why a lot of corporations ignore it. Since most sites allow all outgoing Web traffic to exit their firewalls transparently, the spy ware is able to report your actions unimpeded.

What is the significance of spy ware when you're talking about federal computers that might be being used to research sensitive information? Nobody even wants to think about the consequences.

you should know

A CTO of a computer security products company promulgated a policy that everyone was to install a standard antivirus product. The company had licensed enough copies for every employee in the company, and everyone was told how to obtain and install it in their new employee packet. Apparently, however, the policy did not apply to the new CEO, whose first official action was to open a virus that automatically emailed copies of itself to all resellers and customers.

IF ONLY THERE WERE NO USERS...

The state of the art in interfacing users with security systems is not good. To say that it needs work is an understatement.

When we hear of things like the CodeRed worm taking entire federal agencies offline for days, we have to wonder what's going on with federal IT. The vulnerabilities that CodeRed exploited were widely known months before the worm came out. Most competent system administrators had already fixed them. If you'd already had an antivirus program on your machine with an *old* signature database, you would have been immune to CodeRed on the day it came out. Antivirus vendors had signatures to detect and block CodeRed within a very short time of its release; anyone using an auto-updating antivirus product would have emerged unscathed from the attack. Yet, instead of CodeRed being an insignificant blip on the radar screen, it became a gigantic disaster resulting in major service outages and tremendous amounts of lost time and effort. Hundreds of thousands of computers worldwide were infected on the first day of the CodeRed outbreak and the outbreak continued infecting machines for months.

What's the problem? Many government agencies have brokered agencywide licenses for antivirus products; there is no excuse for not having that protection installed. When I challenge people on this topic, their answer is, invariably, "I was just too busy to install it." This begs the question: Why do we *let* our users have the option of not having antivirus software installed automatically on their machines? In fact, I'm amazed that we haven't *solved* the problem of viruses yet. It's not rocket science, yet we appear to be unwilling to pay the cost of solving the problem completely. Rather than solving it completely, we seem to be happy to spend hundreds of millions per year on antivirus products and to lose billions of dollars per year in lost productivity.

The fact that we still have outbreaks like CodeRed or SQL Slammer is a sign of apathy on the part of end users, and misprioritization on the part of managers. Obviously, people don't think this stuff is serious, and they're too busy doing other, more important things to get around to it. What they don't understand is that five minutes spent securing your foundation can save you days of pain later on.

DAMAGE BY POOR PLANNING

When it comes to computer security, we are at much greater risk of damage through apathy and ignorance than we are through enemy action. While the threat of cyber war is largely a boogeyman to scare up funding for vendors, there is a real threat that we will continue to build an infrastructure that is badly designed, incompatible, and obsolete before it is completed.

We're seeing the beginning of this incompetence already in the number of cases where federal IT systems are massively over budget, late, and ineffective. You can see the roots of the problem when you look at the FBI with its 10 or more different incompatible databases that contain antiterrorism-related information: They cost a fortune to build, and they'd cost 50 fortunes to integrate successfully.

When I was researching this book, I found references at various times to 6, 10, and 12 crucial antiterrorist databases at the FBI. So I asked a few people I know who work within the intelligence community — the answers I got back were mostly along the lines of "Nobody really knows." So, one big hurdle to overcome in integrating the FBI's various databases would be *finding* them all. But the real hurdles to such

> **" One big hurdle to overcome in integrating the FBI's various databases would be finding them all. "**

integration are bureaucratic and political, not technical. To be the "owner" of an important database confers importance on the person who maintains and controls it; merging it into a central database would reduce the organizational importance of the former owner and would therefore provoke resistance.

you should know

During the Timothy McVeigh's Oklahoma City Bomber trial, the FBI nearly bungled the case at the last minute. It was discovered that the FBI had neglected to give the defense thousands of pages of documents that had been collected that might contain evidence. Under U.S. law, such documents must be provided to the defense in a criminal trial. Some legal experts feared that this procedural mistake might ruin their case. How did it happen? It happened because the FBI had more databases of information about the bombing than it knew until it was almost too late.

Doing it right the first time wouldn't have taken more work or cost more money; it would have taken more vision, and a bit of attention to detail. Americans are capable of both of those; it's time to start using those capabilities to make sure our information society is built on foundations that will last.

Imagine if the plumbing in your house had a different type of pipe for every room: different threads, different materials, and different inner and outer diameters. Sure, you could still make the plumbing work; you'd just buy a lot of adapters and you'd spend a ton of time trying to figure out how to connect things so they didn't leak as much. But the result would be inefficient. Worse, it would be impossible to maintain. Unfortunately, if you were the proud owner of such a house, you'd need to either keep working with exotic and complex plumbing or you'd have to spend the money to replace it all. In the long run, knocking it down and rebuilding from scratch is probably cheaper. That's pretty much the state of affairs with the various disparate, misdesigned, incompatible government information systems. We probably should be euthanizing them, rather than upgrading them.

> " What we've bought is a much bigger supply of duct tape, spit, and baling wire with which to hold the existing crap together. "

This is, to me, one of the biggest tragedies of Homeland Security: The DHS and all of its budgets enshrine the status quo. There's no sign that the fundamental problems are going to be worked on; what we've bought is a much bigger supply of duct tape, spit, and baling wire with which to hold the existing crap together.

FEDERAL PROCUREMENT: AN OLYMPIAN FAILURE OF VISION

Throughout the government, procurement practices guarantee incompatibility and cost overruns. Attempts to make sense of procurement have, arguably, made things worse.

The practice of selling to the government on large contracts has created an entire priesthood of experts who understand the various obscure regulations regarding pricing, Government Service Administration (GSA) schedules, and how to get products listed on certain purchasing contracts. If you're a company trying to sell to government agencies, you need to find experts who know how to navigate all the legal and procedural hurdles for procurement.

When I was working at a small software startup selling an intrusion detection system for computer networks, we had a government customer that wanted to buy about $100,000 worth of our product. Unfortunately, for them to do so, they would have had to issue a request for proposals (RFP) for products of that particular type, and hold a contracting bake-off to see whose product they would finally buy. However, the agency already had an open arrangement with a larger "beltway bandit" defense contractor that was providing a blanket purchasing agreement for security goods and services. So, we had to negotiate with the contracting company for them to carry our product and to offer it to the agency through their existing blanket agreement. By the time all was said and done, the federal agency was paying nearly $150,000 for $100,000 worth of goods. Not a particularly good deal, by any measure.

Procurement regulations and policies exist for the obvious reason: to prevent graft. That certainly makes sense, but unfortunately the extra layers of bureaucracy add substantially to the price tag. To prevent inequities from happening, further regulations restrict vendors from offering different prices to different branches of the government, virtually guaranteeing that nobody ever gets a discount and every agency pays the same inflated price. You almost have to pity the government: It seems that every time they try to do the right thing, it just creates another expensive bureaucracy. Even attempts to save money result in costly money-saving efforts.

BUYING POWER GONE WRONG

Take firewalls as an example: If all the various federal agencies were to standardize on a single firewall technology, the government could dramatically increase its buying power and negotiating position with that vendor. It would be safe to say that they'd have the vendor's undivided attention. Indeed, the vendor would need no other customer than the federal government. Unfortunately, in order to keep things fair, we don't do things that way. Each department that needs a specific technology has its own procurement process, makes its own suitability studies, and then buys its own licenses for the products.

Imagine if a corporation bought its IT the same way — what a mess! But the U.S. government does this across the entire enterprise: Army, Navy, Air Force, Marines, FBI, CIA, Department of Education, and on and on. There's no centralization of even basic, standard technology.

you should know

The military, at least, has managed to standardize reasonably effectively on a few items such as rifles, uniforms, and small arms. That's because the military understands the need for standards in a visceral way that the rest of the government has not had to face. When you're in a firefight, you do not want to worry about whether or not you can effectively share ammunition with the guy next to you. That's just a bad idea.

Many other nations recognize that certain crucial infrastructure processes such as arms manufacture are best performed "in-house" rather than "outsourced" to third parties. It's a huge trade-off. By having a semiprivatized weapons development effort, the United States gets the advantage of competition and competitive hunger among its suppliers. In return, we have the disadvantage that some critical suppliers might fail financially and that if they succeed, they will want to be able to sell their technology on the open market.

So far, with defense technology, this trade-off appears to be working. But that's primarily because the department of defense is *somewhat* focused in what it wants. If the Air Force bought aircraft the way the government buys IT, each fighter wing would get its *own* unique kind of aircraft, none of which would have interchangeable parts. Not only that, each fighter wing would make up its own rules of engagement, because nobody had ever thought to standardize those, either. Remember I mentioned earlier in this chapter the firefighters and police whose emergency radios don't work together? Imagine a government with an information infrastructure that's built the same way. What are the effects on homeland security of having such an infrastructure? First and foremost it reduces the ability to react quickly in an emergency. When computer systems are compatible and designed to work together, they can operate at full speed and don't require additional effort in order to share information. There's also less of a chance of data getting lost in the translation or being difficult to locate. These factors might be the crucial difference that turns a homeland security disaster into a manageable incident.

IN A PERFECT WORLD

Technology is becoming more and more a part of every system in our world today. The impact that inefficient deployment of technology has in a homeland-security-minded world is profound. Could we turn things around and make all the patched-together systems work together?

STAYING STATE-OF-THE-ART

Security practitioners love to bemoan the horrible state of software security for good reason: It stinks! But what's the solution? Security experts often point to other industries as models for implementing controls through liability. If someone can sue a car manufacturer because its product is flawed and dangerous, why can't the consumers of a software product sue software vendors for damages? I'm terrified of that idea, personally, because the inevitable result would be that lawyers would make a lot of money and software companies would charge dramatically more for their products to cover their additional legal expenses. Everyone would lose in the long run.

What's a reasonable start? Perhaps we need the software equivalent of a lemon law. We could offer some protections to customers who purchase a product and discover that it does not perform as advertised. It's probably not necessary to legislate this kind of thing, however, since a sufficiently astute customer buying products in volume can put nonperformance refund clauses in a purchasing requirement.

I don't think we need any legal or bureaucratic structures above and beyond what we already have in contract law. People who are buying high tech need to remember one of the fundamental laws of commerce: *The customer is always right, because the customer has the money.* I believe a tremendous amount of headway can be made by exercising a little more diligence in product selection — it takes more expertise and time, but expertise is the best tool for getting the job done right than anyone's ever seen.

BUILDING EMPIRES

The way that government agencies choose and deploy technology is due for a complete reassessment. Right now, standards in government computing are largely accidental or the result of industry dominance (the extent to which Microsoft Windows is a "standard") rather than any kind of rational plan. The current approaches encourage waste, empire building, and inefficiency. The government needs an Office of the CTO that would be responsible for coordinating planning of technology deployment across agencies. In order for this approach to work, the

CTO would need real authority over spending and deployment, as well as the power to set stringent standards.

My suspicion is that the position of U.S. CTO's office is already in the process of evolving, albeit slowly. Most government agencies have CTOs and many CTOs in related agencies work together, so long as that cooperation doesn't cross lines in the bureaucratic turf.

Building an office of technology leadership for the federal government would run the risk of that office itself becoming a huge unwieldy bureaucracy in its own right. In fact, the power inherent in such an office would be considerable, which would make it an attractive position for exactly the wrong kind of person. Avoiding turning it into a political plum or, worse, a marketing pulpit for vendor lobbyists would remain a difficult challenge. These are problems we already have to deal with at every federal agency. Oversight and accountability would go a long way toward preventing abuse.

There would be massive side effects if the U.S. government had a strong centralized technology direction. Product selection would become an enormously important process, because a vendor whose products were selected government-wide would do very well, indeed. Of course, this would completely rewrite the rules of pork and would almost certainly result in the failure of a significant number of the businesses that did not win in the selection process.

> " Perhaps a deeper concern is that, if competition was reduced, it might result in vendors becoming lazy and stupid — much like the telephone company in the 1950s and 1960s. "

What kind of ripple effect would that new selection process have on our high-tech industry? My belief is that it would dramatically accelerate the Darwinian processes that control the rise and fall of high-tech startups. As with all Darwinian processes, it would be a good thing and a bad thing: Your perspective would depend on whether or not you were one of the survivors. Perhaps a deeper concern is that, if competition was reduced, it might result in vendors becoming lazy and stupid — much like the telephone company in the 1950s and 1960s.

The U.S. government is one of the most significant — if not *the* largest — consumer of high tech on Earth. It seems to me that its current high-tech procurement processes are oriented toward incubating new technologies and fostering competition more than they are oriented toward building a seamless and well-designed electronic government. In a very real sense, the United States' efforts toward building an electronic government are the prototype that the rest of the world will follow. My guess is that in 5 to 10 years the rest of the world will be watching to learn from our mistakes. The real question is this: Can we?

The Manhattan Project, IT Style

Software maintenance and computer system management is the dirty, hidden secret of our computing infrastructure. Dealing with system software installation alone is a gigantic waste of personnel resources, worldwide. Worse, the resources that are wasted are usually highly skilled and often expensive.

It's amazing to me that we've never really made an effort to attack the problem of reliability and the human factor in computer maintenance. It's not rocket science, but we seem paralyzed by these challenges. Every time we see a new Internet-borne worm clogging up computers and networks, it seems to be exploiting our inability to maintain or patch system software fast enough.

> *" It's not a capability we can expect to see produced by commercial software vendors — they have no vested interest whatsoever in producing good software that doesn't require intervention. "*

On a government computing level, right now that problem is literally unsolvable because of the disparate nature of computing systems between federal agencies. There is no need — including security — that is greater than trying to get humans out of the process of system management; too much of the future depends on getting this all-important foundation right. If I were the CTO of the U.S. government, I'd start a computing "Manhattan Project" devoted to reducing system and software administration manpower costs by two orders of magnitude within five years. I believe it's utterly feasible, but it's not a capability we can expect to see produced by commercial software vendors — they have no vested interest whatsoever in producing good software that doesn't require intervention.

As we face the twenty-first century, we can look forward to a future where high tech will continue to gain in importance. As we saw in the recent war with Iraq, high technology is *the* force multiplier of the future. It's not an area where we can afford to lose our dominance, which means that the government needs to look at high tech and our technology strategy as a crucial component of national security for the future. Our government's infrastructure — a foundation of duct tape and sand — is what's going to have to hold that future together. We *cannot* afford to keep getting it wrong for very much longer.

11

The Business of Computer Security

"Just as ghouls take advantage of a fire or disaster to prey upon the property of the unfortunate victims, so many of the exploiters are taking advantage of the present temper of the public mind and are attempting to slide their pet projects through as national defense measures.

"It's time to call a halt and comb off the national defense bandwagon those opportunists who have attached themselves to it like leeches in an attempt to further their own selfish interests."

Izaak Walton League Executive Director Kenneth A. Reid
writing in *Outdoor America*, November 1940

Most of my professional career has been spent working on computer security, in some fashion. It's an interesting discipline, and it's taught me the value of being an idealist about certain matters and a realist about others. For example, computer security is an area where sloppiness is punished; clear thinking is crucial, and you're dealing with an enemy that really doesn't negotiate with you, or care about your agenda.

Fortunately for computer security practitioners, our enemies aren't out to kill us or thousands of innocent people, but the dynamics and balances shared by terror and computer security are interesting. You're trying to defend an infinite border, which may have been infiltrated by malefactors that can take advantage of a single hole to completely bypass all your expensive defenses. Your enemy can choose the time, place, and method of an attack, and has a huge population of noncombatants that they can hide among to use as unwitting camouflage or for an escape route. And, of course, they aren't forced to play by any rules, but you are.

Computer security practitioners, whether government or civilian, also have to deal with the ethical and technical problems of counterintelligence: How much can we learn from the hackers who attack our systems? Is it justified to pretend to be a hacker in order to learn what the real hackers are working on? And, of course, financial interests are always in play: Computer security is big business, and many fortunes have been made by people offering solutions that vary in their effectiveness.

But there's an expression that applies very aptly to the worlds of counterterrorism and computer security: "Lie down with dogs; wake up with fleas." The closer you get to the bad guys, the more likely you are to get tainted by their methods, their mind-sets, and their reputations. Our intrepid security practitioners from DHS are going to have to navigate their way through not merely nightmarishly complicated technical problems but business development and ethical problems as well.

LYING DOWN WITH DOGS

Computer security has some problems in regard to loyalties. As the security products market reached its peak during the 1990s, a lot of hackers switched sides and went into business helping to defend networks against their erstwhile buddies. Some of these people got quite wealthy.

you should know

One ex-hacker got a position as a "consultant" to some of his former victims and was billing them $4,000/day to do what he used to do for free before he got caught and earned a criminal record. Another ex-hacker whose main claim to fame was getting caught, breaking parole, going on the lam, getting caught again, and becoming a consultant now gets $15,000 for a speaking engagement in which he basically tells his ex-victims what suckers they were to be his victims. I'm sure glad that the other classes of criminals out there haven't figured out how to market themselves as well as the hackers do! Otherwise, we'd be paying pedophiles thousands of dollars to teach us how to run our day-care centers more efficiently, or taking self-defense classes from ex-convicts.

Some established security practitioners began dabbling in the skills of the bad guys, and overtly or inadvertently helped to drum up business by making the problem worse in order to charge money for making it better. To add insult to injury, instability in the computer security industry has served the customer poorly; corporate finances, mergers, and acquisitions conspire to make it harder for a customer to actually get a secure computer system.

What's interesting to me is the obvious analogues between the problem of computer security and the problem of dealing with terrorism. Do you make access restricted and more secure, or leave it open and less secure? Do you inconvenience your users and have better security, or just wave people and their luggage onto the airplane? Fundamentally, there are broad categories of problems in all forms of security that appear to be the same regardless of what you are securing, or what you are securing it against.

> **" There are broad categories of problems in security that appear to be the same regardless of what you are securing, or what you are securing it against. "**

Fortunately for computer security practitioners, our enemies are mostly just annoying, rather than lethal. Unless they are targeting top-secret military databases, with terrorist intentions, that is.

BLAMING THE SOFTWARE

Security software has had a rocky road to traverse, trying to keep up with consumer demand and the threats it was created to disarm. Along the way, there have been some fundamental problems in efficiency and effectiveness. To understand the challenges, you first need to understand how software comes to be.

IN A COMPLEX WORLD

One of the factors that most strongly influences computer security is *complexity*. The applications we use are written by human beings, using programming languages like C, C++, and Java. Humans don't handle zillions of complex details and interactions very well, and software is literally nothing *but* complex details and interactions. Major applications like a Web browser may include hundreds of thousands of lines of source code (the raw description of what a program is supposed to do when it's running). In fact, when you're writing software, there really isn't anything *there* — until it starts running to the point where you can interact with it; you need to literally *imagine* it into existence.

With larger projects that dynamic gets harder and harder to deal with because you need to bring more people into the team and get them all to share a common vision of something nobody can see. If that sounds contradictory, that's because it is. Imagine trying to write a symphony on the fly, by telling the cellists you wanted them to create this part, and the violinists this other thing, and then somehow we'll try to pull it all together later, and it will magically work.

We're talking about dealing simultaneously with three things that people do badly: dealing with lots of complexity, dealing with effective egoless management and delegation of tasks, and dealing with something that is (at least initially) only in the imagination of one individual. Have you got a headache yet?

Now imagine that you have to do that whole process for *each and every symphony you perform*. Remember, every piece of software is a unique performance of a unique score; no knowledge other than the programming skills used can be carried from one task to the next.

Imagine being expected to understand the contents and layout of a 10,000-page book and the reasoning behind the contents of every paragraph. When writing software, it's not simply a matter of instructing the computer what to do; you have to understand *how* all the instructions fit together. This is where the complexity comes in. If this book were a software program, an out-of-sequence sentence *right here* could cause the book to crash and cease functioning on the second page, and you'd have to trace through the entire book's underlying logic in order to figure that out.

My friend Rob Kolstad used to run around at computer research conferences solemnly intoning, "It's a miracle it works at all!" (in reference to the Internet). He was right. We're dealing with things so complicated that it's a massive task to understand even small parts of software — nobody can understand the big picture. And yet, somehow, we need to secure it! Secure it, hell, we can't even *see* it!

MICROSOFT BASHING

One of the great traditions of computer security practitioners is bashing Microsoft for producing poor-quality products that are full of security vulnerabilities. If I had a dollar for every time I've heard some customer complain about Microsoft products, I'd be richer than Bill Gates, if you can imagine that. Yet, those same customers are part of the 99.99 percent of the computerized world that relies on Microsoft's products. I've got sad news for you: Microsoft didn't achieve such a level of industry dominance by producing terrible products. In spite of all the ideology and marketing from its competitors, Microsoft does not have any means of forcing its customers to buy its products. It got where it is by producing perfectly adequate products that appear to satisfy the computing needs of 99.99 percent of the computerized world. Unfortunately for us all, "adequate" is not a good measure of security.

IT GETS TRICKIER

When you're writing a piece of software, you group sets of instructions that are used frequently into what are called "procedures" so they can be referred to from anyplace in your software. For example, imagine you've taught your child how to clean up his room. Suppose the process involves several subcommands, namely, "clean up the floor," "make the bed," "and put away your toys." You can dub that procedure "cleanup-yourroom"; next time you need to invoke it, you can avoid giving the detailed instructions and simply invoke the top-level procedure.

Procedures are ordered into a hierarchy and called in specific sequence to make up a complete program — for example, "cleanthe-house" might call "cleanupyourroom" and then "cleanthelivingroom" followed by "cleanthekitchen."

On top of these layers of commands, it's crucial to understand the dependencies between the elements of a program, because some things might be order-dependent, others might be resource-dependent, others time-dependent, and so on. Programming is hard.

SECURE IS HARDER

Writing secure programs is even harder than regular programming. When you're writing a nonsecure program, you need to worry about all

TERRORIST ANALOGIES

Hostile intent is also one of the fundamental issues in dealing with real-world antiterrorism. Building a skyscraper is *hard* — you need to worry about load, foundations, materials, power, water, heat, rust, earthquakes, floods, fires, and so forth. When you add *deliberate* attack, the menu of problems gets rapidly unmanageable.

I heard a fascinating discussion by a civil engineer who was explaining how the Oklahoma City bomber's blast inadvertently took advantage of some of the structural elements of the Alfred Murrah building's façade. The façade was designed to protect people from rain and keep water from getting into the front of the building; unfortunately, this design channeled the explosion upward and inward, causing more serious damage.

The architect who designed the building did a good job, but his mandate did not include dealing with attacks involving explosives. This is exactly the same problem many security software engineers face. When they write their software, it never occurs to them that someday it could become a mission-critical application that software terrorists could take advantage of.

---

the application's complexity in order to keep a mistake in the code from crashing the program. When you're writing security-critical software, you have to worry about someone *deliberately* trying to crash the program. Suddenly there's another whole added layer of complexity: hostile intent.

Security software engineers needs to understand not only how to write code that is resistant to normal mistakes; they need to write code that is resistant to deliberate mistakes. To anticipate any number of possible attacks, a security software engineer needs to be something of a seer, a paranoid, and a compulsive — all at once.

No Application Is an Island

Unfortunately, complexity in software bites us not just at the level where the code is written; it also comes into play when applications coexist on a computer. For example, there have been numerous security holes in which applications have been able to call each other in unexpected ways that allow attackers into the computer system.

Back in the 1990s there was a fairly famous hack involving an online banking application that got compromised using an email message. The attack worked when the hacker sent his victim a message that contained a small piece of software that checked the user's hard disk and invoked the online banking application. Unfortunately, it didn't invoke the *entire* banking application; it just invoked a little subroutine from a dynamic library — a subroutine that accessed the user's stored password and sent it to the hacker.

How did this happen? Because the programmer who wrote the online banking application never thought "What happens if something other than a human being invokes my online banking application?" Nor did he consider what would happen if only a piece of the program was invoked, instead of the whole thing. In the online banking programmer's mind there was simply no possibility that his program would be invoked in any way other than the one he expected.

Meanwhile, the programmer who wrote the email application thought "Wouldn't it be nice if, when a user gets an email with an attached image file, we just call the image viewer application and it'll automatically run?" The hacker exploited this situation by sending his chunk of attack code and telling the email program it was an image, but that it should be viewed using the online banking application instead of the normal image viewer. So, when the victim got the email, instead of seeing a pretty picture, the mail program invoked the banking program and stole his bank passwords.

Both programmers' reasoning was perfectly good *in isolation*, but taken as a whole, the results were a dangerous security hole. This pattern has repeated itself literally thousands of times in the recent history of computer security. The World Wide Web has produced a culture of computer users who understand that in order to make things happen, you click on them; unfortunately, they'll click on *anything*. And today's applications are so interdependent that it's often extremely hard to tell what you actually just clicked on, and what it's going to do to you.

Most commercial operating systems and software products doubtless contain scores of such holes because, when the core operating systems were written, they were never designed to be secure. There are applications that assume that only a trusted user would invoke them, and there are the new crop of Internet-enabled applications that are set up to provide service to anyone who

> " *If you consider the hundreds or thousands of applications and crucial files on a given computer or network, you can imagine that the number of possible combinations for mayhem is literally astronomical.* "

SMILE FOR THE CAMERA

One of my favorite recent examples of an unintended software design flaw was a digital camera that came with a remote-control program that would allow the user to download pictures from it. What very few people realized was that the remote-control program also, in an attempt to be helpful, started a mini Web server so that the pictures would also be available on the Internet while the camera was connected. So, some users who left their cameras hooked up all the time were potentially sharing their personal photographs with nameless, faceless creeps on the Internet. Why did the programmer who wrote the remote-control program add that feature? He probably thought it would be convenient and helpful. He just didn't think a few steps further to see if that feature might have unintended consequences.

contacts them over a network. If you consider the hundreds or thousands of applications and crucial files on a given computer or network, you can imagine that the number of possible combinations for mayhem is literally astronomical.

CONTRADICTING AGENDAS

After 9/11 there was a great deal of discussion in some circles about engineering buildings to be resistant to terrorist attacks. After all, the reasoning went, we can build earthquake-resistant buildings, why not bomb-resistant ones?

The problem is that building structures that are earthquake-resistant, bomb-resistant, fire-resistant, and everything-resistant is *really* hard and *incredibly* expensive. If we insisted that buildings be everything-resistant, they would mostly be two stories high, with angled 15-feet-thick concrete side-walls, no windows, and only two doors (so you could get out if one was blocked). Remember, when architects are designing buildings, they don't put a lot of work making them earthquake-resistant if they aren't near a fault line. They don't make them flood-resistant if they're on a hilltop. They can take into account local conditions to make the structure cost-effective and attractive for its location.

Just like the architects who decide what threats a building needs to be built to resist, programmers design their programming to suit the perceived environment in which the program will be run. When writing security-critical software, programmers are expected to successfully juggle dozens of contradicting agendas. People want to be able to install their favorite software on their computer, but they want their computer to be virusproof. Well, the easiest way to make a computer virusproof is to not allow new executable programs to be installed on that system. People want their browsers to be able to execute nifty Web sites with cool programs that play fancy graphics and sounds, but they don't want hostile programs to be downloaded and run.

I'd like to eat 3 pints of ice cream every night and still be slim and attractive while I'm at it. But certain desires are inherently contradictory.

COMPLEX INTERACTIONS

I'm not saying that conflicting goals such as these are impossible to achieve; but rather they must be achieved *carefully*. Each time a new requirement is levied on a project (be it a program or a building), it increases the cost and complexity of its implementation.

Microsoft Windows, for example, is made up of tens of millions of lines of code, each of which is (arguably) necessary and provides some specific functionality. Understanding the interactions between all of the procedures in a program that's so large and complex is utterly impossible. By extension, securing it all is also utterly impossible. It's like asking one person to secure the entire U.S./Mexican border single-handedly: Even if he tells you he's going to try, you're a fool if you seriously think it'll happen.

People will continue to complain about Microsoft's products, but they aren't going to get any better. Why? Because as much as we're complaining, we're simultaneously asking for newer features in the next version of the software. We're asking for new devices, better games, more powerful video-player software, and on and on. We're asking for ice cream with all-natural ingredients, loaded with chocolate and sweets — and we want it to have no calories and taste good at the same time. Surprisingly, we complain when we don't get it.

We're asking for homeland security, but we're not willing to suffer the irreversible changes in our society that we'd have to accept to get it.

BUYING SECURITY

Before the hackers even enter the picture, software manufacturers and their demanding customers are making a mess out of security. Customers buy products based on the nifty features they want, not based on whether or not the product has good security. If security was the selection criterion for products, 99.99 percent of the world wouldn't use Windows — they'd be using something much less complex, much more reliable, and less feature-rich.

It's convenient to blame the vendors for the poor security of products, but the customers that reward those vendors of overcomplex, buggy software by buying it have to shoulder some responsibility: You get what you pay for.

For years, vendors kept security very far down on their list of priorities. Largely, that was because every time they spent engineering resources to make software more secure, their customers bought software that had more whizbang features. Finally, the vendors got the message and started spending their engineering resources on whizbang features.

In the late 1980s, security got a big black eye with the vendors because of a government program intended, ironically, to promote security. In this program, the government established a standard for operating system security (known as the Trusted Computer System Evaluation Criteria, or TCSEC) that enumerated the features considered to represent desirable security properties for a federal computer. The theory was that, in a few years, all federal computer systems would have to have TCSEC features at a level known as C2. The C2-level features were actually a pretty reasonable set of security properties to expect, and a lot of vendors made sure they met the standard. Even Microsoft added C2 features to Windows NT so they could meet the government's expectations and not get disqualified from procurements.

So far, so good. But then a strange thing happened: Nobody bought the C2 systems. Government procurements sailed on, with nobody ever getting disqualified for *not* having C2 features, and the C2 features went completely by the wayside. At that time, I was working for an operating systems vendor, and I remember that a *lot* of work was put into C2 functionality. Probably several million dollars' worth of engineering resources were utterly wasted by each vendor. Now the vendors are continually skeptical about government attempts to require security features.

THE HACKER CONNECTION

The overused term "hacker" has become merely a handle for a stereotype. You're probably familiar with the pasty-faced, overweight or scrawny-looking boy-child, the "misunderstood whiz kid" the media like to portray. In fact, a *lot* of hackers match that stereotype, but most of them go on to get jobs, girlfriends, and eventually grow up.

There are a smaller number of hackers that never seem to be able to let go of that "rush" they get from penetrating into places where they don't belong or weren't invited. Those few, the geek-elite, are, ironically, the ones the media most like to talk about: the Kevin Mitnicks of the world. These are individuals who seem to have made it their life's work to go where they aren't supposed to be. Hacking becomes such a part of their self-definition that they just can't let go of it.

MARKETING HACK

Somehow, during the 1990s, the hacker culture all changed: Being a hacker was now marketable.

In the early 1990s there were only a handful of companies devoted to computer security systems and software. When the Internet boom began, the more forward-looking of the security companies began producing the first-generation Internet firewall and antivirus packages. During the IPO craze that followed, most of the first-movers went public, making large fortunes for their founders and backers, and putting Internet security on the map for the venture capital and investment banking communities.

Soon after, the lines between "good guys" and "bad guys" blurred quickly, as the hacker elite began applying in droves for jobs at the newly formed and rapidly growing security companies. Imagine if the CIA announced that it was forming a special unit for Middle Eastern terrorism specialists and would overlook past history for all applicants — and 95 percent of the applicants *were* "ex-"terrorists.

You wouldn't think that anybody would buy products and services from the people that were causing the problem, would you? Yet, somehow, that's exactly what has happened. The media gravitated toward these colorful characters and swallowed what they offered hook, line, and sinker.

The government and military have followed suit — during the late 1990s there were a series of media-circus hearings before Congress, where hackers were brought in to attempt to terrify lawmakers into taking security more seriously. Of course, the agenda was to uncork congressional mandates for security spending. But the hackers put on a grand show, giving testimony in their ill-fitting suits. With their long hair and crazy-sounding hacker aliases, they announced that they could "take the Internet down" in 15 minutes if they wanted to. The same hackers that were giving the testimony had day jobs as security consultants.

you should know

At hacker conventions in the late 1990s, we saw senior government officials paying court to the tattooed and body-pierced hacker elite, implying that they could find interesting jobs working for agencies like CIA, NSA, or the FBI. It was kind of pathetic, really. The government had allowed itself to become enamored of the very people who had victimized it.

THE NEW OXYMORON: ETHICAL HACKING

Companies that had hired lots of reformed hackers needed to find something for them to do that fit their skills, and thus *ethical hacking* and *penetration testing* were born. The idea of ethical hacking is basically this: have one of our domesticated pet hackers take a crack at your network before one of the wild ones does it.

The customers ate it up. Guys I knew who had criminal records for electronic breaking and entering were making $80,000 in a week, doing exactly the same thing they were doing for free before they'd gotten arrested and gone legit. Part of the beauty of the scheme was that a hacker could come back and do another penetration test the next year, to see if the customer had managed to fix all the vulnerabilities he or she had identified during the last test. All the hacker needed to do to ensure a steady gravy train was to find a new problem every so often.

On the surface, this sounds like a reasonable idea, but really it's almost useless to the organizations performing the penetration test. When a hacker attacks a computer system, one of three things will happen:

- The hacker knows a bunch of tricks for breaking into that particular type of system, and the system has not been patched or configured to prevent them working, and the hacker gets in.
- The hacker knows a bunch of tricks for breaking into that particular type of system, and the system has been patched or configured to prevent them working, and the hacker gets frustrated and gives up.
- The hacker knows a trick for breaking into that particular type of system, and nobody else knows about the trick, so the system cannot be protected and the hacker gets in.

You'll notice a couple of things from this analysis. First, the hacker has the advantage of battlefield knowledge and initiative. Second, barring secret knowledge, the hacker is not going to get into a well-managed and maintained system. These facts hold true regardless of how many penetration tests you run before a hacker attacks you. Unless, of course, your penetration tester is an ex-hacker who stays up late at night working the other side of the fence to develop new secret forms of attacks that can be used to demonstrate to your company that its systems are insecure *no matter what you do.*

> **❝ Your penetration tester is an ex-hacker who stays up late at night working the other side of the fence to develop new secret forms of attacks that can be used to demonstrate to your company that its systems are insecure no matter what you do. ❞**

THE RIGHT WAY

There's a right way to improve security, and that's by designing computer networks and systems carefully from the outset. Unfortunately, that takes a rare set of skills that few organizations are willing to acquire or invest in. After all, most companies expect that the software they paid good money for would be secure enough not to need a ton of expensive security consulting on top.

CUSTOMIZED VICTIMS

I worked at one site that was subjected to such a penetration test. The "ethical" hacker doing the test spent two days developing a special attack that would work against that customer, and then used it to break in. That attack would have worked against virtually any system of that particular type, because it had never been seen before and nobody knew how to defend against it. Of course, the customer was impressed; they had been victimized in an utterly unique fashion — how flattering. It's a great way of generating business, certainly. But does it help the customer?

C

[handwritten note: And can many + other do test that way ↓]

Security-conscious n[   ] ministrators work to design security into their [   ]ning, rather than by adding it on later as a resu[   ] This is a well-known engineering approach: Ur[   ]s and their breaking points, and use them withi[   ]ctices.

Imagine if ethical hack[   ]ey'd build the bridge and then destructively test an individual strut of the bridge until it failed. Do you think once you've replaced that strut you can assume you're okay? I've worked on dozens of security systems that have withstood the test of time because they were designed against *categories* of attacks and not individual, specific attacks. Unfortunately, designing systems in that from-the-ground-up manner requires a greater commitment of expertise and resources than most people are able or willing to make.

About the only way that penetration tests and ethical hackers have been able to help customers improve their security is by providing a nondestructive way of getting corporate IT managers to take security seriously. Many organizations have trouble dealing with the constant balance between securing things and leaving them open, and need this kind of reality check. I've seen a lot of corporate computer security specialists use penetration tests as a way of getting security-illiterate CIOs or CTOs to listen to them about what really needs to be done.

TAKING ADVANTAGE OF FOOLS

One brokerage that I worked with had a business unit that had consistently ignored security as they set up a Web site, and an online reporting site that included some potentially sensitive information. Every time the security people complained and raised alarms, they were shouted down because the business unit was very profitable and was run by people who were very experienced at office politics. In that case, being able to go to the CEO and explain that well-known and widely available hackers' tools had cracked their site in 13 seconds was a real eye-opener. Unfortunately, though, when you're dealing with situations such as these, it's because of bad or indifferent management, or office politics, and seldom has anything to do with security at all. Perhaps such organizations truly are suckers that deserve to be parted from their money, but I don't think so: Taking advantage of fools is never ethical.

THE BUSINESS OF COMPUTER SECURITY: BREAKING EACH OTHER'S CHOPS

Ethics in the business of security continued to plummet in the late 1990s as the market grew and even more money was at stake. In order to make customers aware of their products, an increasingly large number of vendors began adopting an approach of marketing vulnerabilities either in Microsoft's products or in other security products.

By 1999 there was a huge underground trade in locating and disclosing security vulnerabilities in mission-critical products. The justification for this was based on the successful justification used for ethical hacking: It's best if you know about this stuff right away so you can fix it before the bad guys use it against you.

Of course, the fact that the vulnerabilities were *found* just so that they could be used as marketing tokens was never mentioned. The fact that the vulnerabilities wouldn't have been used if they hadn't been discovered by the vendors and disclosed by the vendors was never mentioned. Oh,

> ❝ *By putting this information out where it was available to anyone, an entirely new crop of hackers was created.* ❞

certainly, if hackers searched, they'd find the vulnerability, too, but by putting this information out where it was available to anyone, an entirely new crop of hackers was created.

you should know

Known popularly as "script kiddies," these hackers are basically ignorant as to the details of the tools they use, but they break into sites and cause mayhem just the same. The "scripts" that the kiddies run are often attack tools developed by the same security professionals who research and publicize the bugs that they exploit.

THE CHICKEN AND THE EGG THING

In most industries, if you had a situation where the people selling the solution to a problem were also able to *cause* the problem, there would be public outcry and a demand for some kind of regulation. In the computer security industry, customers are sufficiently naïve, or have been swayed by the "hackers are on your side" logic to the point where nobody appears to even understand what is going on.

For years, there was a running joke that antivirus product makers were the ones writing and releasing the viruses. Having worked closely with antivirus product makers, I don't believe that's true, but it's a sobering thought. Many security products companies, however, are engaging in activity that is distressingly close to that. They're keeping their hands somewhat clean by not developing and distributing the attack tools directly, but they're publishing the location and types of the vulnerabilities.

Imagine if the companies that provide airport security came up with new ways of defeating airport security, for example, announcing [that certain] machines could be circumvented by using any [cer]tain material. Some enterprising manufacturer [makes s]uitcases. This information reaches the terrorists [around] the world, and when the airport's security is [breached, they] rush to provide an expensive upgrade to their [device]s to overcome the problem they had identified. [Does this make yo]u uncomfortable? If it does, then be wary of the [computer security indu]stry.

[handwritten marginal note: They didn't create the vulnerability, they merely identified it (?)]

SMART (?) CARDS

A smart card is a credit-card-sized device containing a tiny computer that can be used to store identification data, electronic cash, or whatever suits a company's particular application. A few years ago, one company identified a generic flaw in how smart cards operate. Basically, this flaw allowed certain types of smart-card applications to be defeated by an attacker who invested the resources to commit a mathematically intensive attack. The discoverers of the attack published a splashy article about it in the popular press, and the technology illiterate trade journals took up the article, scaring customers about the overall security of smart cards.

Coincidentally, at the time when this happened, I was the chief technology officer at a company that produced smart-card-enabled applications. I got a call from a representative of the company that made the announcement. They were offering us consulting services at a hefty rate to help us ensure that our smart-card application was adequately resistant to the attack they had just identified. Really, it amounts to drumming up business for yourself at your customers' expense. We'd hardly tolerate that in another industry, but for some reason, we accept it from computer security practitioners.

A VULNERABLE BUSINESS

The vulnerability disclosure game has become so popular that there is a constant drumbeat of new bugs being announced, often on a daily basis. A network or system administrator responsible for security is expected to download and install patch after patch, on a several-times-weekly basis for each mission-critical system.

Because the vulnerabilities are real, the administrator can rest assured that if the company doesn't dance to the tune of the vendors, it'll get hacked in short order — or worse. The CodeRed and Nimda worms, for example, were devastating to a number of organizations, as they rapidly spread across the Internet using a series of email and Web-based vulnerabilities. All of the vulnerabilities that were used in those worms had been published weeks or months before by "security experts" out to build their reputations. Did the administrators of the affected sites get any sympathy? Actually, no; many of them were ridiculed for not keeping up-to-date on their patches.

The insanity doesn't stop there. For many security startups, the single most effective means they have of marketing themselves is to find holes in other vendors' products and publicize them. I can think of a half dozen security companies whose only marketing has consisted of finding flaws in Microsoft's products, releasing details about how the flaws work, waiting for the explosion of panic, and then doing interviews about it on television. I've also seen this used as a competitive marketing tool: One company that made a particular security product found a vulnerability in one of its competitors' products and "outed" it to the press in an attempt to embarrass the competitor and steal their customers. Compared to traditional advertising and marketing, this fault-finding is amazingly cost-effective, and it provides better media coverage, since the media is always looking for a new disaster to promote.

I've debated the ethics of this with some of the perpetrators, and, away from the microphones, they'll often admit that they're doing it all for the marketing. "It's free marketing; it's a great way to make a reputation for your company," and so forth. But nobody seems to be willing to ask what *kind* of reputation these companies are trying to establish. They've managed to whitewash their activities so effectively that their victims respect them because they think they're being helped by these clowns. The media, of course, buys the whole line about vulnerability disclosure being for the good of the community because they're basically ignorant about computer security and their "go to" sources in the security industry are exactly the same people who are causing the problem.

BRINGING THE POINT HOME

Imagine that you are a homeowner and your house has a tile roof. Peri-odically, roofers come through your neighborhood and give the local kids bricks and suggest casually that they could break tiles off if they threw the bricks at neighboring houses. The kids, of course, try this for themselves and discover that indeed they can knock down tiles. What fun! The roofers come through the neighborhood, offering everyone a good price on steel roofing shingles to replace the tiles ("those darned kids!"). Now, you're faced with a dilemma. If you replace your roof, you're spending money you didn't really need to spend, but if you don't, you're going to suffer even more damage. Worse yet, imagine that, whenever the topic comes up in the media, you have representatives from the roofers saying, "What a sloppy, lazy homeowner who doesn't take better care of his roof." We call this "blaming the victim," and it's never an acceptable ethical position, yet somehow the security industry has managed to blame the very people who are supporting it financially. The hackers? They're the ethical heroes, remember?

HEY, LOOK AT THE EMPEROR, GUYS!

We have established a self-perpetuating chronic state of crisis. Hackers have convinced an entire industry that they're helping their own victims. People such as me who speak out against it are easily cast in the role of the bad guys who want to inhibit freedom of speech and information. After all, it's information that is necessary so that system administrators can protect themselves against attack!

Well, yes, the information *is* necessary — once it's been released. Now that armies of hackers know a particular trick for breaking into your Web site, it's important that you know it, too, so you can block it. But you're also expected to be grateful to the professional hacker who started the whole ball rolling by publicizing the vulnerability.

Personally, I am shocked and dismayed by the level of intellectual dishonesty shown by many notable industry figures; they all know where their financial interests lie, and nobody is going to interrupt the feeding frenzy because it keeps their bellies happily full.

DELIBERATE INCOMPATIBILITY

During the mid-1980s an interesting thing happened: Computer programmers realized that their systems were going to be important in the future, so they began to standardize various aspects of how they operated.

It's hard to even describe this grassroots effort as a "movement," but a lot of programmers and early networkers realized that a lot of the value of the then-new concept of networking was the ability for users on disparate systems to collaborate and communicate. Email was probably the largest motivator behind early standards efforts; everyone wanted to be able to send and receive messages with their friends, so standard protocols and formats for mail delivery quickly evolved.

EARLY STANDARDS

Largely, the standards effort had its roots in the early Internet and UNIX operating system user community. UNIX was important because it was the first significant operating system that ran pretty much the same on a wide range of hardware platforms. The C programming language, which developed in parallel with UNIX, was popular in that environment because C code written on one "flavor" of UNIX could usually run unchanged on another, providing a previously unheard-of degree of portability for applications and utilities.

At the same time, early Internet researchers were discovering the value of compatibility between networked devices. Anything that could talk TCP/IP could participate in the Internet application suite, and the applications (FTP, Telnet, SMTP, and so on) that provided crucial services were also standardized. These standards were ad hoc and usually based on a "reference implementation" (geek speak for something that pretty much works). In other words, one programmer would solve a problem, then describe the problem and his or her solution, and if enough people had the same problem and adopted the programmer's solution, it was a new standard. From then on, everyone tried to be compatible with the reference implementation, and thus the Internet grew.

As a result of these efforts, if you wanted to send and receive email, all you needed to do was find or write server and client software that talked the SMTP protocol and you were able to become a part of this revolution in communications. Those were fun times for computer programmers; you could spend a weekend or two and hook all your company's systems together to use email and really impress your boss. Back then, the most popular PC operating system, MS-DOS, didn't support TCP/IP as a built-in, but if you were persistent enough, you could find TCP/IP code and make it work sufficiently for your PC to participate.

ORGANIZING FOR STANDARDS

By the late 1980s two influential organizations had come to the fore-front in helping to channel all the positive energy: The Internet Engineering Task Force (IETF) and Interop.

The IETF was originally a kind of social club for geeks, who'd get together, decide what needed to be done, decide how to do it, and exchange information on how they had solved various networking and system problems. These implementations became the reference implementations that led to a standards process whereby the Internet worked. The IETF was a collegial group, in the academic sense, which meant that there were a lot of intense emotional battles over obscure issues. As one IETF participant described it, "The battles were particularly ferocious because there was so little at stake." IETF standards, issued as Request for Comments (RFCs), became highly influential, since RFC compliance was the litmus test for being a good member of the small, but significant, Internet community.

Interop was a sort of geek party where engineers from various vendors met, usually on their own initiative, to make sure that everything worked correctly between the various implementations. So, at any given Interop, you'd see engineers from Sun Microsystems and Digital Equipment Corporation (two fierce competitors) trying to help each other debug their systems and smooth out any compatibility hurdles. For most of us who were there, the late 1980s were the high point of the Internet, when technology ruled over marketing, and getting it right was considered important regardless of commercial value.

But the good old days were ending almost as soon as they began; managers at vendors realized that owning a standard gave them leverage and influence over the customer base. So, by 1990, the IETF was no longer just a private club for software engineers; the vendors began sending representatives — software lobbyists — who tried to push their particular agendas.

Eventually the drive for standards broke down entirely, and the engagement became an open war on all fronts. Vendors that didn't get their way would withdraw from the standards process and offer incompatible variants that suited their agenda or product release schedule. Other vendors would try to shove standards through the committees that contained their own patented intellectual property, in hopes that the standard would be adopted and they'd be able to sit back and collect royalties. Microsoft, of course, was never particularly welcome at the IETF (a hotbed of UNIX bigotry) and cheerfully charted its own course paying lip service to standards where necessary and otherwise ignoring standards efforts completely.

When the Internet bubble began in the early 1990s, the standards process began to fall by the wayside as competitive pressures and time-to-market dominated everyone's agenda. Nobody

> " Microsoft, of course, was never particularly welcome at the IETF (a hotbed of UNIX bigotry) and cheerfully charted its own course paying lip service to standards where necessary and otherwise ignoring standards efforts completely. "

wanted to follow standards anymore; everyone wanted to set them. By the late 1990s, nobody cared about standardizing on anything, but everyone still paid lip service to standards because a lot of customers still expected the expensive stuff they were buying to work together.

Nowadays standards are set by market forces: The largest installed base wins. Who cares if your software is compatible with anyone else's if everyone uses your version, anyway? It took nearly 20 years for the computing industry to make a complete circle from the old days, where IBM ruled the roost and set the standards for everyone to follow, to the new days, where Microsoft sets the standards. The fact that we had a period of flirtation with end-user-oriented standards and open standards bodies was just a brief accident of history.

BUT *WE* GOTTA USE THIS STUFF...

Who was missing and without a meaningful voice during the entire run of the standards wars? The customers, of course. The customers remained the poor rubes who were expected to just sit back, shut up, and consume whatever was put in front of them.

Strangely, for the most part, that's exactly what they did. Imagine that happening in any other major multibillion-dollar industry, and it's a little hard to comprehend. It's like the old Betamax versus VHS wars, but instead of two competing versions, there are 2,000, and they compete on 60 different aspects of how they work. The customers probably gave up and just bought what was put in front of them because the sheer pain of trying to understand the options was too great. The fact that the single largest potential customer on Earth, the U.S. government, had no organized technology procurement strategy meant that the only customer with the clout to take the bull by the horns sat helpless in the chaos just like everyone else.

you should know

Many technologists complain about Microsoft's products, but what they don't realize is that Microsoft's greatest appeal is the notion that, at least in theory, Microsoft's products work with *each other*.

SECURITY SYSTEMS ARE NO BETTER

What about the computer security market and security systems in general? While on one hand people talk about protecting the critical computing infrastructure, it's nearly impossible to do that because security products simply don't work together that well. There is not a single firewall product that can be managed by one of its competitor's management consoles. There is not a single intrusion detection system (IDS) that produces alerts that can easily be used by a competitor's console. Every niche security product is a universe unto itself, and only a few vendors have even made their own products work together effectively.

> " Technology is acquired, and a 'Beltway bandit' consulting firm is brought in and paid millions of dollars to integrate technology that should have come integrated in the first place. "

Where is the customer in all this? They've been part of the cause of the problem by pursuing a "best-of-breed" strategy for technology acquisition. That means they'll buy whatever product works best in whatever technical niche they need to address. Usually, this means that the customers spend a small fortune trying to implement their own layers of glue and management to tie everything together. I've seen countless instances where this approach has played itself out at government agencies: Technology is acquired, and a "Beltway bandit" consulting firm is brought in and paid millions of dollars to integrate technology that should have come integrated in the first place. So the cycle continues.

SECURITY VENDORS: DIVIDE AND CONQUER

Vendors have moved to adopt one of two strategies in marketing security products: Divide and conquer or engulf and devour.

The divide-and-conquer approach works best for small vendors that want to achieve dominance in a small niche within a broader market. To succeed with that strategy, the vendor needs to produce the best product in that niche and make no serious effort to have its product work with any other products. After all, building compatibility takes effort, and the vendor that is trying to build the best doesn't "waste" any effort on anything but making its core technology as good as possible.

Customers that are buying best-of-breed products will gravitate to those vendor's products and pay the price later to integrate their systems. This approach has worked very well for several security companies, including most of the market leaders in niches like firewalls, intrusion detection, content filtering, and so on. Wall Street doesn't like this strategy overmuch because the long-term prognosis for such companies is not necessarily good: They are seen as one-trick ponies that will have trouble surviving when their narrow technology niche goes mainstream and bigger competitors with broader product portfolios move into it.

The engulf-and-devour strategy offers the customer the appearance of one-stop shopping — a single place where vendors can meet most of their customers' product needs with a single integrated offering. In a sense, it's almost the opposite of best of breed, because it's an acceptance that the vendor may be offering slightly inferior products but they have the value of not requiring huge integration efforts on the customers' part.

Unfortunately, engulf-and-devour companies seldom develop their own technology. In fact, they usually just acquire the technology from best-of-breed companies by buying them outright. Thus, Wall Street's prediction that the small best-of-breed companies won't survive is fulfilled.

> **"In virtually every circumstance that I have seen, the technology that gets acquired is pretty quickly screwed up by the acquirer."**

But the customers' expectation of continued excellence in products is thwarted by such strategies. In virtually every circumstance that I have seen, the technology that gets acquired is pretty quickly screwed up by the acquirer. Of course, that's after the acquirer's stock undergoes a huge run-up as Wall Street analysts get excited at the prospect of one company finally dominating the entire security market. This usually lasts for a year or two, but when the engulf-and-devour company's customers begin leaving in disgust, these companies start missing their sales projections, the shine on their halo is off, and the stock price quickly plummets. Before that happens, the founders and backers of the small companies have made a ton of money and found careers in another field or gone to another startup.

THE VENTURE CAPITAL CONNECTION

The engine that fuels all capitalist/free market economies is the urge to make money. In the 1990s in Silicon Valley, the venture capitalist was king. VCs operate on the simple principle that they're going to back 10 companies financially, and hope that 1 in those 10 makes them a 15-fold return on investment. If times are good and the VCs hit 2 out of 10, they stand to make obscene amounts of money.

THE GOLD RUSH

During the 1990s, venture capitalists practically had a license to print money. Some security products companies never even bothered to produce best-of-breed technologies; some of them were acquired for tens of millions of dollars based simply on their having a few patents, a good idea, or a compelling technology demonstration. Their success made the venture capitalists slaver uncontrollably. A few of the early venture capitalists in the security market made hundreds of millions of dollars, against investments of tens of millions of dollars, spawning a whole slew of imitators. The gold rush was on.

It's impossible to overstate the effect of investor expectations on a startup. Companies are expected to sell out, eventually; that's how the VCs and angel investors make their money. So startups have three possible fates: (1) go out of business, (2) get bought, or (3) go public. None of those three paths is likely to produce technology with long-term quality and viability.

Obviously, going out of business doesn't make for years of continued product excellence.

Getting bought generally doesn't, either, because the acquiring company usually screws up the technology they just acquired because they don't understand it. (After all, if they understood it, they'd have built it themselves.) Newly acquired companies collapse internally under the pressure of changing corporate culture and the fact that the founders of the acquired company are suddenly distracted by new wealth.

Going public often screws up a successful business too. Newly public companies are distracted by watching the fluctuations in their stock prices, and they suddenly need to show constant quarter-over-quarter growth for their investors. Many newly public companies stumble and collapse dramatically the first time they miss a quarter, and their stock is punished by the market. Their more mobile employees sometimes jump to a competitor or another startup if they find their options suddenly worthless.

The venture capitalists care about making their big kills; everything else is secondary. So if a company is in a position where it can cash out, it will. Whether it results in the "death" of a good technology or company is pretty much irrelevant. When a new market becomes popular, the VCs suddenly fund a ton of startups in that space, which only serves to make the Darwinian pressures even more extreme as they all fight for a suddenly contracted competitive landscape.

Basically, the injection of a ton of venture capital into a small market is like running a small-displacement engine on nitromethane fuel: It goes from 0 to 60 in no time at all, then back to 0 pretty quickly when it all blows apart at the seams. The market niches that VCs "develop" grow so rapidly because of the infusion of capital that, often, they go from newborn to senescence well before their time.

FUNDING FIREWALLS

An interesting example of VC-itis was when Internet firewalls became a "new market" in the early 1990s. The VCs funded at least 15 different companies in one year alone. This served to not only make the market more competitive, it confused the hell out of the customers by offering them more options than they ever would have wanted. It's not as if there were 15 companies selling *good* products, but there were 15 companies bidding for customers' attention, each with millions of dollars in marketing resources, expected to compete ferociously in order to succeed. Of those 15, I think 3 are still in business as independent entities; the rest were acquired.

WHAT'S SECURITY GOT TO DO WITH IT?

By now, you're probably wondering, "Why has Marcus dragged me through all of this?" Well, that's part of the point. None of this stuff has anything to do with security, building good security products, or helping build a more secure infrastructure. A lot of customers don't appear to understand this, and seem to expect, somehow, that security products companies are actually trying to solve security problems. In retrospect, this seems like a silly assumption. Security companies are about making money for their founders, investors, and shareholders, not about making our critical infrastructure more secure.

The dynamics of the security market are especially painful for the federal government and its infrastructure. Since many federal agencies do not have the budget to simply rip out and replace a piece of technology every time the company that produces it gets bought and screwed up, or goes out of business, there are a *lot* of orphaned products and technologies in the federal infrastructure. This has a huge impact on homeland security, though nobody wants to think about it.

Here's a scary homeland security scenario that nobody seems to allow on his or her radar screen: Many crucial federal systems run on products produced by publicly traded companies. How would the federal government react if a controlling interest in Oracle Corporation (the company that makes the database software that holds the bulk of the intelligence community's classified material) were purchased by the

Chinese government? Or, how about if Microsoft was rolled into a European conglomerate and suddenly we were buying our entire federal computing infrastructure from a foreign power? In effect, many of the companies that produce our infrastructure are for sale to the highest bidder. Some of them are already foreign-owned, such as Checkpoint Security, the Israeli company that makes the firewall products used to secure the majority of corporate America.

Countries around the world have been dealing with exactly this problem for years — with varying degrees of discomfort. How can any country consider its electronic infrastructure to be secure if 95 percent of it is running on software purchased from Redmond, Washington? I suspect countries around the world periodically look for signs of back doors in their software infrastructures; with our slipshod practices for building federal systems, would we even know where to begin, if we had to?

Security may be too important a problem to leave to market forces. This observation applies across the board from computer security products to weapons development to homeland security solutions. On one hand, the free market guarantees us innovation, timeliness, and an industry that is responsive to the customers' demands. On the other hand, it gives us product companies that hew com-

> **" Security may be too important a problem to leave to market forces. "**

pletely to their own agenda-of-the-moment, and a structure of financial rewards that virtually ensures that customers won't get the products they need.

So, the state of computer security industry is a true threat to homeland security. It comes back to the federal government having no coherent plan for information technology and no recognition of its ongoing strategic importance. So far, the feds' thinking on cyber security has begun and ended with "How do we keep the hackers out of www. whitehouse.gov?" It's as if there's a hope that if you worry about the minutiae hard enough, the really big strategic problems will take care of themselves.

One thing I can tell you for sure; the really big strategic problems are not going to be tackled effectively by warring bureaucracies.

IN A PERFECT WORLD

The need for a serious improvement in the computer security world is clear. But how can we bring that about and what price will our government pay if that improvement doesn't happen and a serious attacker decides to undermine us by going through all the back doors that exist in the government's computer infrastructure?

THE RISE AND FALL OF STANDARDS

Those of us in the high-tech industry who lived through the rise and fall of the standards bodies got to witness an amazing time in the history of computing. We saw a brief period in which the rules of free market competition were temporarily put on the shelf in favor of a kind of community spirit among geeks. It only happened because the geeks realized they were on to a good thing a few years before their corporate masters caught on. As soon as commercial reality caught up with the Internet, in the late 1980s, the end was inevitable.

What can we learn from the rise and fall of standards? First and foremost, *great things can happen if you let a small number of innovators lead and everyone else gets out of their way for just a little while.* There is no law written that prevents any organization (even government agencies) from showing such a level of leadership. The government almost got it right with the TCSEC and C2 security: They mandated a standard, and all the vendors stood up and saluted. By failing to follow through by actually *requiring* it, they shot themselves and the potential benefit of standards in the foot. The credibility that was lost in that process can be regained — it's simply a matter of willpower and money.

As we've seen from the Department of Homeland Security's budget, the money isn't lacking, though the willpower may well be. If the Department of Homeland Security wanted to plant the seeds for an interesting future, they'd take the budget dollars wasted on NIPC and spend them to spearhead the development of a suite of government-wide standards for security products and services. They'd get an executive order requiring that *any new products purchased by the federal government must meet those standards.* Of course, the vendors would scream bloody murder. But *the customer is always right.* Our government, the largest customer in the world, keeps forgetting that. But if there is one organization anywhere that has the power to set standards, it's the federal government. It's time for some leadership. Will we get leadership from the Department of Homeland Security? Doubtful, but we can hope.

THE HACKER CONNECTION

My guess is that the era when hackers dominated the computer security scene is coming to a close. The computing public is getting sick and tired of the constant stream of vulnerabilities and security alerts, and will be looking for someone to offer a solution instead of more fear, uncertainty, and doubt. Information security has become a sufficiently lucrative field in the last 10 years that a whole new generation of security practitioners has started to enter the workforce. Pretty soon, we'll no longer be suffering from the deficit of manpower and knowledge that gave the hackers their chance to rise to prominence.

It's a shame that the feds (most particularly the FBI) have burned through whatever goodwill they were initially accorded because of their position and reputation. Attempts to bootstrap a security resource by the government have consistently failed to the point where everyone's taking a wait-and-see attitude. Will the DHS be the next NIPC? So far, everything they have done on the computer security front is straight out of NIPC's playbook — I don't think anyone's expecting anything useful or interesting to happen.

THE FREE MARKET AND SECURITY

The solution to the problem of bad security products is simple, really: Let market forces eventually kill off bad products. That is, assuming that we have the patience to wait for that to happen.

If the Darwinian process is too slow (personally, I think it is), then the government or large corporations can help to accelerate it by focusing their economic power and working together. It would make sense to do this by industry groups (or government communities, such as the intelligence community).

I've written elsewhere about the need for a CTO's office for the federal government and how it will eventually evolve — let's hasten that evolution. What do you think would happen if the banking industry, as a whole, decided to join forces and have a firewall product developed that exactly suited its needs? That's how computing was done in the 1970s. Industry groups, taken as a whole, pay tens of millions of dollars for products that could be created from whole cloth for a few million. Many people forget that the ARPANET (the ancestor of the Internet) was a DARPA (Department of Defense Advanced Research Projects Administration) funded effort to create survivable networks for the military and intelligence community. The NSA and CIA were some of the earliest adopters of the new technology; after all, it was made for them.

Our current paradigm is to let the vendors build what they think we need, then reward those that guess right and do a pretty good job of it. I believe we're spending enough money, collectively, on the free-market approach that there may be cases where reverting to a custom-tailored approach may make more sense. That's especially the case with security-critical components of the corporate and national infrastructure.

12

The Price Tag of Fear

As I write this, the homeland security fear-mongers were at it again. The news was full (for a whole day, until new twists in a prominent murder case distracted us again) of the helpful announcement from the government that a "terrorist incident in the United States is 100 percent certain during the next two years." A more useless and foolhardy public announcement is hard to imagine. Why not just tell the public that the sky is falling? What are we supposed to do, live in fear for the next two years? When I turned the TV off and went out to feed the horses, I followed the only logical course of action: I immediately forgot the idiots in Washington, along with the terrorists.

The primary sales tool of the security marketer is fear, uncertainty, and doubt. If I were trying to get you to buy my security device or service, I would conjure up the most terrifying possible scenario and imply that it is likely to happen eventually if immediate action is not taken. Being a prognosticator of disaster is a pretty straightforward proposition: Bad things *always* happen *eventually*. The question you should ask is this: How *likely* are they to happen? The next question should be how badly would it hurt, if it did?

If this were a normal hype-filled book about security, at this point I would try to paint the most terrifying possible picture of what could happen if my good advice goes unheeded. I won't do that this time. Let's look, instead, at what could happen *regardless* of whether or not anyone does anything. Then we'll envision some scary scenarios and ask the all-important question: How likely is it that any of these scenarios could actually happen?

SCARY STUFF?

The 9/11 attack, and most terrorist attacks, have one unique difference from traditional state-sponsored espionage: The terrorists made little or no effort to occupy positions of trust. Essentially, they came from outside with knives. *But the most dangerous attacks come from inside.*

Typically, state-sponsored espionage consists of a long-term project undertaken with the acceptance that there will be no immediately visible results. The agenda and professionalism of the spy is fundamentally very different from that of the terrorist — for now. But suppose that changes?

THE RISK OF RISK ASSESSMENT

Security practitioners love the concept of "risk assessment" — a rational process for evaluating likely risks and adjusting our behaviors to minimize the potential damage. I already introduced you to the fundamentals of risk assessment at the beginning of this chapter with the two all-important questions: How likely is a bad thing to happen? and How much would it hurt if it did? The rest of the process is simply prioritizing which bad things to worry about so you're not wasting your time worrying about low-likelihood threats.

Take an example: What if you're crossing a street in New York City? Are you more afraid of being struck by a taxicab or a meteorite? The damage a meteorite would do hurtling through the air at hundreds of miles per hour is far more severe than the injury you'd suffer from a runaway taxi. You're fairly likely to survive getting hit by a taxi, whereas even a small meteorite hitting you in the head would turn you into a fine pink mist. But most of us would agree that a taxi is far more likely to cross our paths. That's why most of us look both ways before we cross the street rather than walk out into traffic with our eyes fixed on the heavens looking for a highly unlikely meteorite.

That's a slightly silly example, but it contains all the important elements of risk assessment. You're comparing the odds of two different risks against the expected damage they'd cause. You're also taking into consideration the *cost of remediation* or the *effectiveness of remediation* — we're assuming that it's pretty low-cost to turn our heads to look for a taxicab, while there's not a whole lot we can do if a meteorite decides to hit us, anyhow. And, lastly, we're taking into account that we have *limited resources;* assuming we can't both look up and in both directions or we'd take all day to cross a street, we're forced to choose the defensive posture that's got the highest payoff.

Congratulations, you've now mastered security! The rest is just details.

BRINGING RISK HOME

So how does risk assessment relate to homeland security? Consider this example: Which did more damage to the United States, 9/11 or the collapse of Enron? It's impossible to tell in the short term, but look at how we reacted to each of those disasters. In one case we sent under a dozen people in front of a judge, and in the other we have (so far) killed thousands of people and toppled two sovereign nations. Our response to the terrorist threat has been entirely disproportionate. Why? Both situations have cost billions and billions of dollars. But only one of them scared us.

> " *Consider this example: Which did more damage to the United States, 9/11 or the collapse of Enron?* "

Fear, apparently, is good business. On one hand, we have the politicians who want to comfort us. On the other hand, we have the people who are lining up with their hands out ready to make a fortune off our disproportionate reaction to our fear. They want to feed that fear, in fact, and aren't afraid of telling us nonsense like "There is a 100 percent chance of a terrorist event in the United States within the next two years."

But oddly, considering the risk assessment model, it's far more likely that we'll have more cases of corruption in the corporate world than that two landmark buildings will be demolished by a terrorist attack. After all, do you see a "Department of Corporate Greed" being created as an umbrella to oversee corporate fraud? No: Enron was not scary, so our politicians didn't need to do something dramatic to comfort us.

Using your fear, here's how they manipulate you: What if there were a hundred Enrons all within a week of each other? See how I went from one thing that had a fair likelihood of happening and tried to scare you by implying it could happen with a much greater frequency than it is ever likely to? How about the big meteorite that hit Arizona thousands of years ago? What if 100 of them hit at the same time? Don't worry about it — it's not likely to happen during the lifetime of the universe.

But those who specialize in scare tactics use this technique of unrealistic risk assessment all the time.

So let's indulge in a little exaggerated risk assessment ourselves.

THEY CAME FROM WITHIN

What's the risk of massive insider attacks against the U.S. infrastructure? At this time, this scenario is highly unlikely. But, if such attacks happened, we would be unable to prevent them *regardless* of what we tried to do. Background checks wouldn't work against sufficiently deeply buried sleeper agents, also referred to as moles; it becomes a question, simply, of how far back you can check the records to uncover the initial arrival of and infiltration by these invaders. And, if your counterintelligence organizations are also subverted, then you might be unable even to rely on background checks.

So, imagine this scary scenario: The United States finds itself in a lengthy struggle with ideological terrorists who are utterly implacable, well funded, and have the sense of time and perspective that allows for operations with a long-term view. Or, perhaps, the United States finds itself in a second cold war with a nation that is willing to risk its national existence by using professional terrorism as an alternative to normal combat operations. The terrorists begin to infiltrate key positions with approximately 20 to 30 agents and devise a 10-year plan. For maximum effectiveness, they would choose a single target location — say, New York City, which can be geographically isolated during an emergency.

Step One: Sleeper Agents Settle In

First, the terrorist sleeper agents would get jobs at key organizations: the Department of Homeland Security, the electric company, the water company, news organizations, the telephone company, and shipping companies. The job of these sleeper agents is to keep their heads down, be model employees, and work their way into positions of responsibility, while learning everything they possibly can about the target environment.

At this point, the operation is highly secure because *there is no plan to compromise* and there is no need for the sleepers to know each other's identities, targets, or even how many agents are in place. They are all simply put in place and told to move toward their goals with an approximate time horizon for when an attack might happen. As the sleeper agents work their way deeper into their target organizations, they achieve a greater ability to affect the entire organization as their knowledge of procedures deepens and they come to understand the target better.

Some of the sleepers would wash out, or lose their jobs, or not advance far enough in their chosen target organization. Perhaps some targets would be sufficiently important to be assigned a handful of sleepers. These agents might or might not be aware of each other or, if they were, might be able to cover for each other. Imagine, for example, if one of the sleepers, after years of loyal service, asked for the job of administering polygraph tests to new applicants, or coordinating background checks on employees. Or, perhaps, the sleeper gets control over the night watch operation, or is able to decide what guard company gets the security contract. Meanwhile, the controllers of the operation would periodically need to make contact with their sleepers to make sure that they were not becoming ideologically unsound — even sleeper agents might grow fond of their new home country and decide that they didn't want to hurt it, after all.

Step Two: Get Ready, Set....

Eight years into the attacker's 10-year plan, the next stage of the attack begins: planning. An activation signal is sent or posted — perhaps in the form of a spam email — to notify the sleepers that it is time to act. A small handful of operational commanders meets with the sleepers individually at prearranged locations and debriefs them extensively to learn what they know, what levels of access they have gained, and so on.

Next, an attack plan is formulated. There is a slight chance that during the planning stage the controllers will realize they do not have enough access or the right people in place, and the attack would need to be delayed or cancelled. The probability is good, however, that the sleepers already in place would be able to provide sufficient opportunity to further unfold the attack plan.

The planners spend six months formulating and fine-tuning the final plan, preparing to initiate the final deployment. Perhaps a few key people at targets are identified by the sleepers as needing to be "replaced" with attackers via well-timed accidents, job terminations, or hiring changes. They would pay special attention to the security company that provides guards for their high-value targets.

The main attack team, several dozen trained and armed individuals with explosives and other equipment, infiltrate the country or are activated where they have already been residing for years. The sleepers in the shipping companies provide transport and storage for weapons and large amounts of explosives. The sleepers with access to Department of Homeland Security databases continually check to see if any of their members appear on watch lists or if there is any sign that the targets are aware of the impending attack.

Step Three: ...Go!

Finally, the time draws close. Let's suppose the attack involves the delivery of radiological contaminants into the city's water supply, combined with the explosive demolition of two key electrical transformer stations. The security company responsible for protecting the electrical stations has been subverted; several key employees are actually members of the attack team and have provided uniforms and credible procedural practices to the main attack team.

The second team has a small quantity — enough to fill a soda can — of extremely finely ground plutonium. Plutonium is one of the most toxic substances on Earth: Ingesting a single particle is a horrible, lingering death sentence, and it remains hellishly radioactive for a very long time. This team is composed of sleeper agent-workers for the water company, who have had plenty of time to learn their way around the various pumping facilities.

New York City's main water source is a gigantic pipe leading from the Catskills; it's effectively unrepairable because it runs deep under the city. Once the plutonium was introduced into the main water supply, it would be lethally toxic for years. Never mind the short-term damage, death, and terror — the long-term damage would completely dwarf it: How do you replace *every water pipe* in a city that large?

Having the sleepers in the electric company blow out the main power transformers for the city would also have an amazingly debilitating effect. The big transformers are not something that is kept in stock, someplace: They are custom-made and would take months to replace. The city would empty out to become a ghost town.

Suppose the sleepers in the Department of Homeland Security add to the chaos by bursting into the crisis management center and tossing a few hand grenades into the communications systems?

That's just one scenario. You could just as easily imagine that a nuclear reactor was the target, or a transporter ship filled with liquid propane gas, or virtually anything else that explodes, burns, poisons, or costs a billion dollars to replace.

The key to these scenarios is in the assumption that an attacker would be dedicated enough to invest the time to work into a position of trust. All security systems fall on their face if your

" All security systems fall on their face if your enemy can infiltrate positions of responsibility. "

enemy can infiltrate positions of responsibility. Who's going to watch over the shoulders of your security guards? More security guards?

WHAT COULD WE DO TO PREVENT IT?

How can we protect against this type of attack? I don't think we can, in conventional terms. At a meta-level, the best way to protect against such an attack is to make sure nobody hates you enough to want to launch such a time-consuming and costly effort against you. Sadly, in an ideologically diverse world, such globally rosy relations are not likely.

Another way to protect against such an attack is to make sure that any group that would launch such an attack is already dead or otherwise busy worrying about their own survival. The best defense really *is* a good offense. But this raises a troubling question: At a certain point is peaceful coexistence impossible? If a people believe that they might be subjected to such a ferocious infiltration attack, how can they build the trust that is necessary for peace? It is, in fact, these kinds of passionate, long-term hatreds and distrusts that are the root cause of genocidal wars. Sooner or later one side decides it will be war to the death, and eradicates the other completely.

ON OUR RADAR?

Can we hope to even detect such an attack? Correctly compartmentalized and managed, such an attack could be executed with nearly zero chance of being discovered. By inserting agents into the target's counterterror and incident-response organizations, the enemy ensures that any attempt to discover or investigate the plot would be a tip-off to the attackers, who could then simply vanish. I hate to sound cynical, but even if an attack such as I describe was exposed, many people would not believe it was happening at all. After watching the way the worldwide media and the international community reacted to the question of Iraq's weapons of mass destruction, I don't think they'd see a smoking gun if you stuck it right against their foreheads.

Such an attack would also be extremely difficult to defeat because so many organizations' defenses rely on "knowing the procedures." It would be difficult, but not impossible, for a group of terrorists to pretend to be a highway maintenance team with a truck working on a bridge. A substitute maintenance team with knowledge of procedures could easily carry double its number in "extras" as well as extra equipment. If challenged, its members could come up with a credible explanation for their presence on the spot.

Although it would be difficult for a terrorist to successfully pretend to be an airport baggage handler, it would be easy for a terrorist who has been hired as a real airport baggage handler to abuse the use of his access card to sneak a few friends or a bagful of weapons past the luggage checkpoints.

> " Trust-based mechanisms work well against outsiders launching spontaneous penetration attempts, but they fail utterly against enemies who have invested the time and effort to become trusted. "

No matter how much we try to convince ourselves otherwise, 99 percent of the security we have in place relies on *trust* in the individuals involved. Trust-based mechanisms work well against outsiders launching spontaneous penetration attempts, but they fail utterly against enemies who have invested the time and effort to become trusted. Once the trust boundary has been penetrated, it is increasingly easy for the trusted (but not trustworthy) attacker to bring more attackers into the trusted fold.

First, Recognize the Threat

Is it practical to engage in counterterror on a broad scale? Yes. In fact, it's the most cost-effective option that is available to us, if we can stomach it and live with the consequences. One thing that is helpful about the hothead terrorist crazies: They tend to telegraph their intent. Only a completely foolish and self-absorbed culture like the United States in the 1990s would sit by and smile stupidly while radical groups publicly announced their intent to kill and destroy its people.

One reason we had our heads in the sand about the international threat in the early 1990s was that the U.S. government was paying too much attention to "radical right wing militias." This was a sort of vaguely counterrevolutionary movement that tended to like guns, dislike the IRS, and distrust all governments. Mostly, these groups could have been ignored, except that they had a bad habit of not paying taxes.

Because of Ruby Ridge, Waco, and the Oklahoma City bombing, the FBI's attention was closely focused on the interior threat. Though nobody wants to admit it, Islamic fundamentalists were given a lower priority because most of the anti-American attacks took place outside of the United States — the Al Qaeda USS Cole bombing most notably. Once again, the FBI focused on the previous threat and ignored the upcoming threat. Furthermore, the FBI's hands were tied by laws and executive orders (mostly a consequence of the FBI's own abuses during the civil rights era) that prevented them from trying to infiltrate possibly threatening organizations.

> " *Though nobody wants to admit it, Islamic fundamentalists were given a lower priority because most of the anti-American attacks took place outside of the United States.* "

IS THE BEST DEFENSE A STRONG OFFENSE?

What about Islamic fundamentalist terror groups? Can they be infiltrated and compromised from within? It's actually difficult because many of them are "friends and family" organizations. Al Qaeda, for example, is really a conglomerate of small cells of individuals who are well known to each other. It would be extremely difficult to inject a double agent into such a cell.

But there are other options: penetrate and compromise the support structures of the terrorists. Where do they get their weapons? Where do they get their money? Where do they go when they are wounded and need medical assistance? Nobody can operate in an utter vacuum; the trick is to identify places where the terrorists have to step out of their close-knit circles, and begin to penetrate those. It's not a rapid process — we're talking Cold-War–era long-term thinking. But the methods are well-known. After all, the CIA and KGB wrote the book on how to penetrate enemy organizations.

you should know

I sincerely hope that some of my homeland security dollars have gone to bringing back some of the old cold warriors from retirement to stand up operations against the Islamic terrorists. I'll put my money on the cunning old men and women in the trench coats; they did a good job against a smarter, better-funded, better-organized foe than Al Qaeda. Go get 'em!

A nice side effect of penetration operations is the cooling effect it has on its victims. Looking over your shoulder and not being able to trust anyone except your narrow circle is very emotionally debilitating. It makes you paranoid (for good reason) and makes you disinclined to rely on anyone else — which has the effect of dividing an organization without having to take any overt action.

There are numerous examples of this effect happening during the Cold War. Probably the most famous was when James Jesus Angleton, the CIA's head of counterintelligence, got so spooked by KGB disinformation and moles like Kim Philby that he led a series of internal purges that ruined the careers of several valuable senior CIA officers. Organizations that are concerned with being penetrated are immediately operating at a degraded efficiency level, because they're constantly watching each other and looking over their shoulders.

HOW AFRAID SHOULD WE BE?

What is the likelihood that someone will launch an attack that involves sleeper cells of terrorists against the United States? It's certainly possible, but, like the meteorite-versus-taxicab question, I think it's probably highly unlikely. We already have enemies who have the resources necessary to launch such an attack. Those enemies are obviously intelligent enough to figure out how to do it, and they are obviously sufficiently hate-filled to want to cause us massive damage. In some cases, those hatreds have been longstanding, and a long-term plan could have been established and carried out by now. Why hasn't it happened yet?

USEFUL DETERRENTS

I believe that nation-states have been, until recently, deterred from engaging in massive, state-sponsored terrorist attacks because the danger of retaliation at a state-versus-state level is simply too high. Nations with large standing armies array them against each other and rattle their sabers overtly. Those that are not contenders on the battlefield have, until recently, kept their mouths shut, or aligned themselves with larger power-blocs that helped legitimize them militarily and protected them against retaliation from larger enemies.

As we saw from the rapidity with which the United States latched onto Afghanistan and the Taliban following 9/11, states harboring terrorists have a lot to lose if their terrorist allies are successful. There's an interesting problem of balance: State-sponsored terrorism is attractive to those countries that do not have the military power to directly confront their enemies. But those same countries have to understand that their lack of military power means they're doomed if their terrorist attacks are sufficiently successful that they trigger an all-out assault.

I'm pretty sure that if a country executed the kind of terror attack described earlier in this chapter, they would be wiped out in short order as soon as the United States determined who was behind the attack. In fact, that country would pretty quickly find itself isolated on the world stage. Look how many other nations stood up for the Taliban when push finally came to shove. Nations that have a history of sponsoring terrorism were falling all over themselves after 9/11 to make sure everyone knew they had nothing to do with the attack.

This process of alignment among nations has kept state-sponsored terrorism to a relatively low level. It simply would not have done for a Soviet client state to launch a massive state-sponsored terror attack against the United States or a U.S. client; such provocation might have resulted in the next world war. The global alignment between two superpowers tends to have a steadying influence on state-sponsored terrorism. Rather, state-sponsored terrorism has historically been the province of nation-states that are not militarily mighty.

WORLD WAR IV

When the Soviet Union collapsed, what was essentially World War III (the Cold War) was over. World War IV then began, but the United States slept through it, until early September 2001.

World War IV actually began in 1993, when Islamic fundamentalist leaders announced a new holy war against the United States ("the great Satan"). Among those leaders were Saddam Hussein and Muammar Ghaddafi, as well as clerics from Iran, the Sudan, and Afghanistan. America, basically, ignored them.

As Islamic-backed terrorist attacks against U.S. interests began to mount, America continued to ignore them. The U.S. public was more interested in post–Soviet Europe, and spending the "peace dividend," as well as investigating the then-president's sexual escapades with interns and his real-estate investments.

> " *Post-9/11, global terrorism is the well-defined enemy we were missing.* "

America's time for focusing on internal problems was short-lived. Post-9/11, global terrorism was the well-defined enemy we were missing. Now we can play cowboys and terrorists!

A WEAK THREAT

Realistically, however, radical Islam is not the threat it thinks it is. When Ayatollah Khomeini issued a fatwa (religious edict) in 1989 decreeing the death of Salman Rushdie, millions of Muslims did not rise up and take action. A few did — the lunatic fringe — but the vast majority of sensible individuals went on with their lives. Had the Pope preached a new crusade, the reaction from the Christian world would have been similar, I suspect. A few hotheads looking for an excuse to make trouble would feel empowered to kill and maim; everyone else would get on with their lives.

The terrorists remain the unprofessionals, the slightly bent, the fanatical, the mentally broken, and the psychologically unstable. Fortunately for all of us, these kinds of individuals do not lay out coolly professional plans with a horizon of execution stretching 15 years ahead. We don't need to worry about the real professionals because the real professionals have better and more serious things to do. Mostly, the professionals worry about nation-states and keeping their own nations intact.

The hotheads and the nuts are still dangerous — obviously so — but they are not imbued with the kind of professional talent to launch an attack that costs millions of lives. The fundamental fear that drives the

U.S. government's current obsession with weapons of mass destruction is the realization that even an amateur can be incredibly dangerous if he gets his deadly tools from a professional.

HOW ARE WE DOING?

On one hand, we are losing the homeland security war by spending huge amounts of money inefficiently and stupidly; but on the other hand, we are doing quite well.

THINNING THE RANKS

Our offensive operations have been *vastly* more successful than our defensive operations. Through aggressive diplomacy, offers of economic aid, and carrots and sticks, the U.S. government has made terrific headway in getting foreign powers to render Al Qaeda operatives into U.S. hands.

Doubtless billions of dollars are being quietly expended in what amount to blood-payments for information about terrorist whereabouts. This is money well spent, when you consider the number of arrests of terrorists worldwide since 9/11. While the defensive aspects of the Department of Homeland Security have accomplished little or nothing, foreign intelligence lubricated with greenbacks has decimated the ranks of international terror.

Several planned attacks have been prevented, and the would-be terrorists are now being squeezed for information that could lead to the eventual arrest of their companions. One side effect of going on the offensive is that the bad guys realize the gloves have come off and become a lot more circumspect in their actions.

you should know

The overall effect of the war on terrorism on the terrorist community is Darwinian: The dumb ones and the braggarts get weeded out pretty quickly, while the smart ones with a rudimentary level of professionalism improve their tradecraft rapidly. But the isolating effect of going on the offensive is considerable: Divorced from their support infrastructures, they are more likely to slip up. Ideologues enjoy the company of their peers and cobelievers, and if they want to stay under cover, they are forced to become increasingly isolated and, often, more extreme.

GETTING OUR HANDS DIRTY

The war on terrorism has caused a shift in how we deal with intelligence operations. In the late 1980s and early 1990s the United States got squeamish about going on the offensive. We dramatically cut CIA's expenditures on foreign operatives and "feet on the ground" in favor of clean and morally unambiguous satellite and technical reconnaissance. Ever since U.S. Secretary of State Henry Stimson observed in 1941 that "gentlemen do not read each other's mail" and set back U.S. intelligence by several decades, we have been reluctant to get our hands dirty — even when we badly needed to.

President Clinton was horrified to discover that many CIA sources were criminals, gangsters, and drug dealers and implemented strong restrictions of spy recruitment of "unsavory" characters. Consequently, many foreign sources were discarded and dried up. The more expensive and dangerous option — building a network of deep-cover moles around the world inserted in organizations that might spawn terror — has not even been considered.

Other countries have not been so squeamish and have not hesitated to infiltrate agents into crucial locations as a matter of self-defense. Since 9/11 we've been basically outsourcing our counterintelligence by paying foreign intelligence services for their efforts. The FBI and Drug Enforcement Agency (DEA) can have undercover agents in counternarcotic operations, but CIA and the FBI can't have undercover agents infiltrating potentially violent splinter groups. What's wrong with this picture? This squeamishness is the price we pay for the FBI's spying on the civil rights movement and Watergate: In our fear of a shadow government we've blinded ourselves and tied our hands.

> " Since 9/11 we've been basically outsourcing our counterintelligence by paying foreign intelligence services for their efforts. "

Happily, 9/11 seems to have loosened some of those restrictions — the level of cooperation we've received from foreign intelligence agencies that have turned Al Qaeda operatives over to U.S. forces is heartening. Presumably, that cooperation has been lubricated with ample money and arm-twisting. We won't be fully aware of what kind of new initiatives are under way for a very long time, if ever. Are we engaging in active counterterror? Are we infiltrating terrorist organizations and support networks at home and abroad? I hope so!

WAKE UP!

I think everyone who has written something about 9/11 has called it a "wake-up call," so now it's my turn. What 9/11 woke us up to was the realization that political unrest in foreign countries can come home to hurt us. It snapped us out of the indulgent nap we were taking after the end of the Cold War. It made us realize that a decade of having no foreign policy and of repeatedly asking the Israelis and Palestinians to just shake hands and be best friends wasn't going to work. I think it's pretty clear that the current U.S. administration woke up and smelled the coffee on 9/11.

KEEPING THE PEACE

For all of the worldwide talk and hand-wringing about U.S. imperialism, I think that the current administration profoundly "gets it" when it comes to keeping the peace. Implicit in virtually every foreign policy decision of the administration since 9/11 is the awareness that if the hot spots of the world are pacified, we're less likely to have trouble domestically, or to get involved in warfare abroad.

But the learning curve for the Bush administration has been very steep. When President Bush sent Secretary of State Colin Powell to Israel/Palestine the first

> **" [Colin Powell's first trip to Israel/Palestine] worked about as well as it would work if the French sent their foreign minister to ask the United States to return the Sioux their original tribal lands. "**

time, it was a well-intentioned but politically simplistic move. Powell had nothing behind him except the power of his words, and the words were "pretty please." It worked about as well as it would work if the French sent their foreign minister to ask the United States to return the Sioux their original tribal lands. You simply cannot make strides in Middle Eastern peace by asking nicely. Unfortunately for all of us, both the Israelis and Palestinians know this and have long since stopped asking nicely.

The 9/11 attacks gave the United States a moment of moral authority to take sweeping international action, until the shock wore off and everyone reverted to their traditional enmities (even the FBI and CIA). In a sense, we squandered that moral authority by not tackling the Israeli/Palestinian problem head-on.

As long as the worldwide media shows footage of American-made tanks and American-made helicopters crewed by Israeli soldiers attacking Palestinian towns, the U.S. role as an uninvolved peace broker for the Middle East is going to be a tough sell. In fact, it will be a joke. We either need to tackle the Israeli/Palestinian problem head-on and stop saying "pretty please" or we need to accept the fact that turmoil, violence, and terrorism will be an endless presence. The only way to broker a peace in the Middle East is for the United States to become relentlessly even-handed in its dealings with both parties. It may be necessary to suspend lucrative weapons sales and foreign aid to Israel if that's what it takes to achieve some credibility in the region. Arabs justifiably feel the United States is pro-Israel, and that will always be an impediment as long as we don't do whatever it takes to act in a balanced manner.

If we choose the path of failing to act decisively to broker a Middle Eastern peace, our remaining option will be to aggressively pursue counterintelligence and counterterror to try to prevent attacks before they come against or within our borders. My guess is that won't last very long. Sooner or later we'll suffer another damaging successful attack, and it'll be left to the U.S. Marines to bring peace the way they do so well — by waging war. Without an effective foreign policy, however, even the peace that the USMC brings is only temporary.

WHERE DO WE GO FROM HERE?

The United States has a lot of cultural naiveté about terrorism. As a society, it says something good about us, I think, that we prefer to imagine the kind of evil that you can negotiate and reason with. In the movies, the bad guys usually just want money; they are never inflexibly devoted to extremism. Perhaps that's another reason why our foreign policy regarding the Middle East has been ineffective: We keep assuming everyone will eventually see reason. What we don't recognize is that, perhaps, the situation has progressed to the point where reason is no longer an option.

Our view of the future is also charmingly naïve, in a hopeful way. Take, for example, *Star Trek* — a program I devotedly watched growing up. *Star Trek* poses a future in which everyone in the galaxy (human, at least) has pulled together to create an idealized Federation of Planets. As I look at the problem of terrorism, I can't help but think how simplistic the galaxy of *Star Trek* is when, with the kind of technology represented in that fictional world, terrorist events could wipe out planets or species easily. I guess the Federation of the future learned to say "pretty please," or perhaps none of the bad guys in that distant future are sore losers.

The Federation in *Star Trek* also hasn't learned the foreign policy lesson that the Bush administration is learning right now: If there is unrest at the borders of your territory, it can follow you home.

We're not comfortable with confronting implacable enmity in others. I think, as a society, we sense that hatred makes you do stupid things — we've certainly done our share in the past — and so there are some hard-learned lessons informing our cultural consciousness. The crusade of good against evil is an easy sell to the American public. Perhaps we've simply watched too many John Wayne movies,

> **" The crusade of good against evil is an easy sell to the American public. "**

and that is why the President's regime-changing missions in Afghanistan and Iraq garnered such overwhelming popular (if not international) support.

It's been fascinating for me to watch the reactions of my international friends change in the last two years. Prior to the war against Iraq, I had several friendly discussions with European friends, and invariably I was presented with the argument: "But you Americans nearly committed genocide against the Native American tribes; why are you so high and mighty you can take it upon yourselves to overthrow a sovereign power just because you think its leadership is corrupt?" The fact is that we're embarrassed about that episode in our history, which is why we did our best to stop it a long time ago. Now we're comfortable exporting those values to other parts of the world. Even if it sometimes means letting the USMC do it.

If we're going to be the good guys of the world, we do have to be evenhanded and fair, and that means that eventually we'll have to deal with the Israel/Palestine problem in a way that doesn't increase resentment toward us. Our long-term ties to Israel have always served to blind us to the fact that the Israeli regime has committed horrible atrocities, and continues to do so on a regular basis. The cycle of self-justifying violence appears prepared to continue indefinitely in the Middle East. But sooner or later the Palestinians and Israelis need to learn that "an eye for an eye, a tooth for a tooth" is not a viable negotiating position. Both parties are blind and toothless after years of debasing themselves to the point where they have become interchangeable with that which they hate. It's sad to think that the real secret to homeland security lies in the hands of such twisted, angry, agonized, violent people.

IN A PERFECT WORLD

How can we break out of the cycle of being surprised by the next thing because we're too busy worrying about the last thing? The simple answer is this: Don't let yourself get surprised. Be on top of what the bad guys are doing and make sure something awful happens to them, first.

With terrorism or in a cold war, the only viable answer is active counterterror. It's a nasty, dirty business, but so far it is the single most effective tool against organized attacks. We've avoided it for years. Indeed, we've had a number of laws against domestic counterintelligence since the FBI targeted individuals who were opposed to the administration's policies but were not an immediate military or civil threat. The big problem remains: How do we infiltrate organizations, which have known associations with assassins and terrorists, without also compromising the next Dr. Martin Luther King? We need to be realistic about allowing counterintelligence against self-declared threats without instantiating a police state.

Personally, I don't think the balance between staying alert and a police state should be particularly difficult. Many of the organizations we're talking about have members that do indiscrete things such as standing in the street chanting "Death to America." I don't think it's a moral leap to justify investigating their after-hours behaviors and hobbies. The challenge is to keep administrations from using espionage services to their political ends, as Richard Nixon attempted to do.

Our founding fathers understood the importance of separation of powers, and I believe that the threat of abuse of authority can be mitigated through careful planning. Compartmentalizing information is one technique that might work, separating authorities is another. Our government has not adequately explored the use of opposing controls in intelligence. For example, an office of ombudsman could be established and staffed with properly cleared members of the anti-establishment. The very idea would terrify the spooks, but I believe that there are always a sufficient number of people who can exercise good judgment and display strong morals at the same time. We just need to get them in the right places within the organizational structure.

THE LAST WORD

The challenge of homeland security is a tough one filled with difficult problems. Simple solutions? I don't have any. I think that true homeland security requires massive changes that we, as a society, are not going to be willing to make. I'm actually happy about that, because the resulting secured society would be something that would terrify our founding fathers and impress George Orwell. That particular solution, I believe, would be worse than the disease.

Index